Sustainable Development Through Global Circular Economy Practices

This is a very important and timely book in a growing area of interest in business schools and among practitioners globally. The book explores the conceptual roots of circular economy, setting out the theoretical strands and areas of application with clarity and interest. Case studies are most welcome in this field as there is a dearth of applied material. The case studies in the book are wide and varied, integrated seamlessly into the text and offer crucial insights into what and how CE can be embraced and implemented. The addition of content relating to organisational context, resistance to change and leading change in CE is very useful, opening up questions and answers to both researchers and practitioners. The final chapter considers a progressive research agenda in the field which is very welcome for the academic community. There is something in this book for everyone, from teachers, researchers to practitioners and general interest audiences. The writing style is very accessible and the authors pull no punches in setting out the need for immediate action. A great read, a well-researched and presented book and core reading for anyone interested in social and environmental sustainability.

—Professor Colin Dey, Professor of Social Accounting, University of Dundee, UK

The development of the Circular Economy is probably the most important in management research. It transcends all disciplines, sectors and geographies.

This book provides an excellent overview of the managerial challenges in transitioning from the linear to the circular with a perspective that emphasises the role of digital technology. The authors rightly emphasise the radical over the incremental and thus provide a comprehensive account of 'how to' for practicing managers.

—Roger Maull, Professor of Management Systems, University of Exeter's Business School, UK

Sustainable Development Through Global Circular Economy Practices

BY

STUART MAGUIRE

University of Sheffield, UK

AND

IAN ROBSON

University of Dundee, UK

United Kingdom – North America – Japan – India – Malaysia – China

Emerald Publishing Limited
Emerald Publishing, Floor 5, Northspring, 21-23 Wellington Street, Leeds LS1 4DL.

First edition 2024

British Library Cataloguing in Publication Data
A catalogue record for this book is available from the British Library

ISBN: 978-1-83753-591-0 (Print)
ISBN: 978-1-83753-590-3 (Online)
ISBN: 978-1-83753-592-7 (Epub)

Printed and bound by CPI Group (UK) Ltd, Croydon, CR0 4YY

INVESTOR IN PEOPLE

Contents

Introduction: Sustainable Development Through Global Circular Economy Practices

Almost every private and public sector organisation will be affected by the elements of this book. They will be aware of national and international debates on global sustainability issues. A significant majority of these firms will know they will have to change their business plans to incorporate sustainable and green changes to their activities. If they do not engage in this agenda for change it may have a detrimental effect on their business or department. This will be especially true if sustainability/green targets are imposed from above. Our book will be relevant to these individuals/firms as they strive to grasp quite rapidly changing business activities. Nearly every undergraduate and almost as many postgraduates will undertake a module that is focussed on environmental and green issues as part of their university's commitment toward adhering to a sustainable agenda. This book will underpin these agenda for sustainable behaviour change.

Sustainability and green issues are being extensively discussed in schools across the world. We have strong evidence within our universities that new starters are much more environmentally aware than previous cohorts. This is affecting their career choices. Graduates are much more likely to join organisations that have sustainability and green agendas. This is also having an influence on how firms are formulating their websites. Understanding how the circular economy (CE) can influence changes in areas such as global warming will be beneficial in the near future. This book, through its focus on current and future projects, will provide metrics on how the CE is helping to meet national and international targets, that is, carbon emissions.

The battle to preserve the environment is only just beginning. It would be a big mistake for any organisation or government to underestimate the public outcry for cleaner environments and an end to increases in global warming. These words were said over 45 years ago (Van Gigch, 1978). We have some catching up to do. There is no doubt that there is a groundswell of opinion to solidify this behaviour change in the next few decades. The authors have reviewed the literature on the CE through the lens of paradigm change. This book will identify the level of purposeful activity in the CE and what policies will be required to cement circularity into mainstream business and management practices in the future.

Sustainable Development Through Global Circular Economy Practices, 1–8
Copyright © 2024 by Stuart Maguire and Ian Robson
Published under exclusive licence by Emerald Publishing Limited
doi:10.1108/978-1-83753-590-320231009

The CE, like many previous initiatives, has been able to tap into the current zeitgeist and is being coveted by many academic disciplines, that is, logistics management, economics, ethics, logistics, behavioural science and industrial ecology. There is still time to ensure that the academic and business communities work together to make this a real success story. Just having contributions from many disciplines is not enough. Ideally, these groups would bring their own particular visions and competences and work together in an effective way towards positive CE outcomes. At the very least, these different stakeholders would complement each other when researching or working on CE projects. We definitely need more certainty in the CE enterprise; it should not be a leap of faith. This book will reinforce the key areas that need to come together to make CE projects successful. In view of ambitious climate change targets and COVID-19, we may have to design CE frameworks that work not only in 2022 but 2035 or later.

Decoupling production and consumption for certain research and analysis could be a positive outcome of these collaborations. Executives in the era of the CE will need to deal with a raft of ethical dilemmas. Increased and improved supply chain (SC) activity will lead to an increase in the availability of products, that is, food, cars, and white goods. This will increase the potential for waste. A much better balance is required between production and consumption. There is currently a significant amount of purposeful activity trying to link SCs with the CE.

A really positive aspect of the current sustainability debate is that it identifies key strategic issues from behavioural change through the potential symbiotic business activity within the CE. It is also able to visualise the really positive aspects of research in both sustainable production and consumption. This exciting research area was always going to become more complex as the number of intricate and crucial relationships increased. In this situation, where the number of key stakeholders increases dramatically it is often a good idea to take a holistic perspective on the whole enterprise. Closed systems don't work.

Chapter 1: The Origins of the Circular Economy

There is an implicit understanding that the CE will help firms, SCs, and countries meet global warming, carbon emissions, and sustainability targets well into the future. We are not the first generation to identify a pressing need for change as a precursor to 'saving the planet'. It is imperative that we realign our priorities; carefully plan all human endeavours to anticipate their short- and long-term consequences for the planet; bring a genuine end to waste; bring about a significant retrenchment in our levels of consumption; increase recycling, environmental restoration, and repair; ensure conservation through changes in social and economic patterns of development and life control of natural surroundings, primary agricultural land, open spaces, etc.; and protection and enhancement of environmental quality. This previous list seems to resemble a set of demands that might have emanated from COP-26.

Fligstein and McAdam (2014) undertook some important research into business structures and fields that seems to give an insight into how the CE may develop. It was underpinned by social management theory and the political theory of markets. They stated that social order is constructed through a process of interactions among stakeholders who are competing for advantageous business positions. They identify the dynamic of how new systems and institutions emerge, remain stable, and are transformed. They also investigated how individuals and groups come to compete with each other in social arenas where something important is at stake. One of the most exciting aspects of planning the CE is to address the potential methodological impasse that exists in CE design. The authors believe that the future design of the CE may need to be radically changed as the moral compass for choosing such systems is reset. This should be a positive, not negative, outcome from the future design of the CE. The move to a CE is undoubtedly a major sociological change.

The dynamic of SCs within the CE will be sufficiently different to make them problematic for a significant number of organisations. The CE is likely to open up new business markets for many of these companies. Markets are generally socially constructed arenas where repeated exchanges occur between buyers and sellers under a set of formal and informal rules (conventions) governing relations among competitors, suppliers, and customers. These arenas operate according to local understandings and rules that guide interaction, facilitate trade, define what products are produced, indeed constitute the products themselves, and provide stability for buyers, sellers, and producers. However, with governments signing up to ambitious targets in areas such as carbon reduction across the globe it is more than likely that this stability will disappear. Marketplaces are also dependent on governments, laws, and cultural understandings supporting marketing activity. If we add ethical and ecological aims and goals to this list the future is certain to be more complex and uncertain in SC and CE transactions.

Chapter 2: Sustainability and the Circular Economy as Part of a Global Environmental Strategy

A significant amount of recent debate has suggested that the CE can be given certainty through a mix of laws, policies, risk reduction (tax levies), and strict governance. As citizens, organisations, and governments across the globe increase their interest in environmentally and socially sustainable means of production and consumption, the idea of a CE has been at the forefront of recent discussions held at organisational, national, and global levels (Hazen et al., 2020; Hussain & Malik, 2020). A significant amount of debate has focussed on the need to ensure improved sustainability in SC management endeavours with operational excellence in the CE (Sehnem et al., 2019). They stress that the CE is not only concerned with a reduction in the global environment being used as a receptacle for waste but also with the creation of self-sustaining production systems with reusable materials as the norm. A useful addition to this debate is that several of these articles highlight the need to focus on the long-term requirements of environmental sustainability (Genovese et al., 2017). It is interesting to note that there still tends to be a real focus on production rather than consumption (Georgantzis Garcia et al., 2021). The authors will return to this discourse later in the book. A very positive stream of work focusses on the need to view CE as a way of reducing pressure on the environment.

Chapter 3: Sustainable Production and Consumption Within the Circular Economy

The CE has received global attention because it has the potential to optimise and promote sustainable production and consumption through new models based on continuous growth and limitless production (Govindan & Hasanagic, 2018; Ludeki-Freund, 2019; Tseng et al., 2020). The recent outcome from COP-27 shows that change in global sustainability cannot always occur by just issuing edicts and laws. In certain areas of the globe, it would certainly be more beneficial to rely on conventions rather than laws. A more realistic suggestion may be to develop and implement a set of desirable and feasible international rules and regulations that can facilitate the promotion of an effective CE. The chapter considers the more holistic model of strategic action fields (Fligstein & McAdam, 2014) in surfacing potential key drivers for sustainability from both a policy/structure and an agency/behaviour perspective.

A pressing need for all firms given these global changes in SCs is a requirement to further understand the sociology of consumption. Given the international potential and scope of the CE, it would be a positive step for organisations if they took a systems perspective when developing new alliances and markets. Historically, we have understood economic values for thousands of years (use of coins/currency); however, we have much less or no understanding of social, aesthetic, or ecological currencies. Despite the wealth of literature in the area over the last 70 years, it is not clear how analysts in the private sector introduce the important element of social responsibility into their design-making equation. It has been understood that the executive should try to maximise profits for the firm and shareholders, though they should always take into account the responsibility of the organisation towards the public, the community, the preservation of the environment, and aligned goals. This usually depended on the perceptions of the manager towards different situations. It is often believed that the executive will always seek the short- and long-term profit of the company and that he/she will automatically take into account their responsibility towards wider society. This shows the uncertainty of this position. Is it always in the self-interest of the firm to carry out social obligations, and by doing so, it is maximising its profits in the long run. This position leaves the executive open to criticism uncertain how far to pursue either profits or the welfare of others.

The ability to decouple production and consumption will be a positive aspect of CE and should lead to improved resource efficiency. With the CE gaining impetus as a concept and practice, the ability to promote closed material processes with strategies for material recycling and product reuse will become more important (Hussain et al., 2020; Moreau et al., 2017). SCs acting as district energy systems should be viewed as a viable method of moving towards a circular industrial economy (Mignacci & Locatelli, 2021; Pan et al., 2015). This framework can be practically transferred to several business and industrial areas, for example, construction (Leising, 2018).

The current linear 'take-make-waste-extractive' model leads to the depletion of natural resources and environmental degradation. CE aims to address these impacts by constructing SCs that are restorative, regenerative, and environmentally benign. This may require the need to deploy a multi-objective optimisation strategy for trade-off analysis within the CE (Baratsas et al., 2021). Waste management and the requirement for sustainable packaging need a radical overhaul and drastic improvement to move towards a zero-waste CE (Meherishi et al., 2019; Zhang et al., 2019). This is just as important when assessing people-driven issues for small and medium-sized enterprises (SMEs) or short SCs in the CE (Kiss et al., 2019; Sawe et al., 2021). The chapter draws on a powerful case study in H & M, the Scandinavian fashion manufacturer and retailer to illustrate SC complexity and begin to draw out the organisational response to the CE challenge.

Chapter 4: Supply Chain Management and the Circular Economy

It is claimed that digital SCs facilitated by big data analytics (BDA) capabilities have become of business significance to developing a competitive and sustainable SC. CE practices and flexibility in the sustainable SC are significant mediating variables between BDA capabilities and SC performance (Cheng et al., 2021). A significant number of practitioners and academics have investigated the possibilities of using decision support systems and blockchain to improve CE practices in post-COVID-19 SCs. In these debates, a breadth of theoretical practices and perspectives are considered by industry and academia in addressing future research directions to develop knowledge and understanding about CE operations, principles, and theory in areas such as energy analysis and marketing (Alkhuzaim et al., 2021; Batista et al., 2018; Li et al., 2021). The authors argue for moving away from a prescriptive set of practices and definitions for the CE towards a set of key goals to allow for the inclusion of future practices, technologies, and techniques. It is possible that we do need research to go beyond meso-level to consider a wider social and institutional environment needed to solve current challenges (Masi et al., 2017).

Other research investigates the function of *remanufacturing* principles and the adoption of green and sustainable manufacturing practices. There is a strong possibility of improving the capability to influence and reinforce SC resilience in the CE. A dynamic remanufacturing capability can have a positive effect on SC resilience (Bag et al., 2019). Complex SCs need to determine the optimum amounts of specific elements, such as pricing strategy, remanufacturing (rework) policy, delivery time, and sales effort to reduce the conflicts between different stakeholders. This should enhance the economic and CE objectives of the SC (Alizadeh-Basban & Taleizadeh, 2020). There is a pressing requirement to acquire a more detailed understanding of how innovative and flexible solutions can be incorporated into food SCs in order to feed the world (Mahroof et al., 2021; Mehmood et al., 2021). Other recent research in food SCs shows that important learning can be gained from problematical projects when severe challenges impede the smooth development of CE-driven sustainability practices (Sharma et al., 2019). Methodological frameworks for CE enhancement will be introduced later in the book. The identification of circular food waste flows can maximise the sustainability of food SCs (Batista et al., 2021).

Chapter 5: Business Innovation and Change for Circular Economy

It is very important that practitioners in the CE are able to implement robust business models. They will need to take a much wider perspective in planning and implementing their business activities. Scoping endeavours in the CE will be a difficult but necessary ambition. Putting a partial plan in place for single aspects of a CE project could have serious negative repercussions. Executives in these areas will need a concise vision of the whole system. This issue, in itself, may need a radical change in staff competences and capabilities as firms struggle to envision the bigger, more complex business relationships that will emanate from their new working environments. SC management will move from largely binary contracts towards multi-stakeholder negotiations. The control that many organisations had over the SC process may seem to disappear as decision-making becomes much more complex. Plans that were being made for the immediate future must now be made for the longer term. SC management's financial negotiations will dramatically change in the CE. Presently, companies and suppliers have quite a clear idea of what their contract is. Many supplier contracts are for several years, a significant number are rolling contracts. There is a certainty within the transaction and process, potentially a complacent attitude. A fee is agreed upon by both parties to provide services at a certain price that can be renegotiated at a pre-defined date.

In today's business environment, there is not even certainty about the 'currency' that will be used in negotiations. There is every probability that these contracts will move from being purely financial, to where the 'deal' is a combination of finance and corporate social responsibility (CSR) benefits from these alliances. This will be the most basic element of the negotiations in these new, turbulent business environments. Organisations might want to sign contracts with you because you are greener than your competitors. You may not even become part of a particular CE because you do not have the requisite CSR credentials. Your firm may not be able to attract graduates with the appropriate skills and competences because your record on carbon emissions has been poor for several years. No company wants to be viewed as a weak link in what is otherwise seen as a relatively virtuous circle. If firms do not currently have the appropriate capabilities in-house, they will have to set up a training regime to ensure they reach a level of competence sufficient for the new environment. This environment will probably require a different blend of staff to achieve agreed business objectives.

The organisational reality of the CE challenge requires innovation and change on a large scale to drive and implement new systems and processes and to create a new mindset of circularity across SCs, in integrated regulation and government systems and the end users themselves. The vision to change and the drivers to do so have many origins, and organisational leaders are required to interpret and map these phenomena into a coherent strategy. This strategy requires stakeholder engagement at all levels of the company, externally in terms of customer groups and across the SC. This chapter begins to illustrate the full nature of the organisational challenge, the nature of change, the models of planned change, and the leadership role in this setting. Technology and adaptation are at the heart of CE business model innovation, and some of the issues of implementing tech-driven change are explored in the chapter. Excellent case studies of Ricoh and Adidas are included to illustrate some of these points.

It is important that we put in place a coherent set of systems and frameworks to facilitate the integration of circular business models and circular SC management in a way that promotes the growth of sustainable, flexible, and collaborative practices (Bai et al., 2019; Geisdoerfer et al., 2018; Ripanti & Tjahjono, 2019; Tassinari, 2020). However, a comprehensive, integrated view of circular supply chain management (CSCM) is still absent in the extant literature. This prevents a clear distinction when compared to other sustainable SC concepts and may be a hindrance to the further development of this field of study (Farooque et al., 2019). However, several authors have seen the importance of undertaking comparative studies in this area, especially with linear and circular SCs in the construction and electronics industries. It is posited that an integration of CE principles within green and sustainable SC management can provide real advantages from an environmental perspective (Bressanelli et al., 2021; Nasir et al., 2017).

The dynamic of SCs within the CE will be sufficiently different to make them problematic for a significant number of organisations. The CE is likely to open up new business markets for many of these companies. Markets are generally socially constructed arenas where repeated exchanges occur between buyers and sellers under a set of formal and informal rules (conventions) governing relations among competitors, suppliers, and customers. These arenas operate according to local understandings and rules that guide interaction, facilitate trade, define what products are produced, indeed constitute the products themselves, and provide stability for buyers, sellers, and producers. However, with governments signing up to ambitious targets in areas such as carbon reduction across the globe it is more than likely that this stability will disappear. Marketplaces are also dependent on governments, laws, and cultural understandings supporting marketing activity. If we add ethical and ecological aims and goals to this list the future is certain to be more complex and uncertain in SC and CE transactions.

With regard to the CE, it is important that firms have a much better grasp of pricing policy in complex CE contracts. Looking further ahead, organisations will need a much broader and deeper insight into the vagaries of national and international trading regulations which will be further complicated by climate change targets. Global treaties to govern the flow of capital, trade, and more recently and into the future global warming and carbon emissions have historically been difficult to validate.

Chapter 6: A Review and Research Agenda for the Circular Economy

Moving to a CE at a time of increased global ecological awareness may require a change in the ethical and moral standards of existing and future staff. This may manifest itself in different ways in different organisations and circumstances. This may include a different sense of personal responsibility, possibly deriving from one's own beliefs; a sense of official responsibility, including CSR, acting in the interest of one's employees, customers, and shareholders; standards stemming from personal loyalties, including organisational loyalties; technical morality dictated by standards set by one's professional enterprise; and legal responsibility to abide by the law, court decisions, and administrative orders (adapted from Steiner, 1975). This list of standards does not go anywhere near far enough to meet the ethical and moral standards required by employees and companies to meet the requirements of business and ecological change in the CE into the 2030s.

It must be stated that this is not an academic discipline as such. This is a major industrial, business, and management initiative with global consequences. However, there is no doubt that the academic community can play an important role in its effective development. New intelligence will need to be rapidly acquired as firms need to gain an advantage over their rivals. In such business environments, effective routines are those that are highly adaptive to changing circumstances, giving the firm the opportunity to move quickly to a more optimum competitive position. It has become clear during our preparation for this book that radical change is required regarding the research agenda for the CE. One of the main positive reasons for this particular book was to clarify the scope and relationships within the future CE. How and why are the goals of the CE being set? Are these goals underpinned by ethical and ecological standards? Who are the main drivers of the CE? Is this a push or pull business scenario? There has been a significant amount of purposeful activity in these research areas in the last few years. There is potential for positive collaboration across many academic disciplines as well as with practitioners in these fields.

Chapter 1

The Origins of the Circular Economy

1.1. Introduction

There is an implicit understanding that the circular economy (CE) will help firms, supply chains, and countries meet global warming, carbon emissions, and sustainability targets well into the future. We are not the first generation to identify a pressing need for change as a precursor to 'saving the planet'. It is imperative that we realign our priorities; carefully plan all human endeavours to anticipate their short and long-term consequences for the planet; bring a genuine end to waste; bring about a significant retrenchment in our levels of consumption; increase recycling, environmental restoration, and repair; ensure conservation through changes in social and economic patterns of development; and control of natural surroundings, primary agricultural land, open spaces, etc.; and protection and enhancement of environmental quality. This list seems to resemble a set of demands that might have emanated from COP-26.

Fligstein and McAdam (2014) undertook some important research into business structures and fields to give an insight into how CE may develop. It was underpinned by social management theory and the political theory of markets which stated that social order is constructed through a process of interactions among stakeholders who are competing for advantageous business positions. They identify the dynamic of how new systems and institutions emerge, remain stable, and are transformed. They also investigated how individuals and groups come to compete with each other in social arenas where something important is at stake. One of the most exciting aspects of planning the CE is to address the potential methodological impasse that exists in CE design. The authors believe that the future design of CE may need to be radically changed as the moral compass for choosing such systems is reset. This should be a positive, not negative, outcome from the future design of the CE. The move to a CE is undoubtedly a major sociological change.

The dynamic of supply chains within the CE will be sufficiently different to make them problematic for a significant number of organisations. CE is likely to open up new business markets for many of these companies. Markets are generally socially constructed arenas where repeated exchanges occur between buyers and sellers under a set of formal and informal rules (conventions) governing relations

Sustainable Development Through Global Circular Economy Practices, 9–35
Copyright © 2024 by Stuart Maguire and Ian Robson
Published under exclusive licence by Emerald Publishing Limited
doi:10.1108/978-1-83753-590-320231001

among competitors, suppliers, and customers. These arenas operate according to local understandings and rules that guide interaction, facilitate trade, define what products are produced, indeed constitute the products themselves, and provide stability for buyers, sellers, and producers. However, with governments across the globe signing up to ambitious targets in areas such as carbon reduction, it is more than likely that this stability will disappear. Marketplaces are also dependent on governments, laws, and cultural understandings supporting marketing activity. If we add ethical and ecological aims and goals to this list, the future is certain to be more complex and uncertain in supply chain and CE transactions.

1.2. Circularity and Nonlinearity – Moving from a Linear to a CE

The economy is key to fighting climate change. That is why we must continue the shift from a linear to a CE to make sure society progresses in a way that is environmentally friendly. The earth's resources are finite so it is crucial that citizens, governments, and organisations work together to use them more responsibly. We need a new model that provides an alternative to the traditional linear economy. We are currently concentrating on a traditional model where raw materials are collected and transformed into products that consumers use until they as waste, usually with no concern for their ecological footprint or environmental consequences (Santander.com).

The key difference between a linear and a CE is that a linear economy focusses on profitability, irrespective of the product life cycle (PLC), whereas the CE targets sustainability. With CE design, production, and consumption are based around sustainability and production must keep energy consumption to a minimum, using renewable sources and non-polluting raw materials where possible. Ideally, products must not have a limited shelf life and should be built so they can be repaired or recycled (Santander.com). A CE (also referred to as circularity) is a framework of production and consumption which involves sharing, leasing, reusing, repairing, refurbishing, and recycling existing materials and products for as long as possible.

It is important that we understand how to transform the current linear and degenerative socio-economic systems into ones that are circular and regenerative. We must know how these systems grow and develop – what are the limits to their robustness and can these limits change by moving to a CE? The circularity rate has been defined by Eurostat and there may be a move towards a maximum circularity rate. High circularity rates will most likely result in higher export rates which in turn seem to lead to brittle networks. This means that 100% circularity rates seem unlikely, even unwanted, for improved sustainability (Zisopoulus et al., 2022).

What are the advantages of measuring the circularity of firms (research.aimultiple.com 21/12/22):

It enables the determining of a CE *strategy*: You may identify present pain points in your organisation's resource and waste management by measuring the circularity of your business and then design plans to address these issues. Remember that CE is typically associated with efficiency since it strives to better allocate resources via the use of innovation and technology. As a result, calculating the CE level can help improve your operating efficiency.

It promotes proactive business practices: 67% of firms consider that revealing their CE advancements will attract customers, investors, and suppliers. The easiest strategy to communicate these accomplishments is to use measures which are understood and to compare regular reports to indicate progress.

Help to achieve certificates: There are universal certificates, such as the cradle-to-cradle (C2C) certificate that certify a firm's high CE requirements. Companies must measure the circularity of their business and enhance areas of necessity based on these results in order to earn such certificates.

It measures the legal cost of your business practices: Countries quickly changed their legislation after the Paris Agreement[1] to penalise corporations with non-sustainable business practices. Extended producer obligations and plastic taxes can be seen under this umbrella and soon such regulations will be widespread – measuring CE will be a matter of compliance.

1.2.1. Measuring Circularity

Over the next few decades, a high proportion of organisations across the world will need to benchmark their environmental and sustainability activities against standards set by international committees and national governments. This is already happening. In some instances, these activities have been raised to moral principles of behaviour. These firms will be constantly focussed on these standards and comparisons, often benchmarking against rivals working in the same sector. What is required is a general set of accepted measurements to try and identify the environmental progress of companies striving to improve their sustainability credentials. The following metrics and table provide a framework that enables organisations to go a significant way to addressing this goal (adapted from The Ten Metrics for Successful Corporate Circularity – research.aimultiple. com 21/12/22). Knowledge of this list may prove prescient for many firms and will help them to be proactive as they attempt to meet the various environmental challenges. It also helps to set up the following Case Study on the Worldwide Glass Industry. It highlights the percentage of recyclability of a product, where glass excels, and where for many decades, milk and soft drink bottles were recycled. There are strong signs that consumers are once again willing to use glass containers more extensively because of their recyclable properties.

---

[1]The Paris Agreement or the Paris Climate Accords is an international treaty on climate change. Adopted in 2015, the agreement covers climate change mitigation, adaptation and finance. The Paris Agreement was negotiated by 196 parties at the 2015 United Nations Climate Change Conference near Paris. As of September 2022, 194 members of the United Nations Framework Convention on Climate Change (UNFCCC) are parties to the agreement. Of the four UNFCCC member states which have not ratified the agreement, the only major abstainer is Iran. The United States withdrew from the agreement in 2020 but re-joined in 2021.

The Ten Metrics for Successful Corporate Circularity Strategy

Metric	Description	Algorithm
Resource productivity (RP)	Effective use of natural, finite resources such as copper ore	RP = Total sales in \$, £, etc./mass of virgin material inflow. The higher the ratio the more circular the resource usage
Percentage of non-virgin (renewed) material used	Use of renewed/recycled raw materials	Percentage of non-virgin material inflow for production = mass of renewed raw materials/mass of total raw materials × 100. Increasingly high sustainable resources indicate high circularity
Percentage of recyclability of product	Use of recycling systems to improve circularity	Number of recycled, reused, repaired or repurposed products
Percentage of circular water consumption	Reducing water content and increasing recyclable water usage in industry. Rescuing production and consumption, particularly in consumer markets	All water should be recycled and reused to the point of irretrievable toxicity as per environmental standards like GRI 306
Percentage of circular water discharge	Industry and government ought to have water recycling capability and technology. Consumers require a mindset change	As above though both push and pull factors will enable this to take place. Legislation, regulation are required as well as internal CE drivers to drastically improve water recycling
Percentage of renewable energy consumption (REC)	Use of renewable energy throughout the supply chain and in end-use product design	Target net zero carbon emissions. REC% of REC = annual REC/total energy consumption × 100
Estimated environmental savings of rentals	Mindset shifts towards 'pay as you use' approach	Increased usage of products and services reduces carbon footprint and capital investment. Allows for investment in CE technology for example
Repairability of a product	Shift in timescale for obsolescence in products. Provision in design for easy repair and repair services	Increased length of use in the market. For example, H & M case in Chapter 3 and the Adidas case in Chapter 5
Warranty period	The increased warranty comes with increased usage and increased circularity	This is an implicit statistic that provides information about a firm's CE level
Progress towards goals	Circularity auditing and reporting. Tracking CE strategy success through Industry 4.0 (I4.0) digitisation	

Source: Adapted from Dilmegani (2023).

1.2.2. Case Study – The Worldwide Glass Industry

One of the authors of this book (Stuart Maguire) used to work in the glass-making sector (Britglass.org.uk). Glass is one of the most sustainable materials on earth – it is 100% recyclable and can be remelted endlessly without ever reducing its quality. In fact, it's the perfect CE material, and making new glass from recycled glass reduces CO_2 emissions and energy use. British Glass is working with firms to increase recycling at every point in the life cycle of glass products. Closing the loop on glass recycling reduces CO_2 emissions, saves energy, and drives down costs – so it benefits all stakeholders, manufacturers, brands, retailers, consumers, waste processors, and ultimately, the planet. In fact, increasing the recycled content of glass packaging is a key part of the UK's Glass industry decarbonisation action plan.

However, it is a complicated and complex journey from shop shelves to homes and then, via waste processing, back to a glass furnace. Achieving meaningful change will require coordinated, evidence-based interventions. British Glass has set up their free 'Close the Loop' network – an informal group of organisations and professionals from across the glass packaging life cycle who want to improve the UK's glass recycling rate. Joining the group means you will be kept in the loop with:

- Email updates on glass sustainability news, data, and developments.
- Opportunities to discuss British Glass policy positions on packaging recycling and sustainability.
- Ways to shape the future sustainability agenda and practices for glass packaging.
- Invitations to take part in round tables and working groups with glass manufacturers, waste processors, and other key stakeholders (when appropriate).
- Access to British Glass packaging expertise.
- This initiative could act as a useful benchmark for other sectors where recycling is a key priority.
- Waste glass that has been processed and ready for recycling is called cullet and demand for good quality cullet is always high. Glass manufacturers commonly use it to manufacture new bottles, jars, windows, and fibreglass, as well as tiny glass beads for industrial uses. Increasing the use of cullet in glass-making is a priority in the British Glass–Net Zero Strategy.
- Every tonne of glass remelted saves 246 kilogrammes of carbon dioxide emissions as well as decreasing the energy needed to make glass and reducing reliance on virgin raw materials. Even when cullet is too poor for remelt (i.e. it contains too high a level of certain non-glass materials), it can still be used for a range of secondary applications, such as aggregate, an additive in building materials (including eco-cements and concretes), water filtration and blast cleaning.
- This is open-loop recycling (or down-cycling).

As remelting back to glass (closed-loop recycling) is usually the best environmental option, British Glass advocates, in line with CE principles, that remelt uses should be prioritised and glass maintained at its highest material value for as long as possible. The UK glass sector has an excellent recycling record of 76%, one of the highest rates of any packaging material. British Glass has set out an ambitious target to achieve a 90% collection rate by 2030.

Glass is infinitely recyclable, yet at the moment around half of household glass packaging is not remelted; much is recycled as aggregate or is lost to landfill or incineration. Even though window glass can be recycled indefinitely, most glazing refurbishment and demolition glass waste currently ends up as aggregate, if indeed it avoids landfill. Ideally, more of this would be remelted, making new glass, saving energy, and reducing CO_2 emissions. There is certainly potential for knowledge transfer from the Glass Industry to other enlightened sectors.

This research presented an in-depth case study. It detailed the history, experiences, and wider practitioner and policy lessons from a CE business model over a 30-year period, highlighting the successes, difficulties, and conflicts of adopting a CE model (*Ricoh General Principles on the Environment*). The case was based on interviews, key documents, and customer insight. The findings demonstrated how sustained CE business practices can deliver significant new revenues, RP, and business continuity benefits, but at the same time require practitioners and managers to develop competencies and capabilities, such as balancing linear and circular systems to address complex and highly dynamic factors, including rapid technological shifts and market volatility (Hopkinson et al., 2018). The CE concept works on the principle of replacing the open-loop setup, comprising a linear pattern of production and consumption, with a closed-loop circular system. The value of products, materials, and services is maintained with their active use as long as possible via the recycle, reduce, and reuse principle (Goyal et al., 2016; Lieder & Rashid, 2016; Merli et al., 2018).

CE has recently been put forward as an economic model that can replace the previous 'linear' model. In some quarters, it is claimed it can achieve this while addressing issues of environmental deterioration, social equity, and long-term economic growth and while having the ability to act as a tool for sustainable development. Despite the individual prominence of sustainable development and CE in the academic and wider literature, the exact relationship between the two concepts has neither been thoroughly defined or explored. This has resulted in several inconsistencies occurring across the literature as regards how CE can serve as a tool for sustainable development and as regards incomplete understanding of how its long-term effects differ from those of the 'linear economy'. There appear to be numerous challenges concerning conceptual definition, economic growth, and implementation that inhibit the use of CE as a tool for sustainable development (Millar & McLaughlin, 2019).

Generally, linear systems come to an end because of rising consumption, production, and economic growth, all of which make the system run out of resources and result in economic crises and often environmental pollution. Any signs of this downward spiral must be closely monitored. As an example, utilising a 'rolling-window' approach in the Netherlands, carbon emissions were compared alongside the CE over 20 years. The findings showed that, due to a variety of causes, the CE had a negative influence on carbon emissions in certain sub-samples. However, carbon emissions have improved CE's ability to address environmental challenges. Transitioning to the CE framework requires comprehensive development of models for controlling emissions (Khan et al., 2022). There is certainly a need for improved life-cycle thinking for sustainable consumption and production towards a CE. Sustainability is the most important global initiative in the 21st century. Sustainable development goals (SDGs) deal with responsible consumption and production and could play a key factor in increased sustainability. This could bring an end to the linear economy and a closure of unsustainable end-of-pipe waste treatment. There is a need for life-cycle-based tools such as life-cycle assessment and costing to meet the requirements of SDG 12 (ensure sustainable consumption and production patterns) and thus provide responsible production and consumption (Gheewala, 2020).

Even though the undercurrents of CE date back more than 50 years (i.e. Boulding, 1966), the concept has gained potency due to the urgency of mitigating climate change (Korkhonen et al., 2018). The principles of CE emphasise closed-loop material flows by considering product reuse, remanufacturing, reprocessing and recycling. Generally, industrial transformations such as the envisaged transformation towards CE, are about understanding the logic and mechanisms of radical systemic changes. Assuming that CE is a transformative mechanism, it is impossible to talk about the dynamic and evolving aspects of change without taking a systems perspective. It is important to consider CE from an evolutionary perspective in the context of industrial transformation, and it needs to be considered in light of further conceptual and theoretical improvements. The concepts of circular tension and systemic complementarities can be applied to various scopes to identify unpredictable dependencies and tensions within and between the dominant linear and emerging circular economic systems (Chizaryfard et al., 2020).

Linear to circular business models at the company-level introduction of CE is still poorly understood and leave firms without guidelines about changing culture and working practices. Improved capabilities in this area are urgently needed and ten examples have been identified in the textile and clothing industry:

(1) Control positions in the supply chain.
(2) Product orientation.
(3) Prevailing product portfolio.
(4) Identification of the correct customer incentives and benefits.
(5) Prediction of regulatory and technological development.
(6) Optimum management of design trade-offs.
(7) The ability to reshape the current fragmented, fast fashion-oriented supply chain.
(8) Breaking away from a linear buy-and-that's-it culture.
(9) The formation of novel business ecosystems and alignment within them.
(10) Multi-disciplinary cooperation (Salmi & Kaipia, 2022).

There is a certain level of agreement among researchers in this area that the CE needs further investigation in more diverse, unstructured contexts. The informal economy and the CE are gaining traction, especially in Global South countries. The Global South is made up of Africa, Latin America and the Caribbean, the Pacific Islands, and Asia (excluding Israel, Japan, and South Korea). These are countries where social factors, such as high inequality, tend to collide with environmental factors, such as high natural bio-diversity. It is possible that their significant informal economies could hinder, or at least complicate, their transition to a CE (Dewick et al., 2022). Further research on CE has focussed on communication campaigns, and there is certainly a need for behavioural change in the search for an effective move towards CE. Efficient communications campaigns are urgently needed to move from linear to circular models of working (Romero-Luis et al., 2022).

Packaging production and consumption waste is a significant share of urban solid waste generation (20% by volume in Europe and the USA). This has had wide-ranging negative impacts on interconnected Earth systems. From linear to circular, compostable cassava starch-based material has far better societal and environmental outcomes than petroleum-based packaging. Grow-make-use-restore redefines the significance of waste, products, services, markets, natural capital, and growth. The previous way of addressing greenhouse gas (GHG) emissions from petroleum-based packaging can move effectively to a promising climate change mitigation strategy (Garcia-Casarejos et al., 2018). Maximising the plastic recycling rate is a reasonably easy goal for enhancing material circularity. However, the conventional mechanical recycling method requires improvement because chemical additive release and contamination rates act as obstacles to achieving high-quality plastics for future reuse and should be mitigated through chemical recycling and additive extraction. There is a clear requirement for a safer closed-loop plastic infrastructure to handle additives in a strategic way to support sustainable materials management efforts and transform the USA's plastic economy from linear to circular (Chea et al., 2023).

The adverse impacts of electronic-waste (e-waste) disproportionately affect low-income communities and marginalised ecosystems in countries with economies in transition (Singh & Ogunseitan, 2022). However, a corporate social responsibility (CSR) initiative on solid waste has the potential in an emerging economy to transform a linear flow into a circular one. That being said, funding needs to be put in place before these aims can be achieved (Thongplew et al., 2022). Further research into designing effective waste management practices in developing economies has revealed how acute the nature of the waste problem actually is. Given there are 9 billion tons of waste annually, small island developing states (SIDS), such as Suriname, on the northeastern coast of South America, lack a structured and formal waste management system. People, especially in villages, have positive attitudes towards the environment but they still need appropriate schemes to be put in place. Having the general public on side is a positive basis from which to face future sustainability projects (Oke et al., 2022).

This chapter has presented an in-depth case study detailing the history, experiences, and wider practitioner and policy lessons from a CE business model over 30 years, and highlighted the successes, difficulties, and conflicts of adopting CE (Ricoh General Principles on the Environment). The case was based on interviews, key documents, and customer insight. The findings demonstrated how sustained

CE business practices can deliver significant new revenues, RP, and business continuity benefits, but also require practitioners and managers to develop competencies and capabilities, such as balancing linear and circular systems to address complex and highly dynamic factors, including rapid technological shifts and market volatility (Hopkinson et al., 2018). It is also possible that waste from bio-refineries could facilitate the transition from a fossil-based linear economy to a sustainable circular bio-economy. This could be achieved by integrating the composition of food waste into the techno-economic analysis of waste bio-refineries for bio-diesel production (Li, 2022).

Some academics have focussed on the laudable aim of using I4.0 as a model for a CE and thus for cleaner production. The onset of I4.0 is progressing extremely quickly and offers a productive output in terms of CE and cleaner production to attain ethical business by achieving accuracy, precision, and efficiency. Until quite recently, manufacturing had been slow to implement I4.0. However, once introduced it should pave the way towards data-driven, intelligent, networked, and resilient manufacturing systems. I4.0 can lead to smart manufacturing to gain self-adaptability, reliability, and flexibility with high-quality and low-cost output using mixed-integer linear programming (MILP). There may be a trade-off between environmental consumption and machine processing which results in ethical business by deploying sensors to capture real-time information/intelligence to establish the I4.0 facility. This is more likely to guarantee the optimised manufacturing of customised, high-end products at lower production costs with minimal/low energy consumption (Rajput & Singh, 2020).

It is certainly very important to identify and measure the effect of the CE on a firm's value chain and overall profitability. Uncertainties with CE design over multiple life cycles and a complex interconnectedness with diverse stakeholders make CE effects difficult to predict. This makes any new knowledge on the implementation of circular economies extremely useful. By analysing the implications of circular solutions for a firm's value chain processes through utilising a literature review and adopting Porter's value chain framework, seven prominent topics were identified. They relate to stakeholder collaboration; consumers' perceptions; I4.0; performance measurement; multiple life-cycle thinking; specific CE skills; and a supportive senior management and corporate culture. Further analysis shows that the linear structure of Porter's framework is not sufficient to reflect circular business practices which require changes that move towards a circular and interrelated view. A circular value chain model is proposed (Eisenreich et al., 2022).

1.3. Conventional Waste Management Driven by Collection and Disposal Costs

Conventional waste management involves several actions: storage in a temporary repository; classification according to the European Waste Code; update and registration according to law; and removal from the plant through authorised transport for ordinary operations of recovery or disposal (Sogin.it). Conventional waste means non-porous, non-asbestos waste that can be cleaned, removed from the work area, and disposed of. The four main types of waste are industrial waste, hazardous waste, municipal solid waste (MSW), and agricultural waste. It is generally accepted that there are four types of waste management: landfill, waste compaction, incineration, and composting (in all its forms). The Ministry of Environmental Protection has also isolated five stages of waste management which are viewed as a hierarchy: reduce, reuse, recycle, recover, and landfill(ing). The seven wastes of lean production are also relevant to sustainability and CE: overproduction, inventory, defects, motion, over-processing; waiting, and transportation. Waste can also arrive in the form of not utilising resources efficiently, for instance, inefficient use of electricity, gas, and water can result in unnecessary expenditure and can have a detrimental effect on the environment.

Recycling rates of plastic waste in 2021 were approximately 32.5% in the European Union (EU). It is important to find a better alternative to plastic which neither degrades land, water or air nor affects living organisms. Can CE lead to sustainable disposal approaches such as pyrolysis, plasma gasification, photo-catalytic degradation and the production of value-added products from polymer waste? These options need to be explored in more detail (Chawla et al., 2022). Deposit-refund schemes are a topical research area in the sustainability domain. It is anticipated that by the end of 2035, a minimum of 65% of glass packaging waste must be prepared for reuse and/or recycled within the EU Member States. Thus, appropriate policies and solutions, such as deposit-refund schemes, should be adopted to meet these targets. Recent findings show that the different waste management systems currently available affect neither the amount of glass packaging consumption nor glass packaging recycling or recovery (Agnusdei et al., 2022).

The basic premises of CE appear to be closing and slowing loops. Closing loops refer to postconsumer waste recycling while slowing is about retention of product value through maintenance, repair and refurbishment, and remanufacturing. Narrowing loops is about efficiency improvements. This is a notion that is already commonplace in the linear economy. Closing loops is about creating value from resources that have formerly been considered as 'wasted'. Exploiting the residual value of such resources is about the collection and sourcing of otherwise waste or unexploited materials or resources in order to turn these into new forms of value.

Business models that contributed to closing loops appeared to be quite commonplace. Industrial symbiosis models seemed to be growing in popularity six years ago. Multiple value models, where sequential cash flows can be generated from waste in biological cycles (McDonough & Braungart, 2002), such as in the oft-cited mushroom growing from coffee waste example, are predominantly conducted by innovative start-ups, given that large-cap companies seem to fail to incorporate such novel ways of creating value (Pauli, 2009). Slowing loops is about retaining the product value as long as possible. Examples of business models include product-service system models, the classic long-life model, sufficiency-driven business models, and business models that extend the product value through remanufacturing (Bocken et al., 2016). Even though remanufacturing as a strategy could significantly mitigate energy use and emissions while contributing to job creation and economic growth, innovation in this field is still lagging behind. It has been suggested that remanufacturing as a sustainability strategy is still undervalued in the industrial landscape (Norton et al., 2015). There appears to be a stark misalignment between the potential slowing loop business models and actual business practice (Bocken et al., 2017).

Fashion brands need to cope with multiple challenges in the process of developing circular business models within their organisations including the diverging perspectives of value and unclear success criteria, poor alignment with existing strategy, limited internal skills and competences, and limited consumer interest (Pederson et al., 2018). Resource constraints and product end-of-life issues have become relevant topics for governments and businesses; both are regarded as an environmental liability and economic opportunity (Lewandowski, 2016). The problems of material waste and resource efficiency are closely linked to the concept of CE, which opposes a linear economy and aims to achieve the decoupling of economic growth from natural resource depletion and environmental degradation through activities that reduce reuse and recycle materials in production distribution and consumption processes (Cooper, 1999; Murray et al., 2015).

The core of CE is the circular (closed) flow of materials and the use of raw materials and energy through multiple phases (Yuan et al., 2006). Current trends, such as increasing consumption, new generations of consumers, urbanisation and employment, tightening legislation and technological leaps, accelerate the transition to CE (Antikainen & Valkokari, 2016). The transition towards CE requires changes throughout many components of an economy and society, from value chains, product design, new business models, and new approaches of turning waste into a resource, to new modes of consumer behaviour, financing methods, and legislation (European Commission, 2014).

To move towards circularity there is an argument that brands must integrate these strategies across supply chains rather than limiting them to the waste stage. The fashion industry is one of the most wasteful consumer industries in the world. Through the advent of fast fashion and trendy, low-cost clothing produced by global fashion brands, clothes have evolved from a durable good to a daily purchase. In recent years, the concept of CE, a framework for a more efficient, closed-loop economy, has emerged as a key way forward in the transition to a more sustainable and less wasteful fashion industry. For this industry to move towards circularity, it is argued that brands must integrate these strategies across supply chains rather than limiting them to the waste stage. It is important we explore in more detail the gaps between CE principles and practice, identifying challenges inherent in fashion brand approaches (Brydges, 2021). This could be the aforementioned closing of the loop.

The management of waste from electrical and electronic equipment (WEEE) has been a novel issue for both practitioners and the academic community. Within a circularity strategy or system, the reconditioning or refurbishment of smartphones is a major part of WEEE strategies. We need to know what determines the green purchase intentions of a refurbished smartphone. This research used discriminant analysis and found that psychological factors, such as perceived green value and environmental knowledge, can lead to the most powerful predictions of green purchase intentions for refurbished smartphones. Social and emotional intentions, that is, collectivism, subjective norms, and environmental concerns, do not appear to influence these intentions (Bigliardi et al., 2022). The bio-refinery based on producing bio-ethanol from waste textiles is economically feasible. This will make it a key cornerstone of the cleaner waste textile movement towards the CE (Farahmandpour et al., 2022).

The building sector has been a rich vein of research in the area of the circular and sharing economy and several strategies in the construction sector have been investigated. A sizeable number of these strategy initiatives remain unexploited even though they have significant potential for climate change mitigation. Substantial reductions in greenhouse-gas (GHG) emissions are highlighted for utilising waste wood in bio-concrete, sharing offices, urban farming, and recycling building facades. Recovery of construction and demolition waste (C&DW) is shown to be economically possible and environmentally beneficial. Urban mining could move beyond concrete and metals with 350 components identified as being economically possible and environmentally beneficial, with more beyond concrete and metal components. Accurate modelling of material and building stocks is required to enable effective planning. Robust methodologies such as life-cycle assessment are necessary to capture the full potential benefits and trade-offs (Harris et al., 2023).

Among all the considerable research on sustainability and CE, there has been a quest to pinpoint benchmarks and identifiers to measure progress. A new circularity indicator for treatment plants (CITP) has been proposed that combines two main components – material recovery efficiency and quantifiable energy recovery. It has been stated that the best Municipal Social Waste (MSW) treatment alternatives must contemplate the intensive recovery of recyclable materials and the energy use of combustible rejects (Rondon et al., 2020). The biological processing of MSW followed by bio-gas and bio-methane generation is one of the innumerable sustainable energy source choices. In the handling of MSW, biological treatment has some attractive benefits such as reduced volume in waste material, adjustment of waste, economic aspects, obliteration of micro-organisms in waste materials, and creation of bio-gas for energy use. In the anaerobic process, the utilisable product is energy recovery (Saravanan et al., 2022).

Valorisation of fruit and vegetable wastes (FVW) is challenging owing to logistic-related problems and their perishable nature and heterogeneity. Food waste valorisation is the conversion of food waste or by-products into higher-value products that give back to the food supply chain. This contributes to the CE approach where useful material, once seen as waste, is recycled into the supply chain to create new products. FVW constitutes an important potential source for valuable natural products and chemicals and it is anticipated that their management can be undertaken following different processing routines. However, in 2020, the best solution may be to find an adequate balance between conventional waste management methods and several emerging valorisation technologies. At present, both conventional and emerging technologies must be considered so that impacts on both food safety and the environment can be minimised, while at the same time saving natural resources. The most efficient emergent processing technologies must be promoted in the long term to the detriment of conventional ones used today. Future integral valorisation of FVW is likely to comprise two stages – direct processing of FVW into value-added products followed by processing of the residual streams, by-products, and left over matter by means of conventional waste management technologies (Esparza et al., 2020).

The oil and gas sector has been a key focus of research into sustainability and CE. Recent research has adopted conceptual modelling of the re-refining process. A CE model is proposed for the oil and gas industry by incorporating re-refining based on an integrated solvent extraction and the hydro-treatment unit has been introduced as a media to revalorise the waste lubricating oil (WLO) generated from crude oil. This CE model achieves 22.67% lower overall annualised cost (OAC) and thus demonstrates financial viability (Lau et al., 2022). Further research focusses on management approaches to maximise the sustainable value of waste from the oil and gas industry. The conversion of waste into economic value-added products, which reduce environmental impacts and support sustainability within the oil and gas industry, is of paramount importance. This includes solid waste (oil sludge), flue gases (CO_2 & SO_2), and liquids (produced water). An important aspect of this process is to ensure that discussions take place with key stakeholders to establish the environmental and economic effectiveness of resource recovery from oil and gas waste on a large scale (Shahbaz et al., 2023).

1.4. Reconciling Ecological Systems and Economic Growth

Ecological economics is a field of study initiated in the 1980s from the conjunction of human ecology and environmental and resource economics. It is a transdisciplinary field of study whose fundamental premise is that the economic system is embedded within a social system, which is in turn embedded within an ecological system – the bio-sphere (*Journal of Cleaner Production*, 2017). The ecological sustainability of the economy is analysed in terms of the energy and material throughput. Thus, the economy is viewed as a thermodynamically open system (www.sciencedirect.com).

Ecological economics is not trying to be a sub-discipline of economics or ecology, but it is, rather, a bridge across not only ecology and economics but also psychology, anthropology, archaeology, and history. This interdisciplinary approach is what is necessary to get a more integrated picture of how humans have interacted with their environment in the past and how they might interact in the future. It is an attempt to observe humans embedded in their ecological life-support system as opposed to separate from the environment. It also includes some design elements in the sense of how we design a sustainable future. It is not just an analysis of the past, it applies that analysis to formulate something new and improved. However, environmental economics is a sub-discipline of economics, and as such it applying standard economic thinking to the environment. Mainstream economics focusses mainly on markets whereas ecological economics tries to study everything outside the market as well as everything inside the market and bring the two together (Costanza, 2010 Yale Insights, Management in Practice).

An optimum methodology for the measurement of performance related to the ecological and ethical transition is still missing from the sustainability armoury. This methodology or framework can have true relevance in several key areas:

(A) With the integration of sustainability, CE and industrial symbiosis paradigms.
(B) The possibility it can be applied at different levels of application, that is, firm-level, the supply chain, or the district.
(C) Adaptability to firms with different characteristics (firm size and awareness), thanks to the development of two different (full and core) scalable systems.

The framework has been tested in four manufacturing firms against its capacity to represent each paradigm, its usefulness, and its ease of use. The utility of the framework should be in its ability to overcome tensions among the three paradigms and encourage firms to consider performance beyond their own boundaries, including supply chain or district, and scalability for different sizes. It should also be beneficial to increase knowledge on ecological and ethical transition (Cagno et al., 2023).

The CE approach promises to reconcile the two goals of ecological systems and economic growth. Even though the notion of circular production systems is at the intersection of different research areas, such as sustainable product design, sustainable supply chains and reverse logistics, knowledge of how these concepts combine to ease or impede firms' transition towards circularity is scarce. To shine a light on these gaps, the authors used multiple case studies from Cradle to Cradle certified companies in the European textile sector. Through the utilisation of qualitative research, the researcher identified a set of factors along the textile value chain – from product design to take-back and reprocessing – that are crucial in expediting or delaying a firm's determination to develop a circular product. The main contribution of this chapter is a dynamic understanding of how certain collaborative supplier–buyer innovation factors (i.e. supply chain position, power balance, and a shared vision) coupled with complex aspects in product design (namely in basic materials, architecture, and functionality), combine to determine the output speed and quantity of circular products to be sold, taken back, and ultimately regenerated (Franco, 2017).

The CE has recently been studied with regard to the co-evolution between science and policy. This seems to reinforce the need to take a systemic perspective with research on CE. It is generally accepted that the CE aims to decouple economic development from natural environmental impacts. Several previous studies have focussed on a single area through qualitative analysis. In most cases, the impact of science-policy interaction has rarely been discussed. However, by using a mixed-method approach utilising big data analytics (BDA), it was found that by two-way feedback and continuous adjustment between science and the policy of CE that progress could be made. In relation to China, there is a focus on a development strategy and policy at a macro level, such as 'ecological civilisation' and 'agricultural circular economy' and hopes for a 'bandwagon effect'. At an international level, the CE seems to focus on implementation at a micro level based on the market and is progressive and coherent (He et al., 2023).

We certainly need to move away from the archaic view of making products with built-in obsolescence to one that changes design and transforms products so that workable relationships can be made between ecological systems and any future economic growth (Genovese et al., 2017). Moving to a CE at a time of increased global ecological awareness may require a change of ethical and moral standards of existing and future staff. This may manifest itself in different ways in different organisations and circumstances and may include: a different sense of personal responsibility, possibly derived from one's own beliefs; a sense of official responsibility including CSR; acting with the interest of one's employees, customers, and shareholders; standards stemming from personal loyalties, including organisational loyalties; technical morality dictated by standards set by one's professional enterprise; legal responsibility to abide by law, court decisions, and administrative orders (adapted from Steiner, 1975). This list of standards does not go anywhere far enough to attain the ethical and moral standards required by employees and companies to meet the requirements of business and ecological change in the CE going into the 2030s.

CE is increasingly being seen as a solution to ecological and socio-economic challenges resulting from increasing consumption of non-renewable resources, waste generation (solid and e-waste), pollution (soil, water, and air), and resource scarcity (Lieder & Rashid, 2016). CE aims at decoupling value creation from waste generation and resource use by substituting the end-of-life notion with restoration and closed-loop PLCs. Greater ecological integrity in fashion should lead to an increase in sustainable clothing. Knowledge of consumer behaviour intentions in this sector has always been crucial. This analysis of 2,694 consumers in Italy revealed some interesting results around environmental concerns, the perceived value of the products, and consumer familiarity with the products. The research found that green consumer behaviour was strongly dependent on the consumers' socio-demographic characteristics. Knowing this could help firms introduce better marketing strategies which would lead to more successful public communication campaigns (Dangelico et al., 2022). Another project explored the customer experience role in influencing satisfaction and reuse decisions. It put forward innovative ecological sanitation systems ideas for urban households (Guyader, 2022). Scientific studies on the decoupling debate have shown that the relationship between economic growth and natural resource consumption is not sufficiently understood to make reliable predictions about whether successful decoupling, that is, funding a dynamic equilibrium in a safe ecological operating space for humanity, will be achieved within an appropriate timescale (Hoffmann, 2022).

1.5. Dematerialisation of the Economy

Dematerialisation is the reduction in the quantity of materials and/or energy needed to produce something useful over time. Dematerialisation attempts to answer the basic underlying question and concern of sustainability – whether humans are taking more from the earth than the earth can safely yield (Malenbaum, 1978). Malenbaum utilised the concept of intensity of use which is defined as the ratio of the amount of materials (or energy) measured in bulk mass divided by gross domestic product (GDP).

Since the first Industrial Revolution we have been living in a linear economy. Our consumer and 'single use' lifestyles have made the planet a take-make-dispose world. This in turn led to a unidirectional world of production – natural resources provide our factory inputs, which are then used to create mass-produced goods to be purchased and, typically, disposed after a single use. This linear economy model of mass production and mass consumption is testing the physical limits of the globe and threatening the stability of our future – it is, therefore, unsustainable.

We have been consuming resources at a rate 50% faster than they can be replaced; by 2030 our demand will require more than 2 planets' worth of natural resources if they are to be met, and by 2050 three planets' worth. In this same time-line, the global middle class will have doubled by 2030 which will drive demand for resource-intensive goods, such as vehicles and other contemporary conveniences that many of us in advanced industrialised countries enjoy today. While many S paradigms revolve around doing more with less, CE is also recuperative. In terms of S, it would be incomplete to say that CE is environmentally friendly. CE is not just about attaining effective business terminologies and emphasising idealistic words like recycling, it can be defined by its focus on maximising what is already in use along all points of a product's life cycle – from sourcing to supply chain to consumption, to the remaining unusable parts for one function and their conversion back into a new source for another purpose. Adopting the CE model requires that firms initiate and develop disruptive technology and business models that are based on longevity, renewability, reuse, repair, upgrade, refurbishment, servitisation, capacity-sharing, and dematerialisation (Esposito Tse Soufani, 2018).

Bernardini and Galli (1993) postulated that the decreasing maximum intensity over time with usage of materials/energy per GDP might be a positive sign of a tangible dematerialising trend, but they eventually conceded that the empirical data at the time were insufficient to draw such conclusions. Dematerialisation fundamentally derives from ongoing increases in technical performance, but it can be counteracted by demand rebound – increases in usage because of increased value (or decreased cost) that also results from increasing technical performance. A key question is to what extent technological performance improvement can offset, and is offsetting, continuously increasing economic consumption. There are indications that there is no dematerialisation occurring, even for cases of information technology with rapid technical progress (Magee & Devezas, 2017).

Many companies, states, regions or cities are currently adopting CE strategies and implementing CE initiatives. The EU has implemented a CE Action Plan that gathers numerous measures along the life cycle of products from eco-design to waste management. Beyond the current popularity of CE, the meaning and destination of this transition often remains vague. Will these projects towards circularity be enough to achieve a truly sustainable economy operating within planetary boundaries? How can individual 'actors' such as a company be sure they are moving in the right direction? (The Laboratory for Applied Circular Economy (LACE) is an interdisciplinary research project from the National Research Programme: 'Sustainable Economy' NRP 73). CE is defined as an economy directed towards human well-being, while operating within clear physical and environmental limits. Given an optimal use of the earth's limited resources, three guiding principles are espoused:

(i) *The use of resources should aim at minimising entropy production.* The idea of CE is often seen as allowing materials to be cycled indefinitely, for instance, the plastic of a bottle being recycled and used in another product. Yet, because of inevitable loss and degradation processes, material cycles cannot be fully cycled, and virgin materials need to be added in the manufacturing process. As every step in a PLC produces entropy, the design of products, and end-of-life strategies should be guided with the aim of reducing it and keeping resources at the lowest state of entropy as long as possible.

(ii) *Durability and Longevity are key to preserve material value.* Since material cycles cannot be fully cycled, the faster a product needs to be replaced the more material is lost in providing the same service. Hence, an important principle of CE is to slow cycles, which means, for instance, to extend the lifespan of products through eco-design, maintenance, reuse, repair, or refurbishing activities.

(iii) *The use of resources needs to be optimised in order to sustain the resource base.* Materials and energy are available in limited quantities and it is therefore critical to decrease material and energy use per product. This applies both during manufacturing and during the use-life of products, for instance, through minimising manufacturing wastes or the energy demand.

Any activities conducted in the economic and social spheres are to be hierarchically submitted to environmental limits. Any violations of these limits mean that activities cannot be considered sustainable because they jeopardise the basis for life of current and future generations. At the level of individual actors such as a company or a country, the key to a sustainable CE lies in deriving all the business and socio-economic decisions from the global limits of the Earth system.

Dematerialisation is a paradigm in resource conservation strategies. Material use should be reduced so that resource consumption as a whole can be lowered. The benefit for humankind should be completely decoupled from the natural expenditure by a definite factor X. Instinctively, this approach is convincing because our entire value-added chain is based on material transformation (Muller et al., 2017). Targets for mass-based indicators are found within the context of justification for ecological carrying capacity and intergenerational fairness, taking into account the economic and socio-political expectation of raw material scarcity. However, in the light of further development of material flow indicators and the related dematerialisation targets, the question arises as to what they actually stand for and what significance they have for resource conservation. Is it fair to assume that pressure on the environment will decline steadily if the use of materials is reduced, whether for an economy or at the level of individual products or processes? A high resource relevance cannot be inferred from high physical material inputs at any of the considered levels. Dematerialisation founded on mass-based indicators without mapping other resources should be critically investigated (Muller et al., 2017).

Economic development and growth depend on growing levels of resource use and result in environmental impacts from large scale resource extraction and waste emissions. Previous research (Krausmann et al., 2013) focussed on the resource dependency of economic activities over several decades for a set of developing, emerging, and industrialised economies. These authors identified a diversity of economic dependencies on material use. Over the longer-term, emerging and developing countries tend to have significantly larger material-economic coupling than mature developed economies, but the opposite is true for short-term coupling. They demonstrate that absolute dematerialisation limits economic growth rates, whereas the successful industrialisation of developing countries inevitably requires a solid material component. In conclusion, alternative development priorities are urgently needed for both mature and emerging economies, thus reducing absolute consumption levels for the former, and avoiding the trap of resource-intensive economic and human development for the latter (Krausmann et al., 2013).

It has been important to highlight the difference between economic growth and development and waste generation. Negrei and Istudor (2018) focussed on the dematerialisation of the economy and concentrated on three key aspects – cyclicality, circularity, and nonlinearity. They came to several succinct and important conclusions: (1) The laws of nature are a source inspiration for economic thinking and practice. (2) Through the way it is formulated, CE contradicts the second law of thermodynamics, namely, the entropy laws. (3) Through its content, in fact, CE aims to close material flows by means of adequate technical-productive processes. This particular issue has been dealt with for a long time when referring to production integration and active circular processes. (4) The options should take into account adaptive socio-economic systems and the rethinking of the idea of production specialisation. It is important to recognise that specialisation and super-specialisation set in motion the productivity crisis because they undermined the innovation and adjustment potential by way of the unidirectional use of human resources (Negrei & Istudor, 2018).

1.6. Social and Institutional Dimensions of the CE – Integration of Economic Activity and Environmental Well-being

It has generally been accepted that social and institutional aspects are important for a successful circular economy. However, it stops short of interfacing with the institutional and social predispositions necessary for societal transitions toward a CE. Often non-competitive and not-for-profit activities are not addressed. Labour conditions, wealth distribution, and governance systems are not usually at the top of the agenda. However, there may be underlying bio-physical aspects to explain the current limits to CE approaches. We need to acknowledge that labour is essential to tackling the large share of dissipated material and energy flows that cannot be retrieved economically, leading to a social and solidarity economy, and adding understanding to the circular economy (Moreau et al., 2017).

Other authors proposed a revised definition of CE as: 'an economic model wherein planning resourcing procurement production and reprocessing are designed and managed, as both process and output, to maximise ecosystem functioning and human well-being'. There have long been calls from the industry for guidance in implementing strategies for sustainable development. CE represents an attempt to conceptualise the integration of economic activity and environmental well-being in a sustainable way. This set of ideas has already been adopted by China as the basis of their economic development and was included in both the 11th and the 12th 'Five-year Plan'. This may have escalated the concept in the minds of Western policymakers and NGOs. This chapter investigated the origins and conceptualisations of CE, tracing its meanings and exploring its antecedents, in economics and ecology. It also insightfully assessed how CE has been operationalised in business and policy. While it places emphasis on the redesign of processes and cycling of materials, which may contribute to more business models, it also includes tensions and limitations. These include an absence of the social dimension inherent in sustainable development that limits its ethical elements and leads to several unintended consequences (Murray et al., 2017).

There has been an increasing interest in the social aspects of sustainability and circular economy. The CE model, where resources are kept in the loop for as long as possible, has been acclaimed for reducing environmental impacts. However, less attention has been paid to the negative consequences of CE. These have been generally underplayed as CE interventions are mainly viewed as a win–win–win situation which can result in a win for the environment, the economy, and the people. This work raises questions about the level to which societal consequences have been considered and whether all relevant stakeholders, especially civil society, have participated in the design of a city's CE strategy. These findings identify possible negative consequences of CE transition (Vanhuyse et al., 2022).

Food organisations are pressing to adopt CE to enhance the economic-ecological-social sustainability of supply chains. Adoption of circular economies is more complex for developing nations. The following authors recognised a significant number of circular economy -led sustainability-related challenges and analysed appropriate interactions among the identified challenges. According to their findings, these include: (1) poor government policies; (2) lack of technology and techniques; (3) lack of farmers' knowledge and awareness; (4) lower productivity; (5) GHG emissions; (6) food safety and security problems; and (7) lack of cold chain (Sharma et al., 2019). CE seeks to rebuild capital whether this is financial, manufactured, human, social, or natural, with the potential to offer opportunities and solutions for all organisations applying CE at industry levels (Stahel, 2016). This next research aimed to articulate the potentially catalytic function CE performs in the waste and resource management debate by creating a cognitive unit and a discursive space that centres around the capacity of a group of waste and resource management. Strategies to extend the productive life of resources.

Through this, the CE concept provides service to this debate by addressing a knowledge gap in relation to what constitutes meaningful and actionable waste and resource management (Blomsma & Brennan, 2017).

There has been quite a debate about the emergence and development of the Umbrella Concept in relation to circular economy. Umbrella concepts typically arise when a field or discipline lacks guiding theories or a development paradigm (Hirsch & Levin, 1999). Firstly, umbrella concepts can act as a catalyst in filling this knowledge gap by creating a new encompassing cognitive unit as well as a new discursive space. Secondly, these concepts typically progress along a predictable trajectory. This starts with the articulation of the umbrella concept by grouping pre-existing concepts, a phase characterised by excitement and enthusiasm as it seemingly resolves the problem of too many unconnected concepts by providing a new framing that binds them together. After this phase, an umbrella concept usually sees this validity challenged when attempts at operationalising bring unresolved issues regarding its definition and assessment to the surface.

Next, a plurality of definitions, a lack of tools, and the existence of different indicators emerge during this stage, raising questions regarding the nature of the binding capacity of the umbrella concept. This leads to further work in the form of additional theoretical development, which ultimately causes the concept to either cohere/gel (theoretical challenges are resolved), collapse (construct demise), or persist as a contention (agree to disagree) (Hirsch & Levin, 1999). It is fair to say that this concept is an ongoing debate and we saw future valid work as being a research agenda for industrial ecology to contribute to the development of CE. We have argued that our understanding of what aids or inhibits socio-institutional change in waste and resource management can be enhanced by paying attention to how material flows are shaped by, and interact with, nonmaterial flows, that is, different forms of social embeddedness.

Several authors have taken a holistic perspective to measure the effects of a circular economy. Policy monitors focus on recycling heavily while neglecting higher circular strategies and environmental and social impacts. This has been developed using a holistic method to compile indicators for policymakers steering the CE transition. Through the use of a societal needs perspective, it is possible to describe the manufactured, social and natural capital via the established driving forces, pressures, states, impacts, and responses (DPSIR) framework. This has proved useful for CE policy in the areas of material flow, environmental and social indicators, and has provided directed feedback on enacted policies (Reich et al., 2023). A recent systematic analysis of the CE in China and Worldwide shows how CE aims to decouple economic development from natural environmental impacts and has been given significant impetus by science and policy. There is two-way feedback and continuous adjustment between the two. However, science can guide policymakers to pay attention to social issues to promote the introduction of relevant policies. This cycle repeats itself until social issues are optimal leading to 'ecological civilisation' and the 'agricultural CE' (He et al., 2023).

Certain aspects of circularity research may have taken a back seat as the rush to put forward beneficial aspects of the CE has been rightly prominent. Several academics have focussed on formal and informal activities within CE, especially health and safety:

(1) What kinds of health and safety problems are companies and individuals facing?
(2) What factors influence CE safety across the various CE activities?
(3) What outcomes are there with various CE safety events and what is the mitigation?
(4) What are the social, environmental, and economic impacts of safety issues in CE?
(5) Who is responsible for safety within CE?
(6) What are the potential ways to improve safety in CE?
(7) What are the impartiality concerns of safety in CE?
(8) What are the issues related to both the formal and informal CE activities? (Chen et al., 2023).

The successful management and implementation of sustainability and circularity projects will require the full support of small and medium-sized enterprises (SMEs). It is interesting to note how innovation may be able to play an important role in these projects. Recent research using Resource-Based View theory has found that research and development and patents are positively related to sustainable performance, and Schumpeter's innovation theories have close links to the development of the CE. The relationship between innovation and social, environmental, and economic performance in achieving sustainable development goals is put into sharp focus (Zhang et al., 2022). This has led to an increase in research in the domain of circular business model innovation (CBMI), especially in the area of consumer-facing corporations (CFCs).

A recent focus on ways to integrate psycho-social factors into definitions of CE has continued to grow – it is hoped it will lead to improved household and organic waste programmes and a more progressive transition towards CE. It is expected that within the European Member States, there will be significant reductions in urban waste through bio-waste separation at source. To achieve this, it is imperative to have the active participation of the general public. It is interesting to note that only 23% of researchers addressed one or more psycho-social factors. Household organic waste separation behaviour is influenced by the level of education, perceived convenience, and social norms. At the moment it is difficult to precisely calculate the effective impact of communication and education campaigns on this particular type of behaviour (Celestino et al., 2022). One particular model could lead to technological innovation and positioning of heterogeneous consumers towards alternative types, versions, and prices of products and related social and cultural issues. It also evaluated the quantities of product types and versions available in the market and sequentially configure and compare sustainability indices for these alternative systems. Findings have shown that remanufacturing provides improved social, environmental, and financial performance compared to when manufacturing alone is allowed. Product updates also outperform manufacturing leading to another financial motive to move towards a CE (Zikopoulos, 2022).

Historically, we have a profit-maximising production system where all the products are produced with a variable circularity level. Consumers need to become more socially responsible about their consumption practices and buying habits than they are at present. Socially responsible consumer behaviour can directly influence a product's circularity levels. This should achieve the manufacturers' joint optimal circularity and production levels with the ambition of environmental protection by reducing carbon emissions helped by appropriate operational amendments. This optimal CE index can satisfy all the key stakeholders (Khan et al., 2022).

A systematic literature review (SLR) of the CE categorised previous research in this area where there are deemed to be three main lines of enquiry: (A) to change the social and economic dynamics at macro and administrative levels; (B) to support firms in circular processes implementation at micro level to spread new forms of consumption and product design; and (C) at meso-level industrial symbiosis experiences are discussed (Merli et al., 2018). The following research is still focussed on CE but concentrates on case study material in the manufacturing sector. The field has moved from purely conceptual work into empirical studies and research into implementation tools. In empirical studies, the sustainability impact of CE practices is generally typically addressed only through the E – economic dimension – neglecting social and economic dimensions.

High-density polyethylene (HDPE) Recycling has been a very hot topic over the last decade. A recent research project has identified that the material cost of recycled HDPE is slightly lower than for virgin. However, the manufacturing costs are higher as well as being dependent on specific value chains. The social risks of recycling were found to be higher than for virgin plastic production and mainly occur outside the country where the recycling takes place. This highlights the need for regular life cycle sustainability assessments (LCSAs). These can assess and compare the impacts and benefits of circular strategies leading to the development of a higher disaggregated social risk database (Pape & Corona, 2022). Recent research is still focussed on CE but concentrates on case study material in the manufacturing sector. The field has moved from purely conceptual work into empirical studies and research into implementation tools. Generally, in empirical studies, the sustainability impact of CE practices is typically addressed only through the E – economic dimension – neglecting social and economic dimensions.

1.7. Conclusions

The transition to a CE will require a fundamental change in many areas of business and society and will result in new collaborations. CE is undoubtedly a form of business structure. Where it may differ from generally accepted definitions is that many of these alliances are likely to be temporary. The 'process of interactions among stakeholders' (Fligstein & McAdam, 2014), will more than likely be an ongoing feature of these strategic alliances. We must make a smooth transition from a linear to a CE where design production and consumption are based on sustainability principles.

The measurement of the circularity of firms has been a prominent feature of certain research in the last decade. However, this focus on CE metrics should not be seen as an end in itself. At a very basic level, we must be certain that a CE-focussed sustainability strategy can deliver the appropriate outcomes at the optimum rate of progress for the planet. All the metrics in the world will not suffice if we are concentrating on a minor area of the overall sustainability agenda. Every country in the world should have the ability to undertake these important measurements.

The Glass Industry case showed how efficient a production process could be when the catalyst for its success is waste from the original process. Having raw materials and products that are infinitely recyclable would be a real boon for sustainability and CE. Incorporating the five stages of waste management and the seven stages of lean production could also provide a boost to the overall project. It has been argued that CE aims at decoupling value creation from waste generation and resource use by substituting the 'end-of-life' idea with restoration and reuse and closed-loop PLCs.

One only has to survey the range of disparate journals that are publishing articles on CE to understand that this is a complex research area. For example, ecological economics bridges across psychology, anthropology, archaeology, and history, in the quest to design a sustainable future. Environmental economics is a subset of economics. Organisations within CE will need to take a systemic perspective as well as several collaborative supplier–buyer innovation factors, including supply chain elements, power-balance negotiations, and a shared vision. Many issues will have to be reconciled in advance before these CE strategic alliances can operate effectively and efficiently. We need to move away from the very-dated concept of making products with 'built-in obsolescence' (refer to the section in Chapter 2).

References

Agnusdei, G. P., Gnoni, M. G., & Sgarbossa, F. (2022). Are deposit-refund systems effective in managing glass packaging? State of the art and future directions in Europe. *The Science of the Total Environment, 851,* 158256.

Antikainen, M., & Valkokari, K. (2016, July). A framework for sustainable circular business model innovation. *Technology Innovation Management Review, 6*(7), 5–12.

Barriero-Gen, M., & Lazano, B. (2020). How circular is the CE? Analysing the implementation of CE in organisations. *Business Strategy and the Environment, 29*(8), 3484–3494.

Bernardini, G. (1993). Dematerialization: Long-term trends in the intensity of use of materials and energy. *Futures*(May), 432–448.

Bigliardi, B., Filipelli, S., & Quinto, I. (2022). Environmentally-conscious behaviours in the circular economy: An analysis of consumers' green purchase intentions for refurbished smartphones. *Journal of Cleaner Production, 378,* 134379.

Blomsma, F., & Brennan, G. (2017). The emergence of CE: A new framing around prolonging resource productivity. *Journal of Industrial Ecology, 21*(3), 608–614.

Bocken, N. M. P., de Pauw, I., Bakker, C., & van der Grinten, B. (2016). Product design and business model strategies for a circular economy. *Journal of Industrial and Production Engineering, 33*(5), 308–320.

Bocken, N. M. P., Ritala, P., & Huotari, P. (2017). The circular economy: Exploring the introduction of the concept among S & P 500 firms. *Journal of Industrial Ecology, 21*(3), 487–490.

Boulding, K. E. (1966). The economics of the spaceship earth. In H. Jarrett (Ed.), *Environmental quality in a growing economy* (Resources for the Future, pp. 9–14). John Hopkins University Press.

Braungart, M., & McDonough, M. (2002). *Cradle to cradle: Remaking the way we make things.* North Point Press.

Brydges, T. (2021). Closing the loop on take, make, waste: Investigating circular economy practices in the Swedish fashion industry. *Journal of Cleaner Production, 293*(April), 126245.

Brynjolfsson, E., & McAfee, A. (2014). *The second machine age: Work progress and prosperity in a time of brilliant technologies.* W.W. Norton.

Cagno, E., Negri, M., Neri, A., & Giambone, M. (2023). One framework to rule them all: An integrated, multi-level and scalable performance measurement framework of sustainable, circular economy and industrial symbiosis. *Sustainable Production and Consumption, 35,* 55–71.

Celestino, E. Carvalho, A., & Palma-Oliveira, J. M. (2022). Household organic waste: Integrate psychosocial factors to define strategies towards a circular economy. *Journal of Cleaner Production, 378,* 134446.

Chawla, S., Varghese, B. S., Chithra, A., Hussain, C. G., Kesili, R., & Hussain, C. M. (2022, December). Environmental impacts of post-consumer plastic wastes: Treatment technologies towards eco-sustainability and circular economy, *Chemosphere, 308*(Part 1), 135867.

Chea, J. D., Yenkie, K. M., Stanzione, J. F., & Ruiz-Mercado, G. J. (2023). A generic scenario analysis of end-of-life-plastic management: Chemical additives. *Journal of Hazardous Materials, 441,* 129902.

Chen, Z., Yildizbasi, A., & Sarkis, J. (2023). How safe is the circular economy?. *Resources, Conservation and Recycling, 188,* 106649.

Chizaryfard, A., Trucco, P., & Nuur, C. (2020, April). The transformation to a circular economy: Framing an evolutionary view. *Journal of Evolutionary Economics, 31,* 475–504.

Cooper, T. (1999). Creating an economic infrastructure for sustainable product design. *Journal of Sustainable Product Design,* (8), 7–17.

Corona, B., Shen, L. Reike, D., Rosales Carreon, J., & Worrell, E. (2019). Towards sustainable development through the CE – A review and critical assessment on current circularity metrics. *Resources, Conservation and Recycling, 151,* 104498.

Costanza, R. (2010). *Yale insights: Management in practice.* Yale School of Management. https://insights.som.yale.edu/departments/management-in-practice

Dangelico, R. M., Alvino, L., & Fraccascia, L. (2022). Investigating the antecedents of consumer behavioural intention for sustainable fashion products: Evidence from a large survey of Italian consumers. *Technological Forecasting and Social Change, 185,* 122010.

Dewick, P., de Mello, A. M., Sarkis, J., & Donkor, F. K. (2022). The puzzle of the informal economy and the circular economy. *Resources, Conservation and Recycling, 187,* 1–2.

Dilmegani, C. (2023). Top 10 metrics to assess the circularity of businesses in 2023. *AI Multiple,* 10 February.

Eisenreich, A., Fuller, J., Stuchtey, M., & Gimenez-Jimenez, D. (2022). Towards a circular value chain: Impact of the circular economy on a company's value chain processes. *Journal of Cleaner Production, 378,* 134375.

Esparza, I., Jimenez-Moreno, N., Bimbela, F., Ancin-Azpilicueta, C., & Gandia, L. M. (2020, July). Fruit and vegetable waste management: Conventional and emerging approaches. *Journal of Environmental Management*, *265*, 110510.

Esposito, M., Tse, T., & Soufani, K. (2018). Introducing a circular economy: New thinking with new management. *California Management Review*, *60*(3), 5–19.

Farahmandpour, R., Karimi, K., Denayer, J. F. M., & Shafiei, M. (2022). Innovative biorefineries for cleaner waste textile management towards a circular economy: Techno-economic analysis.*Journal of Cleaner Production*, *378*, 134500.

Fligstein, N., & McAdam, D. (2014). *A theory of fields*. Oxford University Press.

Franco, M. (2017). Circular economy at the micro level: A dynamic view of incumbents' struggles and challenges in the textile industry. *Journal of Cleaner Production*, *168*, 833–845.

Garcia-Casarejos, N., Gargallo, P., & Carroquino, J. (2018). Introduction of renewable energy in the Spanish wine sector. *Sustainability*, *10*(9), 3157.

Geisendorf, S., & Pietrulla, F. (2018). The CE and circular economic concepts – A literature analysis and redefinition. *Thunderbird International Business Review*, *60*(5), 771–782.

Geissdoerfer, M., Savaget, P., Bocken, N. M. P., & Hultink, E. J. (2017). Circular economy: A new sustainability paradigm. *Journal of Cleaner Production*, *143*, 757–768.

Gheewala, S. H. (2020). Life cycle thinking for sustainable consumption and production towards a circular economy. *E3S Web of Conferences*, *202*, 1003.

Goyal, S., Esposito, M., & Kapoor, A. (2016). Circular economy business models in developing economies: Lessons from India on reduce, recycle, and reuse paradigms. *Thunderbird International Business Review*, *60*(5), 729–740.

Guyader, H., Ponsignon, F., Salignac, F., & Bojovic, N. (2020). Beyond a mediocre customer experience in the circular economy: The satisfaction of contributing to the ecological transition. *Journal of Cleaner Production*, *378*, 134495.

Harris, S., Mata, E., Lucena, A. F. P., & Bertoldi, P. (2023). Climate mitigation from circular and sharing economy in the building sector. *Resources, Conservation and Recycling*, *188*, 106709.

He, S., Wei, W., Ding, S., Zheng, S., & Niu, T. (2023). Co-evolution between science and policy: A systematic analysis on circular economy in China and worldwide. *Environmental Science and Policy*, *139*, 104–117.

Hirsch, P. M., & Levin, D. Z. (1999). Umbrella advocates versus validity police: A life cycle model. *Organization Science*, *10*(2), 199–212.

Hopkinson, P., Zils, M., Hawkins, P., & Roper, S. (2018). Managing a complex global circular economy business model: Opportunities and challenges. *California Management Review*, *60*(3), 5–19.

Khan, K., Su, C. W., & Khurshid, A. (2022). Circular economy: The silver bullet for emissions. *Journal of Cleaner Production*, *379*(14), 134819.

Korkonen, J., Honkasalo, A., & Seppalo, J. (2018). Circular economy: The concept and its limitations. *Ecological Economics*, *143*, 37–46.

Lau, P. J., Ng, W. P. Q., How, B. S., Lim, C. H., & Lam, H. L. (2022). Paving a way towards circular economy for oil and gas industry: A conceptual modelling of re-refining process through solvent extraction and hydro finishing pathway. *Journal of Cleaner Production*, *380*, 134839.

Lewandowski, M. (2016). Desighing the business models for circular economy – Towards the conceptual framework. *Sustainability*, *8*(1), 43.

Li, R. (2022). Integrating the composition of food waste into the techno-economic analysis of waste bio-refineries for bio-diesel production. *Resource Technology Reports*, *20*, 101254.

Lieder, M., & Rashid, A. (2016). Towards circular economy implementation: A comprehensive review in context of manufacturing industry. *Production*, *115*, 36–51.

Magee, C. L., & Devezas, T. C. (2017, April). A simple extension of dematerialization theory: Incorporation of technical progress and the rebound effect. *Technological Forecasting and Social Change, 117*, 196–205.

Malenbaum, W. (1978). *World demand for raw materials.* McGraw-Hill.

Merli, R., Preziosi, M., & Acampora, A. (2018). How do scholars approach the circular economy? A systematic literature review. *Journal of Cleaner Production, 178*, 703–722.

Millar, N., McLoughlin, E., & Berger, T. (2019). The CE: Swings and roundabouts. *Ecological Economics, 158*, 11–19.

Muller, F., Kosmol, J., Kebler, H., Angrick, M., & Rechenberg, B. (2017). Dematerialization – A disputable strategy for resource conservation put under scrutiny. *Resources, 6*(4), 68.

Murray, A., Skene, K., & Haynes, K. (2017). The circular economy: An interdisciplinary exploration of the concept and applications in a global context. *Journal of Business Ethics, 140*, 369–380.

Negrei, C., & Istudor, N. (2018). Circular economy – Between theory and practice. *Academy of Economic Studies of Bucharest, 20*(48), 498–509.

Oke, A., Pinas, C. J., & Osobajo, O. A. (2022). Designing effective waste management practices in developing economies: The case of Suriname. *Cleaner Waste Systems, 3*, 100030.

Panchal, R., Singh, A., & Diwan, H. (2021). Does CE performance lead to sustainable development? – A systematic literature review. *Journal of Environmental Management, 293*, 112811–112811.

Pape, M., & Corona, B. (2022). Life-cycle sustainability of non-beverage bottles made of recycled high-density polyethylene. *Journal of Cleaner Production, 378*, 134442.

Norton, T. A., Parker, S. L., Zacher, H., & Ashkanasy, N. M. (2015). Employee green behaviour: A theoretical framework, multilevel review, and future research agenda. *Organization and Environment, 28*(1), 103–125.

Pauli, G. (2009). 10 years, 100 innovations, 100 million new jobs, inspired by nature. *The Blue Economy: A Report to the Club of Rome 2009.* Paradigm Publications, Taos, New Mexico, USA.

Pederson, E. R., Gwozdz, W., & Hvass, K. K. (2018, May). Exploring the relationship between business model innovation, corporate sustainability, and organisational values within the fashion industry. *Journal of Business Ethics, 149*(2), 267–284.

Rajput, S., & Singh, S, (2020). Industry 4.0 model for circular economy and cleaner production. *Journal of Cleaner Production, 277*, 123853.

Reich/Reike, R. H., Vermeyen, V., Alaerts, L., & Van Acker, K. (2023). How to measure a circular economy: A holistic method compiling policy monitors. *Resources, Conservation and Recycling, 188*, 106707.

Aimultiple.com. (2022). Top 10 Metrics to Assess the Circularity of Businesses. https://research.aimultiple.com.

Romero-Luis, J., Carbonell-Alcocer, A. A., Gertrudix, M., Gertrudis, C., del Carmen, M., Giardullo, P., & Wuebenn, D. (2022). Recommendations to improve communication effectiveness in social marketing campaigns: Boosting behaviour change to foster a circular economy. *Cogent Social Sciences, 8*(1), 2147265.

Rondon, T. E., Lobo, A., & Gallardo Izquierdo, A. (2020). Circularity indicator for municipal solid waste treatment plants. *Journal of Cleaner Production, 380*(1), 134807.

Salmi, A., & Kaipia, R. (2022). Implementing circular business models in the textile and clothing sindustry. *Journal of Cleaner Production, 378*, 134492.

Saravanan, A., Kumar, P. S., Nhung, T. C., Ramesh, B., Srinivasan, S., & Rangasamy, G. (2022). A review on biological methodologies in municipal solid waste management and landfilling: Resource and energy recovery. *Chemosphere (Oxford), 309*, 136630–136630.

Shahbaz, M., Rashid, N., Saleem, J., Mackey, H., McKay, G., & Al-Ansari, T. (2023). A review of waste management approaches to maximise sustainable value of waste from the oil and gas industry and potential for the state of Qatar. *Fuel (Guildford)*, *332*, 126220.

Sharma, Y. K., Mangla, S. K., Patil, P. P., & Liu, S. (2019). When challenges impede the process: For CE-driven sustainability practices in food SCs. *Management Decision*, *57*(4), 995–1017.

Singh, N., & Ogunseitan, O. A. (2022). Disentangling the worldwide web of e-waste and climate change co-benefits. *Circular Economy*, *1*(2), 100011.

Stahel, W. (2016). Circular economy. *Nature*, *531*, 435.

Steinberger, J. K., Krausmann, M., F., Schandl, H., & West, J. (2013). Development and dematerialization: An international study. *PLoS ONE*, *8*(10), 70385.

Steiner, G. A. (1975). *Business and society* (2nd ed., Chapter 13). Random House.

Thongplew, N., Onwang, J., Kotlakome, R., & Suttipanta, N. (2022). Approaching circular economy in an emerging economy: A solid-waste reutilisation initiative in a small fresh market in Thailand. *Sustainability: Science Practice and Policy*, *18*(1), 665–678.

Vanhuyse, F., Rezaie, S., Englund, M., Jokiaho, J., Henrysson, M., & Andre, K. (2022). Including the social in the circular: A mapping of the consequences of a circular economy transition in the city of Umea, Sweden. *Journal of Cleaner Production*, *380*, 134893.

Yuan, Z., Bi, J., & Moriguichi, Y. (2006). The circular economy: A new development strategy in China. *Industrial Ecology in Asia*, *10*(1–2), 4–8.

Zhang, Y. S., Schneider, K., Qiu, H., & Zhu, H. L. (2022). A perspective of low carbon lithium-ion battery recycling technology. *Carbon Capture Science and Technology*, *5*, 100074.

Zhang, Z., Zhu, H., Zhou, Z., & Zou, K. (2022). How does innovation matter for sustainable performance? Evidence from SMEs. *Journal of Business Research*, *153*, 251–265.

Zikopoulos, C. (2022). On the effect of upgradable products design on circular economy. *International Journal of Production Economics*, *254*, 108629.

Zisopoulus, F. K., Teigiserova, D. A., Schraven, D., de Jong, M., Tong, X., & Ulanowicz, R. E. (2022). Are there limits to robustness? Exploring tools from regenerative economics for a balanced transition towards a circular EU 27. *Cleaner Production Letters*, *3*, 100014.

Chapter 2

Sustainability and the Circular Economy as Part of a Global Environmental Strategy

2.1. Introduction

A significant amount of recent debate has suggested that circular economy (CE) can be given certainty through a mix of laws, policies, risk reduction (tax levies), and strict governance. As citizens, organisations, and governments across the globe increase their interest in environmentally and socially sustainable means of production and consumption, the idea of CE has been at the forefront of recent discussions held at organisational, national, and global levels (Hazen et al., 2020; Hussain & Malik, 2020). A significant amount of debate has focussed on the need to ensure improved sustainability in supply chain management endeavours with operational excellence in CE (Sehnem et al., 2019). They stress that CE is not only concerned with a reduction in the global environment being used as a receptacle for waste but also with the creation of self-sustaining production systems with reusable materials as the norm. A useful addition to this debate is that several of these articles highlight the need to focus on the long-term requirements of environmental sustainability (Genovese et al., 2017). It is interesting to note that there still tends to be a focus on production rather than consumption (Georgantzis Garcia et al., 2021). We will return to this discourse later in the book. A very positive stream of work concentrates on the need to view CE as a way of reducing pressure on the environment.

It is generally accepted that the over-exploitation of natural resources required to achieve economic growth and development has negatively impacted the environment and adversely affected their cost and availability. With the increasing velocity of change brought about by the need to meet global sustainability targets, many organisations around the world are struggling to meet these standards. It has become clear that being a green organisation can have benefits for bottom-line profitability as well as brand image. Being aligned with sustainability principles and strategies is almost a given in today's febrile business environment. It had previously been almost enough for many organisations to be perceived as being 'keen' on sustainability and green issues, a short-sighted strategy (known as 'Greenwashing') that led to many well-known firms being exposed for deceiving the public. The following section focusses on some of the actions employed by

Sustainable Development Through Global Circular Economy Practices, 37–57
Copyright © 2024 by Stuart Maguire and Ian Robson
Published under exclusive licence by Emerald Publishing Limited
doi:10.1108/978-1-83753-590-320231002

organisations to try and persuade the public of their rigorous sustainability credentials. This material should be useful to governments, agencies, authorities, etc. who will be monitoring firms across the world to try to ensure that sustainability targets are being achieved.

2.2. The Dynamics of Global Supply/Demand Relationships and the Advent of Greenwashing

Greenwashing is the act of providing the public or investors with misleading or outright false information concerning the environmental impact of a company's products and operations (Investopedia). Also known as 'green sheen', it is a form of advertising or marketing spin in which green PR and green marketing are used deceptively to persuade the public that an organisation's products, aims, and policies are environmentally friendly (Wikipedia). Environmentalist Jay Westerveld coined the term greenwashing in 1986 in a critical essay inspired by the irony of the 'save the towel' movement in hotels that had little impact beyond saving hotels money in laundry costs. The idea emerged in a period when most consumers received their news primarily from television, radio, and print media when it was more difficult to fact-check than it is today. Firms that engaged in wide-scale greenwashing have made headlines over the years – In the mid-1980s, oil company Chevron commissioned a series of expensive television and print adverts to broadcast its environmental dedication. However, along with the now-infamous 'People Do' campaign, Chevron was simultaneously actively violating the Clean Air Act and Clean Water Act, as well as spilling oil into wildlife refuges (Business.com).

The Clean Air Act (1970) was a comprehensive federal law that regulated air emissions from stationary and mobile sources. Among other things, this law authorised EPA to establish National Ambient Air Quality Standards (NAAQS) to both protect public health and welfare and regulate emissions of hazardous air pollutants (United States Environmental Protection Agency – US EPA). The Clean Water Act (CWA 1972) established the basic structure for regulating discharges of pollutants into the waters of the USA and for regulating quality standards for surface waters. The basis of the CWA, enacted in 1948 as the Federal Water Pollution Control Act, was significantly reorganised and expanded in 1972. Under the CWA, the EPA has implemented pollution control programmes such as setting wastewater standards for the industry. The EPA has also developed national water quality criteria recommendations for pollutants in surface waters (US EPA).

Greenwashing may have changed over the last two decades, but it has certainly stayed around. As the world increasingly embraces the pursuit of greener practices, corporations face an influx of litigation for making misleading environmental claims. As an example, the Alliance to End Plastic Waste (AEPW) – a Singapore-based non-profit making firm backed by big oil and chemical companies such as Shell, ExxonMobil, and Dow – claims to be spending $1.5 billion to clean up plastic waste in developing countries. Despite this supposed goal, APEW not only failed to honour its promise to clean up the Ganges River in

India, but its member organisations moved forward with plans to produce even more plastic (Business.com).

Greenwashing is firmly in the public consciousness due to the broadcasting of a raft of environmental problems around the world. Over the past decade, increasing numbers of stakeholders, as well as investors, consumers, governments, and corporate customers are intensifying the pressure on firms to disclose information about their environmental performance. In order to react to these very important issues, corporate social responsibility (CSR) has gained significant importance among leaders of business. A number of researchers consider only environmental issues when referring to greenwashing, distinguishing it from the term 'blue-washing', which is predominantly focussed on social issues. Other scholars do not distinguish and consider greenwashing as both an environmental and a social issue (De Freitas Netto et al., 2020).

CSR is a form of international private business self-regulation which aims to contribute to societal goals of a philanthropic, activist, or charitable nature by engaging in or supporting volunteering or ethically oriented practices (Wikipedia). However, there is no doubt that sustainability, green, and environmental issues are increasingly viewed as being a major cornerstone of CSR. We also believe that CSR is not only the domain of private businesses – public sector organisations are also changing their behaviour, particularly with regard to the environment.

Consumers are faced with a barrage of green-friendly messaging from organisations hoping to profit from the increasing global concerns surrounding environmental issues. A significant number of these environmental and sustainability promises do not ring true, and recent research in Europe found that 42% of green claims were exaggerated, false, or deceptive. This points towards greenwashing on a grand scale, a risky path to take as we know that stakeholders punish those firms who misbehave or cause environmental harm, for example, BP's Deepwater Horizon oil spill or Volkswagen's emissions scandal. This research shows that when firms, for whatever reason, fail to meet their stated social responsibility goals, customers perceive them to be greenwashing and judge them harshly. Furthermore, greenwashing negatively impacts a customer's experience with a firm's products or services.

A critical finding of this research that firms need to understand is that trying to fool consumers and key stakeholders is not only a matter of a damaged reputation (as previous research has shown), such as happens when customers believe a firm is greenwashing, but that it directly affects how they experience its products or services well into the future. The consequences of this reputational damage and negative experience are that customers will always remember how certain firms have been responsible for negative impacts on the environment. This research of 202 publicly traded large US firms examined these firms' stated goals and actions related to green product innovation (GPI) for the period 2008–2016. They found that customers are highly likely to be aware of the gap between stated goals and implementation. This disconnect initiates perceptions of corporate hypocrisy, which affects the customers' experience with the product itself (Ioannou et al., 2022).

Multi-national corporations (MNCs) have played a major role in expanding market size, and their behaviour can be unpredictable. Reports of greenwashing have increased around the world since Volkswagen was found to have falsified its automobile emissions data. This research has shown that MNCs tend to engage in greenwashing activities immediately after doing business in local, emerging markets characterised by restricted regulations, clear market opportunities, and low competitive pressure. When greenwashing occurs, it will harm the interests of not only consumers but also society as a whole. This does not justify the short-term gains of corporate shareholders (Yang et al., 2020).

This research states that although greenwashing may sometimes be successfully used to influence consumers' perception about a firm's CSR and deflect attention from negative behaviours, the risk of adverse effects on consumers' attitudes, and more generally on the company's performance is increasing. This has been especially true in the last decade where the business environment is characterised by a high level of scrutiny and scepticism. Greenwashing may finally backfire on the firm and dramatically decrease its corporate reputation, leading to a reduction of corporate legitimacy resulting eventually in a legal or credibility crisis. These authors also highlight the general debate about the voluntary versus mandatory nature of CSR (Gatti et al., 2019).

Greenwashing research has generally supported the inclusion of mandatory aspects in the conceptualisation of CSR that contradict the traditional CSR paradigm exclusively based on the principle of voluntarism. Gatti et al.'s (2019) analysis of the previous literature contributed to the refinement of the theory of CSR. It highlighted the implications and consequences of a totally voluntary approach and it strongly supports the inclusion of mandatory solutions proposed by greenwashing academics, which would favour the implementation of a level playing field and, ultimately, a more credible form of CSR. Interpreting CSR as a quasi-regulation could possibly increase organisations' ability to engage in CSR and thus protect themselves from unwarranted attacks. When CSR regulation is stated as private industry self-regulation and not as public law, it is capable of contributing to the improvement of corporate practice (Gatti et al., 2019).

Actual and potential minimisation of environmental, social, and governance (ESG) risks pose a threat, not only to credibility but also to our collective ability to transition to a sustainable future. While regulation is stepping up with good intentions, investors and consumers need to do significant research, reading the fine print and assessing actions, to determine the truth behind sustainability claims. Identifying meaningful data to support this process presents a challenge as traditional ESG ratings often mask underlying risks and vary across providers.

How can an outside-in approach to ESG help investors identify greenwashing in their portfolios? In this article, Gatti et al. (2019) introduce their own unique perspective on greenwashing risk, review historical trends, and look at greenwashing through the lens of two facets of this issue: climate lobbying and climate compensation. They also found that, in recent years, climate change is increasingly subject to greenwashing and ESG risk data indicated the rising accountability of climate action across sectors. Greenwashing misleads consumers and stakeholders to view a firm's environmental footprint in a more positive light. By analysing public sources and stakeholders for information it can tell us what the world is saying about a firm. This perspective can circumvent greenwashing by capturing the impact of a company rather than its messaging and can thus help investors assess a company to make better investment decisions and move towards a more sustainable capital allocation. Reviewing the last 10 years of data linked to greenwashing, it is possible to observe an increase or decrease in the number of such incidents and a shift in the regions, topics, and sectors involved.

Economists have long attempted to understand the dichotomy between the finite amount of natural resources and the unlimited human needs and wants which has resulted in our current economic systems. The current population, allied to growth rates, increasing inflation, and higher demand and consumption, has led to pressure on the world's economic system. In 2013, Cohen proposed new economic models, that is, peer-to-peer provisioning networks, alternative agro-feed arrangements, community-energy schemes, and worker-owner co-ops which would ultimately lead to less resource-intensive lifestyles. In 1990, Pearce and Turner referred to the CE leading to environmental economics. They addressed the interlinkage between the environment and the production/consumption economic model. The environment provides amenity values and is 'a resource base' and a sink for economic activities. This can provide a fundamental life-support system. The purpose of consumption ends up leading to an increase in consumers' utility and/or enhanced social welfare. There is waste at each stage of the supply chain, not all of which can be recycled, leading to missed opportunities and the basic physical and thermodynamic laws, the finitude of resources, and resource depletion. New production and consumption models lead to two further dimensions – reduce and reuse. Reduction can be achieved on the P side (producing with less) and on the C side (consuming less). Matzler et al. (2015) put forward six ways firms could respond to the rise of collaborative consumption: selling a product's use rather than ownership, supporting customers in their desire to resell goods, exploiting unused resources and capacities, providing repair and maintenance services, using collaborative consumption to target new customers, and developing entirely new business model enablers (Morone & Navia, 2016).

The integrated nature of drivers and barriers to sustainability in Australia require an integrated approach to promoting the purchase of green alternatives. This highlights the important requirement for the need to change organisational culture. However, this will only occur with increased intelligence about the existing alternatives and the benefits of changing purchasing policies and practices both within local government organisations (LGOs) and at the broader governmental level. It is crucial to have intelligence regarding what influences the purchasing of products, with recycled material and recovered content by public sector organisations (Wijayasundara et al., 2022). Transitioning towards net zero manufacturing (NZM) is a key cornerstone of global sustainability and the CE. However, it is necessary to convert abstract sustainability into NZ emissions and the CE into feasible, desirable, and practical actions and achievements which lead to a sustainable competitive edge. Through a resource-based view (RBV) lens, leading to the deployment and redeployment of existing internal resources and core competences, it has been shown that firms can achieve NZM emissions and

CE. The study of thirteen manufacturing firms revealed a critical need for the companies to incorporate intangible asset management and development, including labour and supply chain relationships, as part of their digital transformation strategies (Okorie et al., 2023).

2.3. Systemic Strategies for CE Implementation

The normal business transaction is that the seller has a product or service to sell, and the buyer or consumer makes the decision to buy the product/service. This is referred to as Caveat Emptor – let the buyer beware. Caveat emptor is a common law doctrine that places the burden on buyers to reasonably examine the property before making a purchase. This works much better with new products – the buyer has to assume responsibility for the risk that the product may not be of the requisite quality. With caveat emptor, the principle that the buyer is responsible for checking the quality and suitability of goods before a purchase is made has been instilled in transactions for centuries.

The opposite of caveat emptor is Caveat Venditor – let the seller beware. With regard to business transactions, this would be equivalent to a paradigm shift. The maxim of caveat venditor facilitates consumer welfare by ensuring the seller, manufacturer, and providers of services are responsible for the quality of goods produced or services offered. We believe that this is a vital and necessary change that has to take place for CE to be successful as there are many more opportunities for the products within CE to be remanufactured or refurbished. Increasing numbers of organisations around the world should view this as a real business opportunity. The charity sector has decades of experience in selling second-hand products (refer to the Fast Fashion and Charities Case Study). A significantly high percentage of purchasing transactions in the last century have been of new products/goods. For CE to reach its potential there has to be a change in the psychology of buying used/second-hand products. Transactions within the CE may be affected by resistance to change as these new trading relationships are introduced.

Systems and systemic solutions are the most effective among the efficiency strategies as they enable a reduction of volume and speed of the resource flows (Stahel, 2001). In significant areas of the economy, it will be necessary to take even more radical steps to counter climate change. Is it possible for the CE to mitigate the consequences of extracting natural resources? This research has undertaken an empirical, evidence-based analysis of 28 European economies over the last ten years. Its results confirm that promoting a move towards more circular economic systems and initiatives can reduce the extraction of primary resources. However, the mitigating effects of circular initiatives remain marginal compared with economic growth. Current estimates reveal that primary resources extracted annually and linked to economic growth are roughly four times greater than the resources saved by CE initiatives. The circularity of economic systems should be approached from a systemic perspective that includes both production and consumption as well as waste management. Complementary measures which address behavioural consumption are needed if we want to achieve sustainable development (Bianchi & Cordella, 2023).

The CE has recently been studied with regard to the co-evolution between science and policy. This seems to reinforce the need to take a systemic perspective with CE research. It is generally accepted that the CE aims to decouple economic development from natural environmental impacts. Several previous studies have focussed on a single area through qualitative analysis. In most cases, the impact of science-policy interaction has rarely been discussed. However, by using a mixed-method approach utilising big data analytics (BDA), it was found that by 2-way feedback and continuous adjustment between science and the policy of CE, negative environmental impacts can be abated. In relation to China, there is a focus on a development strategy and policy at a macro-level, such as 'ecological civilisation' and 'agricultural circular economy', and hopes for a 'bandwagon effect'. At an international level, the CE seems to focus on implementation at a micro-level based on the market and is progressive and coherent (He et al., 2023). Pathways to both systemic and micro-scale changes present many challenges to CE. In the short term, we need circular consumers to cement the 'sharing economy'. Work on consumption, C refers to the labour integral to the purchase, use, reuse, and disposal of goods and services who undertake C work. It also relates to how, in its multiple forms and to what ends they are co-ordinated within and beyond the household (Hobson et al., 2021).

2.3.1. Fast Fashion and Charities – A Strategic Alliance?

There are a number of very important ways that charities can really help in relation to sustainability and the CE and provide a template for the rest of the world. These include a number of key issues pertinent to this book: circular and linear economic models, policies for secondary materials, greenwashing, unwanted clothing, sustainable fashion, creating value for people in need, and helping consumers live more sustainably. Textile waste is one of the most polluting items globally, and this is being strongly affected by a considerable increase in the number of fast fashion (FF) products (Farahani et al., 2021). Demand for raw materials is expected to triple by 2050, and this information is provided by a registered charity Waste and Resources Action Programme (WRAP). The charitable sector has a significant presence on most high streets and is able to demonstrate the benefits of reuse and how it can be brought to fruition. Taking the UK as an example, there are over 11,000 charity shops that employ 23,000 staff. Almost 95% of the clothes charity shops receive are either recycled or reused allowing over 300,000 tonnes of textile waste to be diverted from landfill (Osterley & Williams, 2018).

To effectively implement sustainability strategies and the CE will require collaborations and a number of important strategic alliances. The alliance between FF organisations and charities will be very important. Charities could help FF firms increase their capacity in this reverse supply chain as they have been the main collectors and recyclers of unwanted clothes. It is suggested that FF firms and charities should collaborate to solve the aforementioned issues and that this might improve charities' competitiveness (Farahani et al., 2021). However, the fashion industry requires urgent change starting with the need for the renunciation of greenwashing practices. Only this will restore consumer trust. Another radical change would be fashion design with the aim of recycling, leading to a reduction in by-products, lower energy consumption, and wiser purchasing habits through behaviour change (Adamkiewicz et al., 2022).

The rapid mass production of 'fast fashion' around the world is depleting natural resources, polluting the environment, and contributing to negative climate change, thus putting many of the world's poorest people at risk (Cornel et al., 2021). It may in fact be the CE, one significant part of which transforms waste into raw materials for new products, that offers a vital solution to keeping clothing in use for longer, conserving resources, and protecting the climate. However, many charities believe that FF organisations generate quantities of low-quality products that need to be collected and sorted. They are also difficult to sell on and would provide only narrow profit margins (Farahani et al., 2021).

Charity shops are actually helping to promote the CE and sustainable fashion by extending the life of used clothing through reuse, resale, or recycling, helping to close the loop on waste and raise funds to end poverty (Circle Economy). They allow consumers to donate unwanted clothing through these shops, which can be found across the UK, and encourage second-hand clothing as desirable and sustainable. By way of the donation of consumers' used clothing, excess stock, or customer returns to charity shops, businesses can make progress on CE goals, thus mitigating any harmful impacts of FF while creating value for people living in poverty. It is intended to be a sustainable and transparent process, allowing companies to oversee where their clothing goes once received by charity shops, and creating value for people in need. This particular partnership also paves the way to strengthening brand identity, helping consumers live more sustainably, and reducing clothing waste. This section has shown how the CE can be adopted in a number of innovative ways. This particular organisational model is also eminently transferable across the globe.

2.4. Strategic Sustainable Resource Use and Built-in Obsolescence

The vision of sustainability can be compared with the problem of crossing a shallow river in which stepping stones are hidden. The service economy is the junction where sustainable production and consumption (SP&C) meet. Sufficiency solutions are of interest only to economic actors in a service economy where they enable an income without resource consumption. This chapter summarises the key differences between the commercial strategies of selling performance and selling products, which are the differences between the industrial economy and the service economy. It is posited that a new industrial policy can best promote sustainability by removing obstacles that hinder sustainability and by creating incentives that foster innovation towards more sustainable solutions. Sufficiency and prevention solutions are the most efficient strategies to achieve a higher level of sustainability and 'wealth without resource consumption' (Stahel, 2001).

Strategic Sustainability is defined as finding the right sustainability drivers to create or enhance value through risk management, revenue growth, and cost reduction. Furthermore, it is important to define a sustainability vision in order to complement and support corporate strategy and to develop a roadmap and introduction/implementation plans to guarantee value creation.

To take advantage of strategic sustainability, organisations need to:

- Identify their key issues and goals to determine where the business pressures are likely to be and raise awareness of what needs to be done to make their business more sustainable.
- Prioritise these issues from both a sustainability and commercial perspective. This will help them recognise and better manage risks, and thus improve efficiency, revenue potential, and growth, and will bring other opportunities.
- Map the short- and long-term ambitions for their sustainability vision, goals, and values, assess the risks, and address any gaps in delivery.
- Support the alignment and integration of their sustainability vision, goals, and values into their overall corporate strategy.
- Develop and deliver a resilient and robust sustainability programme that includes prioritised initiatives, enablers, milestones, key performance indicators, and measurable targets (PwC Malaysia, 2021).

The need for sustainable development was officially acknowledged more than 30 years ago (Brundtland, 1987) and is periodically reaffirmed by science-engaged society, business organisations, and public institutions. A key role is played by society's difficulty in understanding the urgency of downsizing the material scale of the economy. Recently, the European Union (EU) started several initiatives which included combatting planned obsolescence and increasing product durability, particularly within CE action plans (APs). Prolonging product lifetimes can lead to a tool for downsizing the material scale of the economy (Luzzati et al., 2022).

2.4.1. Built-in Obsolescence

In economics and industrial design, planned obsolescence is a policy of planning or designing a product with an artificially limited useful life or a purposely frail design, so that it quickly becomes obsolete (Wikipedia). This seems to be in direct conflict with the aims and objectives of the CE. Built-in obsolescence can be viewed as making or designing something (e.g. a car or white goods) in such a way that it will only be usable for a short time, in order that purchasers will soon have to buy another one. Apple employs built-in obsolescence to force consumers to buy iPhones every few years. As part of this strategy, iPhones use batteries with 2–3 years of lifespan, after which the battery needs replacing which requires a substantial outlay. However, an alternative view is that planned obsolescence is positive for both goods manufacturers and the economy as it keeps sales stable and year-by-year growth encourages consumption. It is also argued that society benefits from constant investment in research and development. In the USA, the Consumer Product Safety Committee, which administers and enforces Federal regulations regarding consumer rights, could set durability standards for products, but there are currently no Federal laws that prohibit planned obsolescence (31 March 2022).

This chapter argues that businesses may take advantage of rapid technological developments to increase sales by designing products with a short lifespan, thus encouraging consumers to buy a replacement more quickly than they otherwise might have to, that is, planned obsolescence. This research explores planned obsolescence from three different angles – demand, supply, and the environmental side. The chapter argues that the current measures in the fields of unfair competition and consumer protection law, competition law, and environmental law are inadequate to deal with planned obsolescence. Therefore, there is a need for an EU law/measure outlawing planned obsolescence in the context of the CE. In 2015, the European Commission adopted its first ambitious CE AP. This included steps to stimulate Europe's transition towards CE, embracing measures which covered the whole cycle, from production and consumption to waste management and the market for secondary raw materials, thus contributing to closing the loop of product life cycles through greater recycling and reuse, and bringing benefits for both the environment and the economy (Malinauskaite & Erdem, 2021).

Different approaches are currently being undertaken to counter planned obsolescence across various legislation measures, such as unfair competition and consumer protection, eco-design and e-waste, and, potentially, competition law. In most cases, the provisions require businesses to be transparent in communicating the expected lifespan of their products rather than forcing businesses to build more durable products which could be upgraded or repaired. Dealing with planned obsolescence from either the demand side or the supply side is not sufficient, as the current provisions of unfair competition and consumer protection and competition law are not adequately equipped to address it. It is argued by the authors that planned obsolescence should be banned by an EU measure/law to safeguard fair play and achieve consistency across EU Member States to ensure that business strategies are in conformity with a CE. It is suggested that a three-tier approach inspired by the waste hierarchy could be introduced, where the most preferred option would be prevention (owing to durable products), followed by promoting reparability and upgradability, with a further suggestion to promote trade-in options in order to influence recycling (Malinauskaite & Erdem, 2021).

These authors recount that in December 1924, the world's largest producers of light bulbs (Philips, General Electric, Osram, and Compagnie des Lampes) colluded to artificially limit the lifespan of their products. The 1924 market standard of 2,500 burning hours was reduced to 1,000 by 1940, far below the multi-decade intended lifespan for incandescent light bulbs invented by Thomas Edison and Adolphe Chaillet. This event, better known as the Lightbulb Conspiracy (Dannoritzer, 2010) or the Phoebus Cartel, marks the emergence of planned obsolescence. Light bulb producers originally used this strategy to increase their product turnover and thus profitability. Around the same time, New York real estate magnate Bernard London went a step further by proposing a national policy of planned obsolescence to restore the US economy following the 1929 Wall Street crash. Robust products became economic liabilities in a Depression economy, and London proposed products to be declared 'legally dead' after a predetermined period, following which they would be collected and destroyed by the State. In exchange, consumers would receive the item's original sales tax value as a voucher for a new purchase, stimulating consumption and contributing to jobs in manufacturing (Bisschop et al., 2022).

Corporations usually close ranks around their common business strategy of planned obsolescence. Due to this lack of transparency, the public becomes aware of these examples through whistle-blowers, such as The Repair Association and the 'right to repair' movement in the USA, or via lawsuits filed by disenchanted consumers, NGO, and States. Well-known examples of planned obsolescence present in consumer products are those of printers and ink cartridges. Similar lawsuits (in France, Italy, Belgium, Spain, and Portugal) have been brought against mobile phone and tablet producers for their planned obsolescence strategies. Management science has a long tradition of studying planned obsolescence as an economic theory (Bulow, 1986), a business strategy (Iizuka, 2007), and an issue of business ethics (Guiltinan, 2009). While the subject of planned obsolescence has been discussed quite extensively within the business literature and has recently gained traction in law, planned obsolescence has not been studied in criminology to the knowledge of the authors. France was the first country that had explicitly addressed planned obsolescence by defining, prohibiting, and penalising it via the 'Consumer Code'. The code defines planned obsolescence as 'the use of techniques by which the person in charge of placing a product on the market aims to deliberately reduce its lifespan in order to increase its replacement rate' (Bisschop et al., 2022). The authors believe that this Code could become a template for all countries with organisations doing business in circular economies.

The product development process should acknowledge the need for ease of manufacture, ease of distribution, and ease of use. Producers who were once producing quality products started to find ways to make goods that were either more fragile or difficult to repair, in order that consumers would be forced to replace the older version sooner. Processes and devices have been created with a predetermined lifetime to maximise economic outputs. The result of shorter lifespans is inevitably that more waste is produced which, in many circumstances, ends up in landfills. The consideration of product lifetime at the early design stage is therefore recognised as an important factor. This description of a product lifespan demonstrated the need for product life cycle management to better design closed systems. In terms of design approaches, design for 'end-of-life' will make material recovery easier. At the same time, it has striven to make disassembly operations economically feasible in order to allow the establishment of recovery networks and infrastructure. These efforts should lead to lower environmental and social impacts. With positive scenarios, these networks could be established in developing countries to contribute to social development through acceptable work practices and job creation. Optimising material flows is imperative to ensure the sustained operation of these networks. The successful implementation of recovery networks will hence provide ways to mitigate the environmental and social impacts of product obsolescence (Rivera & Lallmahomed, 2015).

This chapter analyses the obsolescence problem from the point of view of the organisation. It essentially considers two scenarios: one where the company can perfectly steer the breakdown time of the product and one where the breakdown time is stochastic. In the first scenario, the following authors found that installing a warranty period does not incentivise a firm to extend a breakdown time. Furthermore, it could even be the other way around: installing a warranty period gives consumers the right to ask for a free item once their product breaks down before that period is over. This reduces the firm's profit and therefore it wants to invest less in increasing the quality of the product, which reduces the product lifetime (Hartl et al., 2023).

This chapter identifies that planned obsolescence can artificially increase sales by stimulating desire or perceived need. Barros and Dimla (2021) show that this can be done in many ways and certain companies are releasing newer models sooner than necessary or engineering the product to fail after a certain amount of use. In recent years, they have observed a change in the pattern of planned obsolescence strategies employed by technological firms, shifting from aesthetic to technological obsolescence. The reaction to this model comes from social enterprises and grassroots movements which address the CE and reparability. They focus on product architecture and product features in the mobile phone sector as a reference point to research the embodiment of strategies, and the degree of control the consumer is given for repairing the products (Barros & Dimla, 2021).

2.5. Global CE Models

Certain countries have found that CE strategies can have a transformative effect on their strategic policy programmes. The introduction of a CE programme in Finland has led to the promotion and acceleration of innovation and the reconfiguration of resource-intensive systems. This has put a sharper focus on policy processes that seek to destabilise and disrupt existing systems and practices, incorporating concentration on social justice aspects of system phase-out policies. Their CE policy programme aims predominantly at niche stimulation and acceleration with lesser emphasis on regime destabilisation or coordination. This has led to a strategy of progressive system change with an orientation shaped by the country's corporatist approach to policy-making and pre-existing plans (Lazarevic et al., 2022).

CE has received increasing attention because it has the potential to break with the existing linear economy of unsustainable production and consumption. A single lighting regulation (SLR) has been formulated within EU Member states based on circular strategies, nutrient cycles, the RESOLVE framework, and circular business models. This led to the implementation of a CE AP proposed in 2015 in numerous sectors which helped to build the required infrastructure and provided a technological push for augmenting sustainable growth. Recycling was mostly used for looping materials back into the system. Waste management, electrical and electronic equipment industries, and the construction sector are pioneers. Macro-level initiatives by governments and/or regional administration can result in CE facilitated by government policies, infrastructure, and technological availability, awareness, stakeholder collaboration, and supply chain integration (Mhatre et al., 2021). This review focusses on micro-level indicators for CE moving away from the three dimensions of sustainability. The three levels of indicators align with macro (global, national, regional, and city), meso (industrial, symbiosis, and eco-industrial parks), and micro (single firm/product). Fewer indicators consider disassembly, lifetime extension, waste management, resource efficiency, or reuse. Fundamentally, there was no way of measuring CE at a micro-level which leads to a biased approach to CE that favours economic aspects over environmental, social impacts (Kristensen & Mosgaard, 2020).

Few previous studies have compared circularity indicators with environmental performance, or have linked the circularity indicators between society levels, that is, at micro- and macro-levels. LCA has been undertaken at the micro-level, and multi-regional input–output (MRIO) analysis at macro-level as a way of tracking CE performance. At the meso-level, industrial symbiosis continues to grow in potential; though several national monitoring programmes exist we do not have indicators on stocks of materials, that is, reuse economy, maintenance, and spare parts. The societal needs and functions framework offers a meso-level link to bridge micro and macro (Harris et al., 2021).

There is increasing enthusiasm in academic circles for the development of a framework for circular business models in the fashion and textiles sector. The textiles production and consumption system is a pressing priority for the product-value chain for the European Commission in its 2020 CE AP. It is anticipated that the CE can facilitate the aim of creating markets for sustainable and circular textile products, services, and business models. The European Environment Agency (EEA) and its Topic Centre on Waste and Materials in a Green Economy (ETC/WMGE) have shown that consumption of clothing, footwear, and household textiles in Europe is, on average, the fourth highest category of environmental and climate impacts from a consumption perspective. There is a need to transform the existing concept of production and consumption with an innovation in business-model design, technology, and social practices. As a starting point, several basic principles could be instituted: models based on product durability; the accessibility of models based on renting, leasing, and sharing; garment collection and resale; and recycling and reuse of materials (Coscieme et al., 2022).

To illustrate the challenges of existing circularity indicators, they have been grouped into four clusters: multi-cyclic longevity; up and down-cycling effects; measuring disruptive change instead of incremental change; and integration into sustainability assessment. Two other novel indicators are derived from this approach: (a) a functional circulatory indicator (FCI) and (b) a cross-functional circulatory indicator (C-F CI) – (a) measures the integral surface of functionality over the use-time of the original product's materials while (b) measures the time a product's functionality is reduced by half (Hatzfeld et al., 2022). Further research examines the potential of the EU's Circular Economy Monitoring Framework (CEMF), which is an established indicator-based framework for measuring national and EU-level circularity performance. In urban areas, data quality is assessed following the pedigree matrix approach. The CEMF has been computed for Umea, Sweden signifying the need for improvements in scope and data availability to be recommended (Henrysson et al., 2022).

Sustainable consumption and production (SCP) tools have been identified either as an aid to circularity or as a supporter of the achievement of sustainable development goals (SDGs). These can incorporate environmental management systems (EMS); green public procurement (GPP); eco-design directive; eco-label; energy label; and environmental technology variation (ETV). They have been identified by practitioners and academics as useful tools to promote CE. More research is required on sustainable consumption and production, and the CE has highlighted: (i) the role of EMS in increasing firms' circularity; (ii) the eco-design directive and ETV in the design and manufacturing processes of the products; and (iii) GPP, eco-label, and energy label in driving greener consumption by setting products' circular criteria (Marrucci et al., 2019).

Light-weight steel, masonry, and wood-framing construction supplemented with bio-based materials are viewed as the three basic construction methods. Environmental impact assessment can be underpinned with circularity tools focussing on the reuse and recyclability potential in end-of-life (EOL) scenarios. The integration of life-cycle assessment (LCA) and circularity tools displayed that bio-based design. Preliminary designs have an increased performance owing to the environmental impact avoided through reuse and recycling within end-of-life scenarios. As a consequence of this research, a novel approach is posited that integrates circularity calculations with an LCA methodology put forward to improve long-term impact analysis on circular buildings with more precision in EOL scenario development (Kayacetin et al., 2023).

Many organisations with a global reach are trying to change perception, not only of their firm but of their business/industrial sector. As recently as 12 years ago, the authors tried to achieve an effective interview with the appropriate sustainability manager of a major player in the multi-billion pound cruise sector. The idea was to gauge where this company was in terms of having a credible sustainability strategy for the future. Suffice to say, it was rather a short interview. However, we were able to impart some useful information with regard to the sustainability progress of global corporations of a similar size which was well received. The following case study is an interesting snapshot of how an organisation in the same sector has grasped the green agenda and is putting a cohesive and credible strategy in place for the next 20 years. As you will recognise from these case studies, not all organisations start from the same level of sustainability experience.

2.5.1. Cruise Ships and Accountability

This particular section is particularly interesting for one of the authors. I tried to interview a member of staff from one of the largest Cruise companies to identify what green human resource management credentials they had within the organisation. It was exploratory research, and it was being undertaken in 2012. However, similar to a number of other sectors, the Cruise industry did not have a cohesive strategy and declined to be involved with the research. It is interesting to note how attitudes to environmental accounting in the sustainability arena have changed over the last decade (Di Vaio et al., 2022).

This particular study (Di Vaio et al., 2023) investigates how Cruise firms with high growth rates address the United Nations (UN) Sustainable Development Goal 17 (SDG 17) which focusses on a global partnership of all countries, both developed and developing, to ensure no one is left behind. It also requires collaboration between governments, the private sector, and civil society to meet the goals of the UN's 2030 Agenda. Currently, organisations are being leaned on to perform sustainably as stakeholders and third parties are increasingly expecting greater accountability from these firms pushing them to prove their social economic and environmental credentials. However, it is true to say that the impact and challenge of the COVID-19 pandemic on global cruise tourism (GCT) industry's sustainable development were profound. Since mid-March 2020, the temporary suspension of cruise ships has resulted in operating losses of over $10 billion. Previously, the number of international cruise passengers increased from 22.34 to 29.67 million from 2014 to 2019 (Lin et al., 2022).

Incontrovertibly, all the studied firms have adopted corporate sustainability policies, and relevant initiatives, and disclosed their sustainable activities through their Reports. On their corporate websites, each Cruise company has a section dedicated to sustainable goals. There is also a high general interest in sustainability by identifying what has been achieved in various key areas on an ongoing basis. It is anticipated that further improvements in the sustainability arena can be achieved through improved cross-sector partnerships. However, this sustainability reporting and the company websites do not actually highlight the effectiveness measures of the training initiatives and practices in changing the beneficiaries' behaviour and perceptions regarding environmental issues. It is still argued that research in the Cruise sector remains uncritical due to the oligopolistic nature of the Cruise market. These authors also suggest that Cruise operators may also tend to disclose their sustainable initiatives for the show, which hints at potential greenwashing (Di Vaio et al., 2023). In relation to global sustainability, to say there is room for improvement would be a gross understatement and everyone would like to know how the Cruise industry is responding to this range of damning environmental figures.

Sustainability principles refer to the environmental, economic, and socio-cultural aspects of tourism development, and a suitable balance must be established between these three measures to guarantee their long-term sustainability. Sustainable tourism development requires the informed participation of all relevant stakeholders, as well as strong political leadership to ensure wide participation and consensus-building. The systemic complexity and multidimensionality of cruise tourism are generally acknowledged (Papathanassis, 2023). At least the UN has provided strong leadership in the environmental arena, and the 17 SDGs provide a solid framework (Di Vaio et al., 2022). The Cruise Sector as a whole is trying to respond constructively to implicating environmental figures. One goal within the sector is to achieve net carbon-neutral operations by 2050. The jury may be out on whether this response is as wide or as quick as is needed in the current situation.

2.6. Managing Complex CE Business Models

The concept of the CE can be very complex and has led to a new discipline at the heart of chemical, environmental, electrical, and mechanical engineering.

This also includes the material sciences and energy engineers. Other disciplines should be introduced for future generations of engineers to design, promote, and establish innovation on end-of-life Photo Voltaic (PV) panels and redesign rather than replace PV modules (Papamichael & Zonpas, 2022). The circular bio-economy is not a simple superposition of two pre-existing concepts, that is, the bio-economy and the CE. We need to know how to successfully continue territorial and value-chain approaches in order to analyse the organisational and technological challenges raised by the deployment of the increasing recovery of organic waste. It is important to reveal whether the circular bio-economy contains singular social science research questions, particularly regarding the agriculture–industry nexus (Girard, 2022).

There has also been an increase in theorising around the principles of SP&C in relation to Industry 4.0 (I4.0) and CE. SP has resulted in new economic and industrial models such as CE and I4.0 using the interpretive structural model (ISM) technique. Principles 5, 6, 9, and 10 help to establish the ideal characteristic of sustainable production:

5 – Prioritises employee well-being - contributes to achieving SDG 12.
6 – Enhances management commitment to sustainability.
9 – Measures and optimises sustainable processes.
10 – Boosts the use of sustainable technologies (Viles et al., 2022).

2.7. Resource-based Taxonomies and Global Strategies for CE Implementation

A Taxonomy is a scheme of classification, especially a hierarchical classification, in which things are organised into groups or types. Among other things, a taxonomy can be used to organise and index knowledge (stored as documents, articles, videos, etc.), such as in the form of a library classification system, or a search engine taxonomy, so that users can more easily find the information they are searching for. Many taxonomies are hierarchies (and thus have an intrinsic 'tree' structure), but not all are like this (Wikipedia). Taxonomy is related to an empirical scheme of classification, suitable for descriptive analysis (Smith, 2002). Even though it is often associated with the biological sciences, taxonomic methods are also employed in numerous disciplines that require categorisation. In the scientific literature related to sustainability indicators, eco-design tools, or even CE business models, the term 'taxonomy' is usually employed when it comes to the classification of such indicators, tools, or business models.

This chapter focusses on circularity indicators (C-indicators). A wide range of C-indicators have been developed in the last decade – 55 sets by 2018. However, as there is not one single definition of the CE concept, it is very important to know what the available indicators measure in order to utilise them appropriately. The 55 sets of C-indicators have been developed by academics, consulting companies, and government agencies and have been isolated, encompassing different purposes, scopes, and potential usages. Inspired by existing taxonomies of eco-design tools and sustainability indicators, and in line with CE characteristics, a classification of indicators which aimed to assess, improve, monitor, and communicate CE performance was proposed and discussed. The developed taxonomy included 10 categories and the C-indicators were differentiated regarding criteria such as the levels of CE introduction/implementation (i.e. micro, meso, and macro), the CE loops (maintain, reuse, manufacture, and recycle), the performance (intrinsic and impacts), the perspective of circularity (actual and potential), they are taking into account, or their degree of transversality (generic and sector-specific) (Saidani et al., 2018).

2.8. Conclusions

For sustainability and the CE to work effectively in the future from a micro- to a macro-level, they must be viewed as part of a global environmental strategy. It will be vital that organisations undertake these sustainability endeavours as part of strategic alliances. Sustainability and CE are inextricably linked. However, CE must be built on strong foundations. There is every likelihood that a range of stakeholders will be involved at all levels of negotiations. Many organisations – who have never done business together before – will be communicating with each other. Similarly, practitioners and academics can form alliances, even if they are only temporary, for the greater good of the sustainability cause. They would most likely prefer to be part of a discipline or movement that is more clearly defined or where future outcomes could be gauged more accurately. They would also like a situation where the outputs of one system can be predicted by analysing the inputs into that same system. In most circumstances, especially with sustainability and CE, this will not be the case. However, the CE AP, proposed in many sectors in 2015, helped to build the required infrastructure providing the right environment to propel sustainable growth.

In reality, most cases and projects within CE will not be well-structured and are more likely to be of a piecemeal nature. Not all sustainability and CE projects will be neatly coordinated, especially at a micro-level. There will be great pressure on project managers, particularly at the global level, to organise these projects for optimum sustainability gains. Some projects may fail. However, the drive to succeed is expected to be intense. The Clean Air Act (1970) and the Clean Water Act (1972) were key landmarks in the push towards sustainability, nevertheless, a number of large corporations ignored them. In the future, more time should be spent making sure that these organisations adhere rigorously to regulations. The real success is actually in the implementation of the acts or laws. There are two global examples of what happens when environmental issues are not adhered to comprehensively – BP's Deepwater Horizon oil spill and Volkswagen's ongoing emissions scandal. There are too many others to include here.

The increasing influence of CSR across the world should certainly help embed CE. Customers are much more likely to be aware of the sometimes-wide gap between stated environmental goals and their actual implementation. There is often a minimisation of ESG risks, frequently aligned with the possible misinformation given about sustainability achievements by organisations. However, there is substantially more scrutiny of environmental statistics, and today's generation is more likely to be aware of any 'double-dealing'. Furthermore, it is much more likely that bright graduates will join a company with excellent green credentials and a very good track record on sustainability and carbon emissions than go elsewhere.

Reduction of output can be achieved on the production side by producing with less, as well as on the consumption side by consuming less. Built-in Obsolescence appears to be the antithesis of sustainability and CE. However, the fact that this manoeuvre can be good for business has often been overlooked. It is nearly 100 years since the well-documented case of a group of international light bulb manufacturers colluded to reduce the market standard of 2,500 burning hours down to 1,000. For CE to work effectively across the world a different perspective must be taken on the notion of, the 'lifetime of the product'. Businesses and the general public need standards and benchmarks to measure whether they are buying quality, long-lasting products.

A radical action might be to move the emphasis on checking quality away from the consumer and onto the producer/provider of goods and services. This would trigger a departure from our long-established reliance on caveat emptor to caveat venditor, where the seller will be responsible for the quality and robustness of their products. This should facilitate good practices and enhance the quality of goods produced or services offered, leading to less built-in obsolescence and will be very important for CE where many more goods will be refurbished and resold. It is highlighted in the rapid mass production of what has become termed 'fast fashion'. International organisations such as charities have many decades of experience in the second-hand clothes market. With CE business models, a taxonomy can facilitate the classification of indicators, providing benchmarks and comparisons to gauge whether targets, either local or international, are being met within agreed guidelines.

References

Adamkiewicz, J., Kochanska, E., Adamkiewicz, I., & Lukasik, R. M. (2022). Greenwashing and the sustainable fashion industry. *Current Opinion in Green and Sustainable Chemistry, 38*, 100710.

Barros, M., & Dimla, E. (2021). From planned obsolescence to the circular economy in the smartphone industry: An evolution of strategies embodied in product features. *Proceedings of the Design Society, 1*, 1607–1616.

Bianchi, M., & Cordella, M. (2023). Does circular economy mitigate the extraction of natural resources? Empirical evidence-based analysis of 28 European economies over the past decade. *Ecological Economics, 203*, 107607.

Bisschop, L., Hendlin, Y., & Jaspers, J. (2022). Designed to break: Planned obsolescence as corporate environmental crime. *Crime, Law and Social Change, 78*, 271–293.

Brundtland, G. H. (1987). *The United Nations Brundtland Commission, Report of the World Commission on Environment and Development.* sustainabledevelopment.un.org

Bulow, J. (1986). An economic theory of planned obsolescence. *The Quarterly Journal of Economics, 101*(4), 729–750.

Circle Economy. (2019). *The role of charity shops in a circular textiles value chain. Case Study.* https://www.circle-economy.com/resources/the-role-of-charity-shops-in-a-circular-textiles-value-chain

Cohen, E. (2013). *Sustainability reporting for SMEs: Competitive advantage through transparency* (1st ed.). Routledge. https://doi.org/10.4324/9781351275644

Cornell, S., Häyhä, T., & Palm, C. (2021). *A sustainable and resilient circular textiles and fashion industry: Towards a circular economy that respects and responds to planetary priorities* [Research Report]. Stockholm University's Stockholm Resilience Centre for the Ellen MacArthur Foundation and H&M Group.

Coscieme, L., Manshoven, S., Gillabel, J., Grossi, F., & Mortensen, L. F. (2022). A framework of circular business models for fashion and textiles: The role of business model, technical and social innovation. *Sustainability: Science, Practice and Policy*, *18*(1), 451–462.

Dannoritzer. C. (2010). *The light bulb conspiracy* [Documentary]. http://freedomlightbulb.blogspot.com.tr/2012/05/lightbulb-conspiracy-documentary-by.html

De Fazio, Bakker, C., Flipsen, B., & Balkenende, R. (2021). The disassembly map: A new method to enhance design for product repairability. *Journal of Cleaner Production*, *320*, 128552.

De Freitas Netto, S. V., Sobral, M. F. F., & Ribeiro, A. R. B. (2020). Concepts and forms of greenwashing: A systematic review. *Environmental Science Europe*, *32*, 19.

Di Vaio, A., Varriale, L., Di Gregorio, A., & Adomako, S. (2022). Corporate social performance and non-financial reporting in the cruise industry: Paving the way towards UN agenda, 2030. *Corporate Social Responsibility and Environmental Management*, *29*(6), 1931–1953.

Di Vaio, A., Varriale, L., Lekakou, M., & Pozzoli, M. (2023). SDGs disclosure: Evidence from cruise corporations' sustainability reporting. *Corporate Governance*, *23*(4), ISSN 1472-0701.

Farahani, R. Z., Asgari, N., & Van Wassenhove, L. N. (2021). Fast fashion, charities, and the circular economy: Challenges for operations management. *Production and Operations Management*, *31*(3), 1089–1114.

Gatti, L., Seele, P., & Rademacher, L. (2019). Grey zone in – Greenwash out. A review of greenwashing research and implications for the voluntary-mandatory transition of C.S.R. *International Journal of Corporate Social Responsibility*, *4*(1), 1–15.

Genc, R. (2016). Sustainability in cruise ship management. *International Journal of Social Science Studies*, *4*(6), 76.

Genovese, A., Acquaye, A. A., Figueroa, A., & Koh, S. C. L. (2017). Sustainable supply chain management and the transition towards a circular economy: Evidence and some applications. *Omega*, *66*(Part B), 344–357.

Georgantzis G., D., Kipnis, E., Vasileiou, E., & Solomon, A. (2021). Consumption in the circular economy: Learning from our mistakes. *Sustainability*, *13*(2), 601.

Girard, L. F., & Nocca, F. (2019). Moving towards the circular economy/city model: Which tools for operationalizing this model?, *Sustainability*, *11*(22), 6253.

Guiltinan, J. (2009). Creative destruction and destructive creations: Environmental ethics and planned obsolescence. *Journal of Business Ethics*, *89*(1), 19–28.

Harris, S., Mata, E., Lucena, A. F. P., & Bertoldi, P. (2023). Climate mitigation from circular and sharing economy in the building sector. *Resources, Conservation and Recycling*, *188*, 106709.

Hartl, R. F., Kort, P. M., & Wrzaczec, S. (2023). Reputation or warranty, what is more effective against planned obsolescence. *International Journal of Production Research*, *61*(3), 939–954.

Hatzfeld, T., Backes, J. G., Guenther, E., & Traverso, M. (2022). Modelling circularity as functionality over use-time to reflect on circularity indicator challenges and identify new indicators for the circular economy. *Journal of Cleaner Production*, *379*, 134797.

Hazen, B. T., Russo, I., Confente, I., & Pellathy, D. (2020). Supply change management for circular economy, conceptual framework and research agenda. *International Journal of Logistics Management*, *32*(2), 510–537.

He, S., Wei, W., Ding, S., Zheng, S., & Niu, T. (2023). Co-evolution between science and policy: A systematic analysis on circular economy in China and worldwide. *Environmental Science and Policy, 139,* 104–117.

Henrysson, M., Papageorgiou, A., Bjorklund, A., & Vanhuyse, F. (2022). Monitoring progress towards a circular economy in urban areas: An application of the EU CE monitoring framework in Umea municipality. *Sustainable Cities and Society, 87,* 10425.

Hobson, K., Holmes, H., Welch, D., Wheeler, K., Wieser, H. (2021). ConsumptionWork in the Circular Economy: A Research Agenda. *Journal of Cleaner Production, 321.*

Hussain, M., & Malik, M. (2020). Organizational enablers for the circular economy in the context of sustainable supply chain management. *Journal of Cleaner Production, 256,* 120375.

Iizuka. (2007). An empirical analysis of planned obsolescence. *Journal of Economics and Management Strategy, 16*(1), 191–226.

Ioannou, I., Kassinis, G., Papagiannakis, G. (2022). How Greenwashing affects the Bottom Line. *Harvard Business Review.*

Kayacetin, N. C., Verdocott, S., Lefevre, L., & Versele, A. (2023). Integrated decision support for embodied impact assessment of circular and bio-based building components. *Journal of Building Engineering, 63,* 105427.

Khajuria, A., Atienza, V. A., Chavanich, S., Henning, W., Islam, I., Kral, U., Liu, M., Liu, X., Murthy, I. K., Oyedotun, T. D. T., Verma, P., Xu, G., & Zeng, X. (2022). Accelerating circular economy solutions to achieve the 2030 agenda for sustainable development goals. *Circular Economy, 1,* 100001.

Kristensen, H. S., & Mosgaard, M. A. (2020). A review of micro level indicators for a circular economy – Moving away from the three dimensions of sustainability?. *Journal of Cleaner Production, 243,* 118531.

Lazarevic, D., Salo, H., & Kautto, P. (2022). Circular economy policies and their transformative intent on Finland's strategic policy programme. *Journal of Cleaner Production, 379,* 134892.

Li, R. (2022). Integrating the composition of food waste into the techno-economic analysis of waste bio-refineries for bio-diesel production. *Resource Technology Reports, 20,* 101254.

Lin, L-Y, Tsai, C-C., & Lee, J. Y. (2022). A study on the trends of the global cruise tourism industry, sustainable development, and the impacts of the COVID-19 pandemic. *Sustainability, 14,* 68–90.

Luzzati, T., Distefano, T., Ialenti, S., & Andreoni, V. (2022). The circular economy and longer product lifetime: Framing the effects on working time and waste. *Journal of Cleaner Production, 380,* 134836.

Malinauskaite, J., & Erdem, F. B. (2021). Planned obsolescence in the context of a holistic legal sphere and the circular economy. *Oxford Journal of Legal Studies, 41*(3), 719–749.

Marrucci, L., Daddi, T., & Iraldo, F. (2019). The integration of circular economy with sustainable consumption and production tools: Systematic review and future research agenda. *Journal of Cleaner Production, 240,* 118268.

Matzler, K., Veider, V., & Karthan, W. (2015). Adapting to the sharing economy. *M.I.T., Sloan Management Review, 56* (2), 71–77.

Mhatre, P., Panchal, R., Singh, A., & Bibyan, S. (2021). A systematic literature review on the circular economy initiatives in the European Union. *Sustainable Production and Consumption, 26,* 187–202.

Morone, P., & Navia, R. (2016). New consumption and production models for a circular economy. *Waste Management and Research, 34*(6), 489–490.

Okorie, O., Russell, J., Cherrington, R., Fisher, O., Charnley, F. (2023). Digital Transformation and the Circular Economy: Creating a Competitive Advantage from the Transition towards Net Zero. *Resources, Conservation and Recycling, 189*, 106756.

Osterley, R., & Williams, I. D. (2018). The social, environmental and economic benefits of reuse by charity shops. *Detritus, 7*, 29–35.

Papamichael, I., & Zonpas, A. A. (2022). End-of-waste criteria in the framework of end-of-life PV panels concerning circular economy strategy. *Waste Management and Research, 40*(12), 1677–1679.

Papathanassis, A. (2023, January 19). *A decade of 'blue tourism' sustainability research: Exploring the impact of cruise tourism on coastal areas.* Cambridge University Press.

Pearce, D. W., & Turner, R. K. (1990). *Economics of natural resources and the environment.* Harvester Wheatsheaf.

Rivera, J. L., & Lallmahomed, A. (2015). Environmental implications of planned obsolescence and product lifetime: A literature review. *International Journal of Sustainable Engineering, 9*(2), 119–129.

Rousseaux, P., Gremy-Gros, C., Bonnin, M., Hennel-Ricordel, C., Bernard, P., Floury, L., Staigre, G., & Vincent, P., 'Eco-Tool-Seeker'. A new and unique business guide for choosing eco-design tools. *Journal of Cleaner Production, 151*, 546–577.

Saidani, M., Yannou, B., Leroy, Y., Cluzel, F., & Kendall, A. (2018). A taxonomy of circular economy indicators. *Journal of Cleaner Production, 207*, 542–559.

Sehnem, S., Jabbour, C. J. C., Pereira, S. C. F., & de Sousa Jabbour, A. B. L. (2019). Improving sustainable supply chains performance through operational excellence: Circular economy approach. *Resources, Conservation and Recycling, 149*, 236–248.

Smith, K. B. (2002). Typologies, taxonomies and the benefits of policy classification. *Policy Studies Journal, 30*(3), 379–395.

Spotting Greenwashing with Environmental, Social, and Governance (ESG) Data, RepRisk ESG Data Science and Quantitative Solutions (2022, July).

Stahel, W .R. (2001). The business angle of a circular economy – Higher competitiveness. *Higher resource security, and material efficiency, E.M.F.*

Viles, E., Kalemkerian, F., Garza-Reyes, J. A., Antony, J., & Santos, J. (2022). Theorizing the principles of sustainable production in the context of circular economy and industry 4.0. *Sustainable production and Consumption, 33*, 1043–1058.

Westerveld, J. (1986). *Tiny Caller – The northern cricket frog.* New York Department of Environmental Conservation.

Wijayasundara, M., Polensky, M., Noel, W., & Vocino, A. (2022). Green procurement for a circular economy: What influences purchasing of products with recycled material and recovered content by public sector organisations. *Journal of Cleaner Production, 377*, 133917.

Wood, R. E. (2000). Caribbean cruise tourism: Globalisation at sea. *Annals of Tourism Research, 27*(2), 345–370.

Yang, Z., Nguyen, T. T. H., Nguyen, N., Nguyen, T. T. N., & Cao, T. T. (2020). Greenwashing behaviours: Causes, taxonomy, and consequences based on a systematic literature review. *Journal of Business Economics and Management, 21*(5), 1486–1507.

Chapter 3

Sustainable Production and Consumption Within the Circular Economy

3.1. Introduction

Circular economy (CE) is a powerful and provocative concept that increasingly provides society with a strategy for human action in the face of environmental disaster. The CE has received global attention because it has the potential to optimise and promote sustainable production and consumption through new models based on continuous growth and limitless production (Govindan & Hasanagic, 2018; Ludeki-Freund, 2019; Tseng et al., 2020). These aspirations, when aligned with sustainable development, produce a potential game-changer in the fight to preserve the planet for future generations. The recent outcome from COP-27 shows that a change in global sustainability cannot occur only by issuing edicts and laws. In certain areas of the globe, it would certainly be more beneficial to rely on conventions rather than laws. A more realistic suggestion may be to develop and implement a set of desirable and feasible international rules and regulations that can facilitate the promotion of an effective CE. Both 'push' and 'pull' factors will be necessary to support a collective trajectory towards CE. This requires complex coordination, collaboration and collusion around the values of CE in order to bring about a virtuous set of inter-related partnerships and relationships throughout society, industry, and government. The quintuple helix, underpinned by innovation, becomes a highly resonant model for delivering CE (Carayannis et al., 2012), as it seeks to integrate into partnership with universities and knowledge hubs, government, industry, civil society, and the media along with the natural environment.

As sustainability has become a pressing agenda for all societies and economies around the globe, CE has become a key model and policymaking tool (Korhonen et al., 2018; Winans et al., 2017). The new emphasis brought to bear through CE thinking is that of the reduction of resources in production and the reuse and recycling of waste throughout production, distribution, and consumption in economies. Japan was among the first of the developed countries to apply CE to

Sustainable Development Through Global Circular Economy Practices, 59–78
Copyright © 2024 by Stuart Maguire and Ian Robson
Published under exclusive licence by Emerald Publishing Limited
doi:10.1108/978-1-83753-590-320231003

industrial development strategies, seeking as it does today to reduce the importation of raw materials through the reuse and recycling of raw materials (UEP, 2011).

Given that production and consumption drive the global economy, it is clear that these networks of activity ought to be the focus of our attention. The understanding of their impact on the natural environment is growing, and economic imperatives are no longer the only drivers for businesses and government to consider. The United Nations Agenda for Sustainable Development goes well beyond responsible and places the long-term protection of the natural environment at the top of its list of priorities (UN, 2015). The United Nations naturally promotes positive environmental and sustainable action across all of its 17 Sustainable Development Goals (SDGs). In this chapter, we focus on SDG 12 that concerns responsible production and consumption.

A pressing need for all firms to further understand the sociology of consumption given the global momentum behind CE and sustainability in supply chains is a requirement. Historically, we have understood economic values for thousands of years (use of coins/currency); however, we have little or no understanding of social, aesthetic, or ecological currencies. Despite the wealth of literature appearing in the area over the last 70 years, it is not clear how analysts in the private sector introduce the important element of social responsibility into their design-making equation. It is understood that the executive should try to maximise profits for the firm and shareholders in tandem with considering the responsibility of the organisation towards the public, the community, and towards the preservation of the environment and aligned goals. This is usually dependent upon the perceptions of the manager towards different situations. It is often believed that the executive, as a matter of course, will seek to maximise the short- and long-term profit of the company and that he/she will automatically consider their responsibility towards wider society. This clearly demonstrates the inherent uncertainty – is it always in the self-interest of the firm to carry out social obligations, and by doing so, is it maximising its profits in the long run? This position leaves the executive open to criticism, uncertain how far to pursue either profit, the welfare of others or the protection of the natural environment.

In this chapter, we consider the gradual implementation of CE principles across the globe and in a variety of settings, accepting that while CE is aspirational, we appreciate that we are at a critical moment in human history, one which demands a radical transformation of our collective action in relation to the ecosystem. We look closely at the nature of CE in production and consumption, including a brief journey into sustainable supply chains – which is covered in depth in Chapter 4. We also consider the sociology and institutional context of CE, looking at dimensions of agency and structure, collaboration, and partnership in delivering the necessary changes in behaviour. Finally, in this chapter, we consider CE adoption and the contextual drivers that will most likely lead to radical changes in business models, priorities, and market behaviours, which address both the 'push' and 'pull' factors alluded to earlier. The chapter case study gives us a detailed insight into fast fashion and the challenges of CE in the story of H & M, the high street fashion retailer, and its supply chain.

3.2. Exploring Sustainable Production and Consumption

The definition of CE continues to develop into a more proactive concept of rebalanced organisational goals that fully embrace and prioritise society-wide benefits, eradication of waste, and a foundation of renewable energy (Ellen MacArthur Foundation, 2020). Production processes need to be transformed and a systemic view taken of resource usage, production, and consumption. The investment paradigm needs to shift towards a balance between social and environmental impact and economic performance, potentially reorienting the financial services sector and business financial management thinking towards sustainability in its various forms – ecological, financial, economic, and social.

The CE field is very broad, and in production and consumption, we begin to open the discussion of what it might encompass. The ability to decouple production and consumption is a positive aspect of CE and will lead to improved resource efficiency. With the CE gaining impetus as a concept and practice, the ability to promote closed material processes with strategies for material recycling and product reuse will become more and more important (Hussain et al., 2020; Moreau et al., 2017). Supply chains acting as district energy systems should be viewed as a viable method of moving towards a circular industrial economy (Mignacci & Locatelli, 2021; Pan et al., 2015). This framework can be practically transferred to several business and industrial areas, for example, the construction industry, which is global, complex, and large scale (Leising, 2018). This breadth of concern includes social and environmental outcomes of organisational activity, the management of materials including reuse, recyclability, biodegradability, repurposing, managing hazardous materials, and the maintenance of CE principles in international trade. Breaking these elements down further, we begin to get an insight into the scope of CE and the challenge of its implementation. Consumption, for example, concerns the demand-pull elements of a supply chain. The complexity of consumption lies in behaviour and usage which in turn is underpinned by culture, beliefs, demographic criteria, and values. Organisational and consumer consumption are clearly different user environments with different purchase systems, processes, and regulations. Culture is appropriated at the industry and the societal levels, respectively, and where drivers of behaviour have differing weightings and roles. In the organisational behavioural purchase environment, industry norms and regulations, accounting processes, quantities, and decision-making processes will drive consumption. At the societal level, consumers are influenced more by beliefs and values, education and religion, online influencers and social media. The agency is perhaps a lesser factor in organisational buying environments than in consumer purchasing. Branding and image will play greater roles in the evaluation of product choices and utility value in consumer markets. Both fields of consumption need to change to accommodate CE and all consumption communities need to be educated and encouraged towards long-term buying decisions, the sustainable qualities of products and, of course, services such as financial. Consumers need to understand the impact of their decisions on the environment and society. The industry supply chains that ultimately bring products and services to consumers need the motivation, innovation, and technologies to switch to CE strategies. For a whole supply chain to be CE orientated, a great deal of integrated, cross-sector, and international work is required. The use of energy, water, raw materials, and impacts on human health all need to be factored in and managed. Social impacts might consider welfare packages, fair wage levels, lower prices for goods and services, and local tax contributions for infrastructure developments such as wind farms, bridges, and highways. All these CE actions are strategies aimed at aspirational goals. In CE, these goals are often pre-determined, SDG-focussed goals, some of which have been previously agreed at environmental summits such as COP-27, and passed down to national economies and their constituent industries.

Fig. 3.1 illustrates the core drivers of CE in presenting production, consumption, international trade, waste management (recycling, treatment, collection, sorting, storage, incineration, and landfill), and social and environmental impact. The links between these elements of CE are complicated and require careful mapping, examination, and management to enable sustainability to take precedence over financial profit and shareholder value. Some of the benefits of CE must simply include cost and waste reduction arising from recycling and lean production systems. This – coupled with an educated workforce, a strict regulatory regime, and political and societal pressure to adopt CE strategies – will push sustainability through the supply chain. The acknowledgment of interacting, holarchic systems is a direct application of systems thinking to the sustainability challenge. An application of systems thinking is required to achieve a strong and clear understanding of how the industrial and market elements of the ecosystem work either together or against each other. Given the difference in organisational types and governance systems, we begin to glimpse the enormity of the CE challenge and the requirements for all stakeholders and all institutions in the system to work together to produce a drive towards sustainability (Bassi et al., 2021).

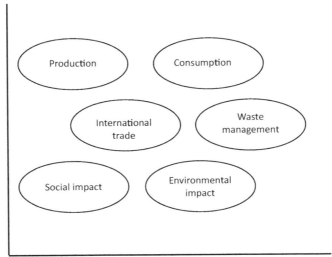

Fig. 3.1.   Core Drivers of CE.

The CE concept is based on the notion of closing loops, completing the circle and, in a very real sense, leveraging the open economic system to minimise waste. We learned in Chapter 1 that the ultimate idea of CE is thought to be unattainable by following a purely scientific rationale. In other words, there will always be resource waste of some sort. Early thinking in this field, Stahel and Reday (1976), for example, suggested that human endeavour ought to replace production systems to recycle or repurpose 'spent' goods. With a background in architecture, Walter Stahel recognised that refurbishing buildings absorbed less energy from the ecosystem than constructing new ones. He then sought to apply that philosophy to the whole economy, citing examples in many industries from mobile phone manufacture to farming. In his concept of CE, models would extend product life through repair, refit, repurposing, and upgrades and would additionally recycle materials to produce new products (Stahel, 2016). This would minimise waste and replace the loss of energy embodied by the constant usage of raw materials with an implementation of human effort in the repair, etc., as stated. Cathartically, this system would also create more skilled jobs in a society where repair and recycling are required. We can see this concept evidenced in the rise of popularity of local repair centres springing up in local communities. The necessary change in mindset is a challenging topic in the CE field – turning consumers and producers, logistics, and primary economic agents into global eco-stewards requires a seismic paradigm shift. Though in digital marketplaces, we can already observe mechanisms that we are beginning to use more frequently to reuse products rather than simply consign them to landfills. E-Bay, Amazon, and AliExpress in China are all examples of platforms that shorten the supply chain, reduce costs of supply, and increase communicative efficiency while supporting the key CE concept of recycling.

Austria is often cited as an advanced proponent of CE and offers a useful insight into the complexity of the challenge at hand. The introduction and social acceptance of stewardship rules in Austria have led to a national drive to reuse, recycle, and repair products and materials, seeking to close the recovery loop. Extracting raw and precious materials from waste is central to this and developing the new technologies to do so is critically important. Ultimately, society needs to be reclaiming materials at the atomic level and this is already happening in relation to precious metal recovery from electronic waste (Ding et al., 2019).

The boundaries of any industry, economy, or society are porous, and any attempt to confine human economic activity would clearly be futile, as history has shown us. As we begin to apply the principles of CE in action, we see that some sense of defining the 'field' of analysis helps in understanding elements of economic and industrial structure such as integrated supply chains, cost structures, and international resource flows (finance, human, and capital), institutional pressure and regulations, legislation, codes of conduct, and so on. We also need to understand agency within the system such as buyer behaviour, and its drivers of culture, values, and beliefs. Studying the field allows us to weigh up the CE implementation challenge and to understand how to influence, educate, and motivate both 'push' and 'pull' factors. Tech-driven innovation is another form of disruptor to traditional socio-economic structures which alters the power dynamics and hopefully increases connectivity with society's demands for responsible, sustainable behaviour. We will consider innovation and CE in more detail in Chapter 5. For now, we need to turn our attention to the analysis of fields, applying Fligstein and Calder (2015) in understanding the elements of power, control, structure, and agency.

3.3. Strategic Action Fields

A strategic action field (SAF) concerns social order and is reminiscent of social systems theory (Luhmann, 2002). Fligstein and McAdam (2012) define social action fields as 'meso level social orders, as the basic structural building block of modern political/organizational life in the economy, civil society and the state' (p. 3). The importance of this contribution can be observed in situations of conflict or disruption in the business community, also at the meso-level (Fligstein & McAdam, 2012). Implementing CE to any traditional industry or economy will lead to major disruption and will be met with many forms of resistance. The key stakeholders in any large infrastructure project, for example, a new motorway development, are often: locally affected communities; local authorities; locally elected council members; members of central government; transport executives (planners, engineers, project managers, etc. employed by the government); media; non-governmental organisations (e.g. Greenpeace and local action groups); and local planning authorities (see Table 3.1).

Field theory considers the *behaviour* of agents rather than simply the *power* of agents as bestowed upon them through the structure. This brings the potential to analyse the tactics and temporality of agency and the fluctuations in concepts of power and saliency. Social actors in conflict scenarios are either forcing a structure onto a context or resisting the existing structure. The inter-institutional context, as represented by the stakeholder array above, is enriched through field theory as it begins to address the complexity of inter-relationships, stability, and rupture. Social actors, according to Fligstein (1997), are part of a complex network of SAF and for the purpose of this chapter, We are focussing on the electronics industry SAF created effectively by the UK central government and manipulated by party politics. What has been developed by electronics industry operating firms, both in the UK and in many parts of the world, richly represents business-community conflict. This economic endeavour represents a new SAF and the hierarchical nature of long-term government energy planning has been a very powerful force in creating the conditions under which it has developed. To understand its emergence, we need to consider the behaviour of key social actors as well as dimensions of legitimacy, which are linked to new institutional theory. This enables us to see how, in a renewable technology environment, a controversial hydrocarbon project of enormous potential scale could be licenced, promoted, and driven through planning regulations.

The core concepts of field theory concern the identification of SAF, incumbents, challengers and governance units, social skill and social actors, the wider field environment, exogenous shocks, mobilisation, and the onset and episodes of contention and settlement. These concepts can be applied directly to the electronics industry SAF as Table 3.1 illustrates.

Table 3.1. The Electronics Industry SAF.

SAF Core Concepts	Electronics Industry SAF Characteristics	Key Social Actions
SAF	The government issues licenses and regulations for manufacturing and distributing electronic goods. Legal framework evolves to protect society and enforce standards	Buyers consume and throw away in landfill or recycle centers due to obsolescence. The electronics industry creates codes of practice
Incumbents, challengers and governance units	UK government issues recycling guidelines. Manufacturers seek to build longevity and self-repair/upgrade into designs, for example, Apple iPhone	Buyers commit to self-repair of electronic devices though a proportion refuse to engage. Business users change preferences for suppliers based on codes of practice and regulations in support of CE
Social skill and social actors	UK political parties enter debate; technical and scientific forms of recycle, repair, and reuse legitimacy are pursued; social and moral legitimacy achieved in the main	Buyers support recycling and self-repair electronic manufacturers. Skills are developed in recycling precious metals from obsolete electronic goods
Wider environmental context	The global economy slows, environmental targets become critical, and buyer behaviour in consumer electronics shifts to longer purchase cycles	The USA is viewed as an economic success due to electronics industry development. The energy at the centre of geo-political conflict and negotiation
Exogenous shocks, mobilisation and contention	Generic products threaten premium brands, innovation declines, investment in recycling increases, and waste levels fall. Efficiency arguments for new technology increase as manufacturers seek to stimulate market growth	China and India capitalise on new tech efficiency and market opportunities for low-cost electronics products
Episodes of contention	Community rejection of landfill. Government rejection of electronics and tech imports. New recycle, repair, and reuse regulations agreed globally	The rise of nationalism and social media propaganda undermines CE ideology and practice
Settlement	Temporary enforcement of government energy policy at the community level. The electronics industry is forced into play by central national governments	The central government exercises control over local interests. Community–industry relationships rupture occurs. Community–political party relationship rupture threatened

The characteristics of the UK electronics industry SAF in Table 3.1 illustrate the viability of this approach to understanding conflict. The social action element requires further explanation as this is the focal point of change and development within the SAF. Fligstein (1997) elucidates the tools available to social actors and links this behaviour to institutional entrepreneurship theory (Di Maggio, 1988). Social action is seen to symbiotically interact with institutions to reproduce, adapt or exterminate SAFs, the focal point of the theory being to analyse social actors' impact on institutions. At the stakeholder or meso-level, social action would depend partially on the social capital of the actors and partially on their social skills. This element of institutional work as applied to field theory is resonant with the concept of saliency in stakeholder theory (Mitchell et al., 1997) and this provides a bridge into considerations of legitimacy later in this chapter. Social skill depends on, according to Fligstein, a knowledge of the core characteristics of the SAF and a strong sense of 'other' to enable a shared sense of social identity and a sustained effort to 'shape and meet the interests of those groups' (Fligstein, 1997, p. 398). Furthermore, an understanding of the position of social groups in the SAF and the types of strategic action that best suit the purpose is critical to the effectiveness of social action. Lawrence et al. (2009) view social actions as those being directed towards institutions, shaping, reshaping, and destroying them according to the level of social skill and the associated impact. Fligstein lists the social skills and tools available to social actors as direct action, agenda setting, taking what the system gives, framing action, wheeling and annealing, brokering, asking for more – settling for less, maintaining goallessness and selflessness, maintaining ambiguity, aggregating interests, trying five things to get one, making another think they are in control, networking with outliers, and so on. All these tools and skills depend on or focus on communication.

3.4. CE and Knowledge Management

A core theme running through this chapter concerns knowledge – both held within the system and that required to transform markets, industries, and interconnected supply chains into CE-driven entities. Diaz et al. (2021) relate strongly to the knowledge dimension of CE in their work, focussing on decision support systems and product life cycles. They argue that sustainability has become the goal of many companies in manufacturing industries around the world and that SDGs are now commonly referred to in industry settings. Following Stahel's (2019) assertion that the CE is fundamentally concerned with decoupling notions of wealth creation and social welfare from resource consumption, Diaz et al. explore value retention options in supply chains where reuse, recycle, and repurpose are substituted for product obsolescence and materials wastage. The SAF concept explored above relates to the decision context of value retention. The action field can be viewed as having three levels which further complicate the role of knowledge in the wider system. Consumers, products, and companies operate at the micro-level. At the meso-level, we have industry bodies and strategic alliances, while at the macro-level are governments, city institutions, regional agencies, and economic cooperation regions such as the EU (Kirchherr et al., 2017).

The degree to which any system can move towards CE is dependent on the availability of knowledge in making product decisions, especially during the design phase. The consequences of these decisions are calculated by Diaz et al. (2021) to represent 80% of the social and environmental impact potential of a product and we assume service design has a similar impact.

Where value retention decisions are concerned, decision support systems involving social and environmental impacts are vital. Product decisions regarding materials, performance, durability, volume, recyclability, and reusability throughout the product life cycle will fundamentally require the following knowledge inputs: regulations and codes of conduct, legal guidelines, international agreements regarding materials, transportation, clean energy in the supply chain, consumer requirements from a CE perspective, ethical sourcing of materials, and human capital. The decision context around production and manufacturing decisions that drive a company or any organisation towards CE is of fundamental importance.

Reike et al. (2018) identified the following strategies, presented in Table 3.2, for CE implementation.

Table 3.2.   CE Implementation Strategies.

Strategy	Definition
Refuse	Avoidance of use of certain materials, substances, products or components
Reduce	Reduce substance or material use
Resell/reuse	Direct or indirect support of user-to-user transactions for sold, returned or unsold products
Repair	Facilitate user, third-party repair services, or manufacturer repair to extend product life
Refurbish	Implement partial repairs or upgrades to prolong product life
Remanufacture	Dismantle, repair, upgrade, replace components to extend product life
Repurpose	Reuse discarded products or components for a new purpose
Recycle	Process post-consumption or post-production waste to capture near-pure materials for reuse
Recover	Utilise waste streams for energy extraction, production, and storage
Remine	Perform selective retrieval of material elements from old products

Diaz et al. (2021) argue that CE strategies such as those above ideally need to be embedded in the whole design of products and services through manufacture, delivery, and abandonment. Supporting these decisions is critical to the successful implementation of CE thinking in the global economy. As we discovered in our

SAF analysis, government, industry bodies, codes of practice, stakeholder group agreement and support must all be factored into the CE ecosystem. Eventually, the whole system and its actors need to support CE implementation, and general agreement around the methods of achieving this must be in place. A great deal of education and support will be required for each and every industry ecosystem, from primary economic activity through to product/service end of life. The complexity of the decision context becomes apparent and adds layers to the field theory analysis we conducted earlier in relation to implementation. This is largely at the micro-level and in Fig. 3.1 is internal to a manufacturer or service provider in a supply chain. For the consumer or end-user, a perspective is required that adds to culture, values and decision-making in support of CE. For the CE philosophy to be implemented, both 'push' factors (through the supply chain) and 'pull' factors (end-user demands and expectations) are required to create a holistic, agreed philosophy of practice. We now develop our discussion in this chapter to consider the 'pull' elements.

3.5. Sustainability and Consumption

Governments around the world seem reluctant to attempt to educate and control consumption despite the clear evidence of the negative effects of buyer behaviour. There is widespread agreement that the way people lead their lives, the choices they make based on the knowledge and values they hold, and have had a catastrophic impact on the natural environment and communities everywhere. The exploitation of the poor by the wealthier nations is well-documented and relates directly to all the 17 SDGs (Tukker et al., 2010). Households contribute over 72% of greenhouse gases according to Dubois (2019) and the response of the international community has been too slow so far to halt the increase in global temperatures that will inevitably lead (are inevitably leading??) to critical changes in weather systems, ecosystems, and habitats. Consumption has been allowed to increase unchecked despite our growing knowledge of the environmental crisis as it unfolds across the globe. SDG 12 is dedicated to sustainable consumption though attention appears to be very firmly focussed on supply chains and private companies (Gasper et al., 2019).

The global picture regarding sustainability and consumption is far from optimistic and key trends are moving counter to responsible consumer behaviour in many parts of the world. We observe stark polemics in the global society of communities with some surviving below the poverty line while the affluent and growing middle or consumer classes are characterised by an over-reliance on car travel, frequent flying, and a startling growth in the consumption of fashion clothing, technological appliances and gadgets, and meat (Moore, 2016).

Swinburn et al. (2019) identify key social phenomena in modern society as comprising obesity, under-nourishment, climate change, and pressure on the fresh-water provision. House sizes are growing and in developed nations, significant numbers of people own more than one home, which places greater strain on resources. The rich–poor divide is growing too, with over 1 billion people living in slum conditions and a similar number having no access to electricity (World

Bank, 2020). The COVID-19 pandemic led to worsening living conditions for the global poor, particularly stark in increasing levels of food poverty (FAO, 2020). The international picture has in recent years become more complicated by the rise of household consumption in Asian communities, where consumer markets continue to boom (Hansen, 2020). Asia has emerged beyond its recent economic role as a low-cost manufacturing provider to foster rapidly growing consumer markets such as electrical appliances, travel services, meat, and luxury goods (Kharas, 2017). Paradoxically, these consumers are expected to form the economic foundations of domestic economies while shouldering the expectation to behave responsibly in implementing sustainable practices such as recycling, reducing resource usage and waste, and so on. Despite the rise of the new consumer classes in Asia, the research focus in the field has continued to be on affluent societies in developed countries. An understanding of the patterns, processes, and interconnectivity of global supply chains in consumer markets is required to help reach the tipping point in CE implementation. Consumer capitalism can no longer be rooted in traditional models of political economy and nowhere is that the case more so than in China, where under a communist government, consumer classes are booming. These 'pull' factors need to be addressed in the global economy and constitute a complex problem to be resolved. Government policy can clearly help 'push' consumers to more sustainable practices and powerful actors in supply chains can help bring about the required change in values and practices. Consumer demand results from complex interactions of social practices, technological innovations, and the cultural contexts in which individuals live out their lives (Rinkinen et al., 2021).

The influence of education, government policy, changes in product characteristics, and changes in supply chain practices will all inevitably impact strongly on social practice and lead to responsibility consumer behaviour. Cultural movements appear to be gathering strength and importance in contemporary society, particularly where young adult groups are concerned. While often regarded cynically and negatively, the growing 'woke' culture is indicative of an increasing awareness of the importance of sustainability and climate issues across the world. Perhaps popularised by the Extinction Rebellion movement (Extinction Rebellion, 2019), it appears that 'pull' factors are increasing in their power and influence. Society is learning to appreciate the difference between sustainable and unsustainable consumption, with fossil fuels and plastics industries coming into sharp focus in recent years. Nevertheless, it will take time, possibly too much time, for the required paradigm shift in consumption practices to take root globally. Developing countries still see merit in consumption-driven wealth creation (Wilhite & Hansen, 2015), while consumerism in historically conservative countries such as Vietnam views consumerism as a counter-culture measure to satisfy a cultural inferiority complex (Taylor, 1993).

The focus in sustainability policy concerning consumers tends to rest on taking sustainable options rather than offering more directive solutions. A good example of this would be solar panel systems in domestic settings where consumers are incentivised to switch home energy and heating systems to solar from fossil fuels. The key consumer decisions that are driving global warming are in the areas of travel and mobility, energy, and housing. These fields are rarely controlled and thus consumption continues to grow unchecked. The solution to this challenge is not only to persuade through education programmes – regulation and legislation are required to arrest growth and emphatically reduce the negative impact these consumer behaviours have on the environment.

The issue of implementing CE becomes wrapped up in how humans behave in the consumption arena. As long ago as the 1950s, authors such as Simmel (1957/1904) considered consumption to be a social phenomenon that involved conformity, competition, and status. Early theories were based on the idea of rational consumption, and many were deeply aligned with utility theory (Dwyer, 2009). Latterly, the alternative position of irrational behaviour (Kahneman, 2011) has supported notions of the phenomena of nudging end-users and consumers towards changing their behaviour. If we begin to understand the ways in which consumers can be moved towards more sustainable patterns and volumes of consumption, we will create and reinforce the market 'pull' dynamic that we feel is required to rebalance the market towards CE.

Taking the example of fashion and clothing, which we later explore in our chapter case study of H & M, the decision of an individual to purchase a specific item of clothing is not the most useful analytical level for researching social behaviour. An individual purchase is based on multiple layers of conscious and unconscious influences and there is a broader pattern or structure in society that strongly influences purchase decisions. This is not to say that rationally orientated explanations of consumption practice are irrelevant – purchase issues concerning brand, packaging, the signs and symbols involved in making decisions, country of origin, recyclability of waste, packaging, and so forth all matter and have weight in the purchase decision (Warde, 2014). The implied agency of the rational model of consumption needs to be tempered by the social structure and perhaps the SAF of operation. In terms of the consumption decision, the structural influences are likely to derive from the socio-cultural setting whereas in the supply chain field, structural influences most likely derive from codes of practice, regulations, and legislation. Agency in both settings exists but is attenuated by these structural entities. A deep understanding of the end-user's behaviour and the motivation to evolve their values and preferences is required to establish a route to CE implementation. The key question is: who would undertake this detailed level of complex research and dissemination of learning? It may be too optimistic to think that a partnership between education, industry, and government might be possible to make this happen. Triple helix thinking (Etzkowitz & Leydesdorff, 1995) is a very powerful idea and there would be no better global issue than this to tackle on a partnership basis.

These complex perspectives on agency and structure add depth to our understanding of the consumption context. We simply cannot leave the implementation of a CE philosophy and system up to the market to pull more sustainable products and services through the supply chain. Nor can we expect the supply chain – manufacturers and designers in particular – to push a CE philosophy through to the end-user. Both are required in tandem and institutions, governments, legal systems, industry bodies, and trade agreements must be aligned with the

Fig. 3.2.   Fast Fashion Waste Creation.

'R-strategies' (listed and discussed in Table 3.2) for CE implementation to come to fruition. The public and voluntary sectors also have their place in his paradigm shift. Procurement strategies can be used as effective levers in pulling CE practice through the supply chain. The hesitancy of the government to use its purchasing power, performance-related policy, and legislative influence is bemusing to onlookers and where it exists this stance must also change. No organisation or end-user is without power and influence in the drive to radically change behaviour and reduce the negative impact of the human race on this planet to the lowest possible levels.

3.6. Chapter Conclusions

For society to grasp CE and drive change throughout the global economy, we must reach a variety of tipping points. The economic system is complex and multiple stakeholders are involved in partnering towards the CE. In recent years, the increasing importance of SDGs has added focus to the benefits of CE. There is yet work to do to convince governments and communities that CE is the way forward and some communities are still not convinced of the big challenges of, for example, climate change, global health, poverty, and clean water and the ways in which we can and must tackle them. Research and innovation are needed to evaluate our options and to embed sustainable design at the heart of industry and society. Reuse and recycle need to become the norm for all markets and the cathartic effect of more abstract entities in the economy, such as the financial services markets, need to be rendered more transparent to aid understanding of, for example, investment impact. Communication strategies should be deployed by governments and global institutions to educate end-users on the environmental and societal impacts of consumption and production and reuse ought to be embedded as the norm, for example, with jewellery, engine parts, electronic devices, the rental of clothes and fashion accessories, and so on. Taxation ought to become the principal tool of dissuasion where non-sustainable products and lifestyle choices are concerned. Environmental taxation on consumption should be increased to reduce negative impacts. Environmental performance and ethical credentials should become the principal performance measures of products and organisations, using emissions and pollution as key indicators. The full costs of pollution should be internalised within organisations and stewardship valued above ownership in the management of companies and resources. Legal frameworks ought to reconsider issues of environmental and social liability and digitisation should be promoted where it brings efficiency, measurement, connectivity, and control over excess usage and pollution. Society requires education to shift our values towards embracing sustainability while shunning environmental degradation and negative social impacts. Rebuilding our natural ecosystem needs to become a top priority for society and governments so that deforestation is flipped towards forestation, plastic pollution is eradicated in our seas and on land, landfill is reduced to almost zero, and all used products are by law, reused, recycled, or repurposed. We require business models that are competitive yet rooted in sustainability and the CE. Many companies are attempting to adopt precisely these values and this book is full of examples. Our case study which follows next considers the fashion retailer H & M and details their strategy for aligning with CE.

3.7. Case Study: The Global Fast Fashion Industry: H & M's Sustainability Strategy

Over the past years, the global media has gathered pace in reporting about the growing waste problem caused by the fast fashion industry. The focal point of the coverage was the dumping of often unused fashion clothing, footwear, and accessories in the Chilean desert where mountains of material were being incinerated each year. Al Jazeera reported in late 2021 that the Chilean Atacama desert was receiving up to 39,000 tons of waste each year [https://www.aljazeera.com/gallery/2021/11/8/chiles-desert-dumping-ground-for-fast-fashion-leftovers (accessed 10 March 2023)]. The waste consists of discarded clothing, manufactured in China or Bangladesh, having passed through Europe or the USA markets and then sent to South America for resale or dumping. Owing to the chemicals used in producing these goods, normal landfill sites can't be utilised and so incineration in the desert is the only option for disposal. Normally criticised for using child labour to keep costs low, the industry has kept this environmental disaster hidden for many years.

The pressure from global institutions, governments, and now consumers to clean up their act has led many fashion and sportswear manufacturers to radically redesign their entire business model from design and manufacture to supply and disposal and to move towards a closed loop, CE philosophy. H & M is one global retailer who has taken steps to employ innovative solutions and technologies in resolving the waste problem. This case study outlines the strategies and operational policies that form the nucleus of this philosophy and integrates this with the core theory of CE.

3.7.1. Introduction to H & M

The company is a fashion retailer with almost 5,000 stores across the world, making it the second largest in the sector (Smith, 2022). Originally a Swedish company founded in 1947, the fashion focus was on women's clothing and it has expanded in recent years into all clothing segments, body care products, and home accessories [https://www2.hm.com/en_gb/sustainability-at-hm/our-work/the-latest.html (accessed 10 February 2023)]. As with IKEA, H & M has focussed on supply chain efficiency, allowing them the flexibility to adapt production to demand and thus reduce inventory and waste. For many years, the company has used traditional manufacturing methods and materials, low-cost labour, and lean supply chains to produce low-cost fashion items for consumers. High chemical content and low durability have led to disposal issues which have become unacceptable consequences of the business model. H & M are now committed to pursuing sustainability having identified several unethical and unsustainable practices in their own supply chain. These are presented in Fig. 3.2.

Production processes in the fast fashion industry require significant energy resources, water, hydrocarbons, and electricity to treat and process raw materials and create man-made materials (e.g. polyester) on a large scale (Earth.org, 2021). Synthetic materials are cheap, durable, and technically superior for use in mass production. However, they are derived from hydrocarbons, extruded from liquid gas in petrochemical plants across the globe and carry the same negative qualities as other plastics in their slow biodegradability. The sustainability challenge for fast fashion is amplified by the perceived need to create new products, styles, colours, and brands on a highly frequent basis, at low cost, and with lean production and supply chains in mind (Stanton, 2021). This form of hyper-competition owes something to the tendency for consumers to increasingly buy online and for the relatively easy access to the digital market for new brands and suppliers. Thomas (2019) claims that consumers only wear each fast fashion item an average of seven times before they discard the product. Despite the provision of recycle, resale, and reuse facilities in most economies, a large proportion of these items end up in landfill (Ninimaki et al., 2020). Under increasingly intense scrutiny by the target demographic, fast fashion companies are looking at ways of embracing CE throughout their supply chain, looking for both technical innovations and behaviour changes to drive a more sustainable business model.

3.7.2. H & M Strategy

The company focusses on internal processes and trumpets its 'White Room' for innovation developments. It owns no productive capacity and outsources all production. Since 2014, its strategic emphasis has been to continuously improve its lean supply chains, eliminating waste, offering creative, innovative designs in its product lines and leveraging agility to respond to trends in the marketplace. Rathore et al. (2019) report that H & M utilise their Hamburg distribution centre for the whole European market, linking suppliers of raw materials in Asia with manufacturers close by to produce an inventory for distribution. The lean supply chain provides a low inventory system which facilitates rapid decoupling when consumption trends dictate changes to production. The outsourcing strategy employed allows H & M to accommodate environmental changes in the market while concentrating on its core strategic strengths of innovative design, customer service, and CE (Johnson, 2020). The strategy has a strong fit with the market in mirroring the need for high responsiveness amid varying degrees of uncertainty. The reputational damage of traditional supply chains with associated additional costs and harmful impacts on the environment have led H & M towards a CE-based strategy. This also aligns strongly with its main target market of late teens to young adults, many of whom are sensitive to sustainability arguments and who support CE-driven organisations.

H & M has transitioned from a traditional linear supply chain model to a circular model in recent years. This has necessitated a significant paradigm shift in the company that is exemplified by Gower and Schroder's (2016) model of circularity. H & M's key internal initiatives are discussed below.

(1) *Business model redesign*: H & M designed and implemented a significant shift in business model orientation in 2015. It created a partnership model in the supply chain to ensure that CE initiatives were understood, co-designed, and shared. These reframed relationships focussed on renewable energy use and materials development to underpin the recyclability of products. A high level of customer service and supply chain agility were coupled with high quality and technological advancements to support the recycling and reuse of products. Water use reductions, reverse logistics, and renewable energy targets (carbon-free by 2030) were underpinned by applications of artificial intelligence (AI) and big data applications along the supply chain to quicken and sharpen decisions and ordering in line with market fluctuations. The tech-driven creation of new materials would add to the reduced environmental impact of the whole supply chain. The key segments for H & M is women with low incomes, students, and responsible consumers and co-users and second-hand shoppers were added to these. The level of sustainability awareness in this segment is very high and provides a viable targeting strategy for the company. The resulting value proposition encouraged reuse, recycle and co-use (sharing is caring), repair, and upcycling as methods of prolonging the life of a product.

(2) *An emphasis on sharing*: H & M subscribes to the CE concept of the sharing economy that has several dimensions. Supporting the practice of sharing and repairing products slows down the life cycle thus prolonging each product's useful life (Williams, 2016). The company also sought to educate consumers through its website with its 'Take Care' initiative (H & M Take Care, 2022). This web information helps customers to care for their products, prolonging useful life, and is bolstered through social media. The CE ideology is reinforced through this initiative which encourages customers to repair, share, and recycle clothing items to slow down life cycles and materials flows, reducing raw materials and energy usage as a result. In-store garment renting has been introduced in some stores to align with low-income customers and support CE. Inter-organisational sharing is also a strong element of the H & M strategy, with co-branding and local supply chain partnerships reducing waste, reducing costs, and promoting diversity. Strategic alliances in the supply chain have also helped H & M to share data and to make collective decisions on products, volumes, and, therefore, wastage. This has assisted in keeping prices low in less affluent markets (such as African countries) and has helped sustain the core business model principles of agility, cost control, and design innovation. Additional alliances in raw materials management and sourcing have produced positive results in reducing pollution and improving working conditions, for example, in the 'Better Cotton Initiative' (Rana et al., 2015).

Additional notable alliances include H & M's circular innovation lab and the technology innovator Fairbrics. This has spawned the development of sustainable fashion products throughout the H & M supply chain, using PET bottle flakes to create clothing fabric. Lastly, the partnership with Bottle2Fashion in Indonesia similarly uses ocean plastics to create fabric for a range of children's clothes.

(3) *Closing the loop*: In utilising the nudge theory (Tagliabue & Simon, 2018) to stimulate responsible consumption, H & M has implemented a garment collection service that encourages the return of its used clothing to stores in return for a 15% discount off new purchases. H & M uses reverse logistics in its collection service to increase circularity and create a multi-faceted consumer relationship. The green technology deployed by the company disassembles old garments and produces the thread to create new fabrics. H & M reports that over 20,000 garments have been collected through this system in 2022 and expects that the system will gain increasing support across a wider geographical area in years to come. In embracing circularity in this way (reuse), H & M has reframed their value proposition around CE. The profitability of the company appears to be heading in the right direction with a 10-year decline in operating profits arrested and turned around. This is a vital element of CE in a capitalist global economy where shareholder value must be balanced against stakeholder value and the requirements of a sustainable future.

3.7.3. Technology and the Fast Fashion Supply Chain

The strategic aim for fashion companies is to reduce inventory and to bake in lean principles. Technology across the whole supply chain has become central to this aim and is driving the evolution of sustainable business models. We consider several dimensions of this in Chapter 5 but in relation to H & M, we see that generative AI is increasingly employed to enhance decision-making (Candelon et al., 2022; Lang, 2021). One of the challenges of this shift to CE and the use of expensive technology is a short-term reduction in profitability. For society more generally, a leaner supply chain means fewer jobs and so the reuse, repair, and repurpose strategies tend to soak up displaced employees (Khanzode & Sarode, 2020). From a CE perspective, AI-driven forecasting creates significant efficiencies in the supply chain, producing and delivering products at the right place, the right time, and in more accurate quantities in terms of size style, colour, and so on. This reduces waste and increases net profit in the longer term.

Radiofrequency identification (RFID) is a second key technology being used extensively in the fast fashion industry. Clothing and other products are tagged and scanned at the point of stocking and sale to help drive a lean supply chain. These real-time data support supply chain modelling and produces efficiency throughout the chain. The only drawbacks of RFID technology concern data ownership issues with supply chain partners. These issues require resolution in many industries and render partnerships overly complex in some instances. Blockchain is an additional technology being implemented in fast fashion (Belhadi et al., 2021).

One of the key areas of waste in fast fashion concerns the return of clothing that has been purchased online. Reagan (2019) found that between 20% and 40% of all online clothing purchases are returned, which causes inefficiencies and additional costs for business operations and customer services (Tian & Sarkis, 2022). Additionally, reverse logistics in H & M's garment recycle system could cause further inefficiencies through an over-complication in the supply chain. For online purchases, H & M has deployed enhanced digital object presentation, including haptics, which utilises simulation to aid the customer's decision to buy or not (Armstrong, 2020). All of these are potential solutions and challenges to implementing CE, and it would appear that H & M, from the very top of the company down, are determined to resolve these issues by creating and implementing technological solutions to underpin their organisational transformation.

3.7.4. Case Discussion Questions

(1) What factors would H & M have considered in gauging the risk of a transformation towards a CE culture?
(2) From a leadership point of view, what would have been the key challenges in persuading employees, shareholders, and stakeholders of the benefits of a CE approach?
(3) What might the hidden costs of the CE transformation be for H & M?
(4) How transferable is the H & M CE model to other countries and other industries? What are the likely barriers to CE adoption outside of Scandinavia?
(5) Is a CE approach a strategic differentiator and how sustainable is the H & M process?
(6) Which SDGs are the focus for H & M and which have they overlooked?
(7) Name five other unrelated industries that you feel could follow the H & M CE strategy.
(8) Thinking of SAF, which external stakeholders could either help or hinder any organisation designing and implementing a CE strategy?

References

Armstrong, M. (2020). *Cheat sheet: What is digital twin?* [Blog]. IBM Business Operations. Retrieved March 24, 2023, from https://www.ibm.com/blogs/internet-of-things/iot-cheat-sheet-digital-twin/

Bassi, A. M., Bianchi, M., Guzzetti, M, Pallaske, G., & Tapia, C. (2021). Improving the understanding of the circular economy potential at territorial level using systems thinking. *Sustainable Production and Consumption, 27*, 128–140.

Belhadi, A., Mani, V., Kamble, S. S., Khan, S. A. R., & Verma, S. (2021). Artificial intelligence-driven innovation for enhancing supply chain resilience and performance under the effect of supply chain dynamism: An empirical investigation. *Annals of Operations Research, 27*, 1–26. https://doi.org/10.1007/s10479-021-03956-x.

Carayannis, E. G., Barth, T. D., & Campbell, D. F. J. (2012). The quintuple helix innovation model: Global warming as a challenge and driver for innovation. *Journal of Innovation and Entrepreneurship, 1*(1), 2.

Candalon, F., Reichart, T., Duranton, S., Charme di Carlo, R., & De Bondt, M. (2022). The AI powered company. In F. Candelon & M. Reeves (Eds.), *The rise of AI powered companies* (pp. 43–52). The Henderson Institute.

Dubois, G., Sovacool, B. K., Aall, C., & Sauerborn, R. (2019). It starts at home? Climate policies targeting household consumption and behavioral decisions are key to low-carbon futures. *Energy Research & Social Science, 52*, 144–158.

Diaz, A., Schoggl, J., Reyes, T., & Baumgartner, R. J. (2021). Sustainable product development in a circular economy: Implications for products, decision-making support and lifecycle information management. *Sustainable Production and Consumption, 26*, 1031–1045.

DiMaggio, P. (1988). Interest and agency in institutional theory. In L. G. Zucker (Ed.), *Institutional patterns and organizations* (pp. 2–22).Ballinger.

Ding, Y., Zhang, S., Liu, B., Zheng, H., Chang, C., & Ekberg, C. (2019). Recovery of precious metals from electronic waste and spent catalysts: A review. *Resources Conservation and Recycling, 141*, 284–298.

Dwyer, R. E. (2009). Making a habit of it: Positional consumption, conventional action and the standard of living. *Journal of Consumer Culture, 9*(3), 328–347.

Ellen MacArthur Foundation. (2020). *What is a circular economy? A framework for an economy that is restorative and regenerative by design.* Retrieved February 17, 2023, from https://www.ellenmacarthurfoundation.org/circular-economy/concept

Etzkowitz, H., & Leydesdorff, L. (1995). The Triple Helix – University–industry–government relations: A laboratory for knowledge based economic development. *Glycoconjugate Journal, 14*, 14–19.

Extinction Rebellion. (2019). *This is not a drill: An extinction rebellion handbook.* Penguin.

FAO. (2020). *The state of food security and nutrition in the world 2020.* Retrieved December 17, 2022, from https://www.fao.org/publications/sofi/2020/en/

Fligstein, N. (1997). Social skill and institutional theory. *American Behavioral Scientist, 40*(4), 397–405. https://doi.org/10.1177/0002764297040004003

Fligstein, N., & Calder, R. (2015). *The Architecture of markets.* Princeton University Press.

Gasper, D., Shah, A., & Tankha, S. (2019). The framing of sustainable consumption and production in SDG 12. *Global Policy, 10*, 83–95.

Govindan, K., & Hasanagic, M. (2018). A systematic review on drivers, barriers, and practices towards CE: A SC perspective. *International Journal of Production Research, 56*(1–2), 278–311.

Hansen, A. (2020). Consumer socialism: Consumption, development and the new middle class in China and Vietnam. *Geoforum, 93*, 57–68.

H & M Take Care. (2023). Repair and Remake. Retrieved January 15, 2023, from https://www2.hm.com/en_gb/hm-sustainability/take-care.html

Hussain, Z., Mishra, J., & Vanacore, E. (2020). Waste to energy and CE: The case of anaerobic digestion. *Journal of Enterprise Information Management, 33*(4), 817–838.

Johnson, P. F. (2020). *Purchasing and supply management* (16th ed.). McGraw-Hill Education.

Kahneman, D. (2011). *Thinking, fast and slow.* Farrar, Straus and Giroux.

Khanzode, K. C. A., & Sarode, R. D. (2020). Advantages and disadvantages of artificial intelligence and machine learning: A literature review. *International Journal of Library and Information Science (IJLIS), 9*(1), 3.

Kharas, H. (2017). The unprecedented expansion of the global middle class: An update. In *Global economy and development working papers.* Brookings Institution.

Kirchherr, J., Reike, D., & Hekkert, M. (2017). Conceptualizing the circular economy: An analysis of 114 definitions. *Resources, Conservation and Recycling, 127*, 221–232.

Kiss, K., Ruszkai, C., & Takacs-Gyorgy, K. (2019). Examination of short supply chains based on CE and sustainability aspects. *Resources (Basel), 8*(4), 161.

Korhonen, J., Honkasalo, A., & Seppaia, J. (2018). Circular economy: The concept and its limitations. *Journal of Clean Production, 175*, 544–552.

Lang, S. (2021). *Future says... amplified intelligence.* Retrieved March 17, 2023, from https://www.linkedin.com/pulse/future-says-amplified-intelligence-sean-lang/

Ludeki-Freund, F., Gold, S., & Bocken, N. M. P. (2019). A review and typology of CE business model patterns. *Journal of Industrial Ecology, 23*(1), 36–61.

Mignacci, B., & Locatelli, G. (2021). Modular CE in energy infrastructure projects: Enabling factors and barriers. *Journal of Management in Engineering, 37*(5), 04021053.

Moore, J. W. (2016). *Anthropocene or Capitalocene? Nature, history, and the crisis of capitalism.* PM Press.

Moreau, V., Sahakian, M., Griethuysen, P., & Vuille, F. (2017). Coming full circle: Why social and institutional dimensions matter for the CE. *Journal of Industrial Ecology, 21*(3), 497–506.

Pan, S. Y., Du, M. A., Huang, I. T., Liu, I. H., Chang, E. E., & Chiang, P. C. (2015). Strategies on implementation of waste to energy (WTE) SCs for CE system: A review. *Journal of Cleaner Production, 108*, 409–421.

Rana, S., Pichandi, S., Karunamoorthy, S., Bhattacharyya, A., Parveen, S., & Fangueiro, R. (2015). Carbon footprint of textile and clothing products. *Handbook of Sustainable Apparel Production, 1*, 141–166.

Rathore, S. M., Maheshwari, K., & Jain, S. (2019). Fast moving H&M: An analysis of supply chain management. *International Journal of Advance Research and Innovative Ideas in Education, 5*(4), 1557–1568.

Rinkinen, J., Shove, E., & Marsden, G. (2021). *Conceptualising demand: A distinctive approach to consumption and practice.* Routledge.

Simmel, G. (1957 [1904]). Fashion. *The American Journal of Sociology, 62*(6), 541–558.

Stahel, W. R. (2016). Circular economy. *Nature, 531*, 435–438. 10.1038/531435a.

Stahel, W. R. (2019). *The circular economy: A user's guide.* Routledge.

Stahel, W. R., & Reday-Mulvey, G. (1976). *Jobs for tomorrow: The potential for substituting manpower for energy* [Report].Commission for European Communities. https://scholar.google.com/citations?user=N9rR7qwAAAAJ&hl=en&oi=sra

Tagliabue, M., & Simon, C. (2018). Feeding the behavioral revolution: Contributions of behavior analysis to nudging and vice versa. *Journal of Behavioral Economics for Policy, 2*(1), 91–97.

Taylor, P. (1993). Digesting reform: Opera and cultural identity in Ho Chi Minh city. In L. Drummond & M. Thomas (Eds.), *Consuming urban culture in contemporary Vietnam* (pp. 138–154). Routledge.

Tian, X., & Sarkis, J. (2022). Emission burden concerns for online shopping returns. *Nature Climate Change, 12*(1), 2–3.

Tseng, M. L., Chiu, A. S. F., Liu, G., & Jantaralolica, T. (2020). *Resources, Conservation and Recycling, 154*, 104603.

Tukker, A., Cohen, M. J., Hubacek, K., & Mont, O. (2010). The impacts of household consumption and options for change. *Journal of Industrial Ecology, 14*(1), 13–30.

UNEP. (2011). *Towards a green economy: Pathways to sustainable development and poverty eradication.* UNEP.

Warde, A. (2014). After taste: Culture, consumption and theories of practice. *Journal of Consumer Culture, 14*(3), 279–303.

Williams, J. (2016). *The reSOLVE framework for a circular economy* [Report]. The Earthbound. Retrieved 12 January 12, 2023, from https://earthbound.report/2016/09/12/the-resolve-framework-for-a-circular-economy/

Winans, K., Kendall, A., & Deng, H. (2017). The history and current application of the circular economy concept. *Renewable and Sustainable Energy Reviews, 68*, 825–833.

World Bank. (2020). *World development indicators.* Retrieved November 5, 2022, from https://data.worldbank.org

Chapter 4

Supply Chain Management and the Circular Economy

4.1. Introduction

There is currently significant purposeful activity attempting to link supply chains (SCs) with the circular economy (CE). A particularly positive aspect of this endeavour is that it identifies key strategic issues from behavioural change through to the potential symbiotic business activity within the CE. It is also possible to visualise the positive aspects of research in both sustainable production and consumption. This innovative research area was always destined to become more complex as the number of intricate and crucial relationships increased – in this situation, where the number of key stakeholders increases dramatically, it is often a good idea to take a holistic perspective on the whole enterprise: closed systems don't work.

In recent research on the CE, authors seek to identify the intellectual contours of this emerging field by conducting a review of the basic conceptual framework and publishing an analysis of articles on the topic of CE and innovation. The results of the study show that eco-innovation (EI) and innovation in business models are highlighted in this field and are operationalised – mainly by activating dynamic, relational, and absorptive capabilities. The most important innovation practices in this context are waste management, eco-design business models, product leasing, and collaborative commerce. The main output of this endeavour is to pave the way for new conceptual developments in organisational capabilities in order to make transition sustainable, serve as a support arsenal for the maturation of CE studies supported by the theory of innovation, and also link management practices with operational processes in the business and production environment favouring the transition to a circular business model. These authors claim that this circular business model generates insights for the scientific progression of studies and demonstrates propositions that can be validated in future quantitative studies (Sehnem & Queiroz, 2022).

There is an implicit understanding that the CE will help firms, SCs, and countries meet global warming, carbon emissions, and sustainability targets well into the future. We are not the first generation to identify a pressing need for change

Sustainable Development Through Global Circular Economy Practices, 79–111
Copyright © 2024 by Stuart Maguire and Ian Robson
Published under exclusive licence by Emerald Publishing Limited
doi:10.1108/978-1-83753-590-320231004

as a precursor to 'saving the planet'. It is imperative that we realign our priorities: carefully plan all human endeavours to anticipate their short- and long-term consequences for the planet; bring a genuine end to waste; bring about a significant retrenchment in our levels of consumption; increase recycling, environmental restoration, and repair; ensure conservation through changes in social and economic patterns of development and life control of natural surroundings, primarily agricultural land, open spaces, etc.; and secure protection and enhancement of environmental quality. This list resembles a set of demands that might have emanated from COP-26 (adapted from Perry, 1976).

As citizens, organisations, and governments across the globe increase their interest in environmentally and socially sustainable means of production and consumption, the idea of CE has been at the forefront of recent discussions held at organisational, national, and global levels (Hazen et al., 2020; Hussain & Malik, 2020). A significant number of articles focus on the need to ensure improved sustainability in supply chain management (SCM) endeavours with operational excellence in CE (Sehnem et al., 2019). They stress that CE is not only concerned with a reduction in the global environment being used as a receptacle for waste but also with the creation of self-sustaining production systems employing reusable materials as the norm. A useful addition to this debate is that several of these articles highlight the need to focus on the long-term requirements of environmental sustainability (Genovese et al., 2017). It is interesting to note that the focus continues to be on production rather than consumption (Georgantzis Garcia et al., 2021). We will return to this discourse later in the book – a stream of recent work focusses on the need to view CE as a way of reducing pressure on the environment.

It is claimed that digital SCs facilitated by big data analytics (BDA) capabilities have become of business significance to developing a competitive and sustainable SC. CE practices and flexibility in the sustainable SC are significant mediating variables between BDA capabilities and SC performance (Cheng et al., 2021). A significant number of practitioners and academics have investigated the possibilities of using decision support systems (DSSs) and block-chain to improve CE practices in post COVID-19 SCs. In these debates, a breadth of theoretical practices and perspectives are considered by industry and academia in addressing future research directions to develop knowledge and understanding of CE operations, principles, and theory in areas such as energy analysis and marketing (Alkhuzaim et al., 2021; Batista et al., 2018; Li et al., 2021). These authors argue for moving away from a prescriptive set of practices and definitions for the CE towards a set of key goals to allow for the inclusion of future practices, technologies, and techniques. It is possible that we do need research to go beyond meso-level and consider the wider social and institutional environment which may be required to solve current challenges (Masi et al., 2017).

Other research investigates the function of remanufacturing principles and the adoption of green and sustainable practices. There is a strong possibility of improving the capability to influence and reinforce SC resilience in CE. A dynamic remanufacturing capability can have a positive effect on SC resilience (Bag et al., 2019). Complex SCs need to determine the optimum amount of specific elements, such as pricing strategy, remanufacturing (rework) policy, delivery time, and sales effort to reduce the conflict between different stakeholders. This should enhance the economic and CE objectives of the SC (Alizadeh-Basban & Taleizadeh, 2020). There is a pressing requirement to acquire a more detailed understanding of how innovative and flexible solutions can be incorporated into food SCs in order to feed the world (Mahroof et al., 2021; Mehmood et al., 2021). Other recent research in food SCs shows that important learning can be gained from problematical projects when severe challenges impede the smooth development of CE-driven sustainability practices (Sharma et al., 2019). Methodological frameworks for CE enhancement will be introduced later in the book. The identification of circular food waste flows can maximise the sustainability of food SCs (Batista et al., 2021).

However, the research by industry into the CE remains limited. In 2018, the following researchers undertook a systematic review of 46 corporate sustainability reports in the fast-moving consumer goods (FMCG) sector. They explored how these firms incorporated the CE concept into their sustainability agenda, focussing on companies' uptake of CE; the relationship between CE and sustainability; and CE practices presented. This work revealed that CE was starting to be integrated into the corporate sustainability agenda. Most reported activities were oriented towards the main product and packaging, focussing on end-of-life management and sourcing strategies, and, to a lesser extent, on circular product design (CPD) and business model strategies. The majority of the identified collaborations were with businesses and almost all of the initiatives focussed on consumers are largely missing although they were considered a critical part of the move towards CE (Stewart & Niero, 2018). In CE, the economic and environmental value of materials is preserved for as long as possible by keeping them in the economic system, either by lengthening the life of the products formed from them or by looping products back in the system to be reused.

In essence, the notion of waste no longer exists in CE because products and materials are, in principle, reused and cycled indefinitely. Taking this description as a starting point, the authors asked which guiding principles design strategies, which methods are required for CPD, and to what extent these differ from the principles, strategies, and methods of eco-design. They argue that there is a fundamental distinction to be made between eco-design and CPD and proceed to develop, based on an extensive Literature Review, a set of new concepts and definitions – starting from a redefinition of product lifetime and introducing new terms such as pre-source and recovery horizon. The Inertia Principle, as put forward by Walter Stahel, describes the hierarchy of a variety of procedures that can be put in place to extend the lifetime of a product while keeping it at its maximum material and economic value. The key to CPD is the aim to keep a product within the upper regions of the pyramid for as long as possible. The following list is a precis of this approach:

- Do not repair what is not broken.
- Do not remanufacture something that can be repaired.
- Do not recycle a product that can be remanufactured.
- Replace or treat only the smallest possible part in order to maintain the existing economic value.

A pressing issue for CE is the development of a typology of approaches for design for product integrity with a focus on tangible durable consumer products. Of high importance is a deeper understanding of CE as a concept (den Hollander et al. 2017). This particular chapter presented an in-depth case study detailing the history, experiences, and wider practitioner and policy lessons from a CE business model over 30 years, highlighting the successes, difficulties, and conflicts of adopting a CE model (refer to the Ricoh General Principles on the Environment). The case was based on interviews, key documents, and customer insight. The findings demonstrated how sustained CE business practices can deliver significant new revenues, resource productivity, and business continuity benefits, but that it also requires practitioners and managers to develop the appropriate competencies and capabilities, such as balancing linear and circular systems to address complex and highly dynamic factors, including rapid technological shifts and market volatility (Hopkinson et al., 2018).

The CE concept works on the principle of replacing the open-loop set-up, comprising a linear pattern of production and consumption, with a closed-loop circular system. The value of products, materials, and services is maintained in their active use for as long as possible via the recycle, reduce, and reuse principle (Goyal et al., 2016; Lieder & Rashid, 2016; Merli et al., 2018). CE is progressively being seen as a solution to ecological and socio-economic challenges resulting from increasing the circularity of non-renewable resources, waste generation (solid and e-waste), pollution (soil, water, and air), and resource scarcity (Lieder & Rashid, 2016). CE also aims to decouple value creation from waste generation and resource use by substituting the end-of-life notion with restoration and closed-loop product life cycles (PLCs).

Understanding which drivers and barriers exist in the development of CE is a relevant and timely endeavour. Recent research aimed to contribute to the on-going debate by analysing evidence regarding the factors helping and hampering the development of CE. It focussed on the eco innovation (EI) pathway towards CE and tried to coordinate available but fragmented findings as regards how 'transformative innovation' can aid this transition while removing obstacles to sustainability. Taking advantage of a new body of both academic and other research, this work offered a framework for analysis as well as an evidence-based survey of the challenges to move towards a green structural change in the economy. It was argued that the combination of the innovation-systems views with the more recent 'transformation turn' in innovation studies may provide an appropriate perspective for understanding the transition to CE. This would include a move towards policy guidelines and organisation strategies (de Jesus Mendonca, 2018).

In the last 15 years, the expression 'circular economy' has gained increasing interest among practitioners and academics, put into clearer focus with the advent of environmental regulations being introduced all around the world. These include the Waste Framework Directive (WFD) in Europe (2008); in the USA the Enactment of the Resource Conservation and Recovery Act (1984) and the Pollution Prevention Act (amended in 2002); in China the Circular Economy Promotion Law (2008); in Japan, the Law for establishing a Material Cycles Society; in Vietnam the Environmental Protection Law (2005), in Korea, the Waste

Control Act (amended in 2007) and the Act on Promotion of Resources Saving and Recycling (amended in 2008). However, even with the rising popularity of the concept of CE among political, industrial, and academic communities a lack of consistency around its definition and scope of action persists. There are many schools of thought regarding CE in production and operations management and cradle-to-cradle products, designs, and sustainable packaging. It is worth emphasising that a product is considered cradle-to-cradle only when it is fully reusable and does not produce any landfill waste while still being competitive and profitable (Elodie et al., 2020).

The structural socio-economic changes introduced by the First Industrial Revolution and two world wars changed the way goods were extracted, produced, delivered, consumed, and discarded (Womack et al., 1990). Those changes, called the 'First Deep Transition' by Schot and Kanger (2016), had severe cumulative consequences for the global environment, including climate change, degradation of ecosystems, and the depletion of natural capital. It is generally accepted that since the industrial revolution, we have been living in a linear economy. Our consumer and 'single use' lifestyles have made the planet a take, make, dispose of world. This led to a uni-directional realm of production – natural resources provide our factory inputs which are then used to create mass-produced goods to be purchased and, typically, disposed of after a single use.

This linear economy model of mass production and mass consumption is testing the physical limits of the globe and threatening the stability of our future – it is therefore unsustainable. We have been consuming resources at a rate 50% faster than they can be replaced, while by 2030 our demand will require more than two planets worth of natural resources, and by 2050 three planets worth. Using the same timeline, the global middle class will have doubled by 2030 which will drive demand for resource-intensive goods, such as vehicles and other contemporary conveniences that many of us in advanced industrialised countries enjoy (Esposito Tse Soufani, 2018). The current linear 'take-make-waste-extractive' model leads to the depletion of natural resources and environmental degradation. CE aims to address these impacts by building SCs that are restorative, regenerative, and environmentally benign. This may require the need to deploy a multi-objective optimisation strategy for trade-off analysis within CE (Baratsas et al., 2021). Waste management and the requirement for sustainable packaging need a radical overhaul and drastic improvement to move towards a zero-waste CE (Meherishi et al., 2019; Zhang et al., 2019). This is just as important when assessing people-driven issues for SMEs or short SCs in the CE (Kiss et al., 2019; Sawe et al., 2021).

While many S (Sustainability) paradigms revolve around doing more with less, CE is also viewed as recuperative. In terms of S, it would be incomplete to say that CE is environmentally friendly as it is not just about attaining effective business terminologies and emphasising idealistic words such as recycling. CE can be defined by its focus on maximising what is already in use along all points of a Product Life Cycle (PLC), from sourcing to SC to consumption to the remaining unusable parts for one function and their conversion back into a new source for another purpose. Adopting the CE model requires firms to initiate and develop disruptive technology and business models that are loosely based on longevity, renewability, reuse, repair, upgrade, refurbishment, servitisation, capacity-sharing, and dematerialisation (Esposito Tse Soufani, 2018).

Several academics have focussed their research on the ability to gain value and profitability from CE loops while attempting to minimise risk and uncertainty. Creating value from CE-led closed-loop SCs in the FMCG sector is an interesting research area. Closing loops in CE and creating successful value ventures is complex and requires the simultaneous reconfiguration of key building blocks to ensure customer acceptance and business viability (Mishra et al., 2018). CE has been a policy initiative for SC looping strategies to reuse, refurbish, recycle, minimise, eliminate, share, and optimise material and energy use while maintaining firm profitability (Nandi et al., 2020). Consumer perceptions of bio-waste products in closed-loop SCs show the breadth of research undertaken in the CE and SCs (Russo et al., 2019; Saif et al., 2017). Other research has highlighted that we desperately need a more informed and evidence-based transition to optimally efficient resource recovery within the realm of CE. It goes without saying, in reference to the CE, that it is never too late to become more informed which will give us increased certainty as we endeavour to set up a resilient CE (Velis, 2015). We will use the above research to discuss this vital area.

Today's business environment does not even offer certainty with regard to the 'currency' that will be used in business negotiations. There is every probability that these contracts will move from being purely financial to the 'deal' being a combination of finance and corporate social responsibility (CSR) benefits arising from these alliances. CSR is a form of international private business self-regulation which aims to contribute to the societal goals of philanthropic activity, or charitable nature by engaging in or supporting volunteering or ethically oriented practices (Wikipedia). A closer link to CE is that CSR is a business model that helps a company to be socially accountable to itself, its stakeholders, and the general public (Investopedia). This will be the most basic element of the negotiations in these new, turbulent business environments. Organisations might want to sign contracts with you because you are greener than your competitors; you may not even become part of a particular CE because you do not have the requisite CSR credentials; your firm may not be able to attract key graduates with appropriate skills and competencies because your record on carbon emissions has been poor for several years. No company wants to be viewed as a weak link in what is otherwise seen as a relatively virtuous circle – if firms do not currently have the appropriate capabilities in-house they will have to set up a training regime to ensure they reach a level of competence sufficient for the new environment. This environment will probably require a different blend of staff to achieve agreed business objectives.

Several other scholars have identified the need for collaboration in these areas. They highlight areas of convergence in the hope of sparking collaboration among practitioners and academics in the areas of CE, SCM and other aligned fields. To show the significant coverage of these areas, the five principles of CE and the eight core SCM processes were also included in this article (Hazen et al., 2020). A significant number of articles focus on sustainable SCM (SSCM), however, it must be pointed out that most articles have more than one focus. Several others are similarly focussed on highlighting green SCM (GSCM). It is important to state at an early stage the need to identify mutual theory applications when studying green SCM and the CE and it is fair to say that green SCM and CE overlap but differ significantly (Liu et al., 2018).

The battle to preserve the environment is only just beginning. It would be a big mistake for any organisation or government to underestimate the public outcry for cleaner environments and an end to increases in global warming (Van Gigch, 1978). We have reviewed the recent literature on the CE and SCM through the lens of paradigm change and this section tries to identify the level of purposeful activity in this area. CE, like many previous initiatives, has been able to tap into the current zeitgeist and is being coveted by many academic disciplines, that is, logistics management, economics, ethics, logistics, behavioural science, and industrial ecology. There is still time to ensure the academic community works together to make this a success story, but just having contributions from many disciplines is not enough. A transdisciplinary approach would be more effective in working positively together towards mutual outcomes. At the very least, these disciplines would complement each other when researching or working on SC projects in the CE as we need more certainty in this CE enterprise, it should not be a leap of faith. In view of ambitious climate change targets and COVID-19, we may have to design CE frameworks that work not only in 2022 but will continue to do so in 2035 and onwards.

It is important that a coherent set of systems and frameworks is put in place to facilitate the integration of circular business models and circular SC management in a way that promotes the growth of sustainable, flexible, and collaborative practices (Bai et al., 2019; Geisdoerfer et al., 2018; Ripanti & Tjahjono, 2019; Tassinari, 2020). However, a comprehensive, integrated view of circular SCM (CSCM) is still absent in the extant literature. This prevents a clear distinction when compared to other sustainable SC (SSC) concepts and may be a hindrance to the further development of this field of study (Farooque et al., 2019). However, a number of authors have seen the importance of undertaking comparative studies in this area, particularly with linear and circular SCs in the construction and electronics industries. It is posited that integration of CE principles within green and SSCM can provide real environmental advantages (Bressanelli et al., 2021; Nasir et al., 2017).

It is claimed that digital SCs facilitated by BDA capabilities have become significant to businesses developing a competitive and sustainable SC. CE practices and flexibility in the sustainable SC are substantial mediating variables between BDA capabilities and SC performance (Cheng et al., 2021). A convincing number of practitioners and academics have investigated the possibilities of using DSSs and block-chain to improve CE practices in post COVID-19 SCs. In these debates, a breadth of theoretical practices and perspectives are considered by industry and academia in addressing future research directions to develop knowledge and understanding about CE operations, principles, and theory in areas such as energy analysis and marketing (Alkhuzaim et al., 2021; Batista et al., 2018; Li et al., 2021). The authors argue for moving away from a prescriptive set of practices and definitions for CE towards a set of key goals to allow for the inclusion of future practices, technologies, and techniques. It is possible that we do need research to go beyond meso-level to consider a wider social and institutional environment required to solve current challenges (Masi et al., 2017).

Other research investigates the function of remanufacturing principles and the adoption of green and sustainable manufacturing practices. There is a strong possibility that the capacity to influence and reinforce SC resilience in CE can be improved: a dynamic remanufacturing capability can have a positive effect on SC resilience (Bag et al., 2019) and complex SCs need to determine the optimum amounts of specific elements, such as pricing strategy, remanufacturing (rework) policy, delivery time, and sales effort to reduce the conflicts between different stakeholders. This should enhance the economic and CE objectives of the SC (Alizadeh-Basban & Taleizadeh, 2020). There is a pressing requirement to acquire a more detailed understanding of how innovative and flexible solutions can be incorporated into food SCs in order to feed the world (Mahroof et al., 2021; Mehmood et al., 2021). Other recent food SC research shows that important learning can be gained from problematical projects when severe challenges impede the smooth development of CE-driven sustainability practices (Sharma et al., 2019). Methodological frameworks for CE enhancement will be introduced later in Chapter 6 of this book. The identification of circular food waste flows can maximise the sustainability of food SCs (Batista et al., 2021).

4.2. SC Resilience for the CE

Business managers face an uncertain landscape. The impact of each decision feels impossible to predict, which is why they need a resilience strategy that is proactive, resourceful, and competitive. From geo-political tensions and SC bottlenecks to soaring inflation, rising interest rates, and decelerating growth, businesses must navigate a range of complicated global headwinds. The COVID-19 pandemic and the conflict in Ukraine are two very prominent examples of this. No matter how laudable the aims and objectives of sustainability and the CE, they will not be immune from these major geopolitical disruptions. The invasion in Ukraine compounded SC adversity in several critical sectors such as agriculture, automotive, energy, and food – all prominent sectors in the CE debate. As the frequency and magnitude of the disruptions increased, the application of previously held robust solutions to try and restore predictability to a complex system became even more difficult. To reimpose the required resilience, SC executives need to seriously consider an updated range of options, including structural reform (McKinsey.com, 2023). Firms that invest in SC resilience may be able to turn disruption into a competitive advantage. Producers can address critical challenges by designing flexible factories, sharing assets, and decoupling factory ownership and use, capabilities that would be of immense benefit to companies that play an active role in CE. If we had to factor in all the unknowns linked to the CE it seems futile to put in place any sort of a business plan (Boston Consulting Group, 2023).

A responsive SC leads to better customer relationships. SCM should be closely linked with customer relationship management (CRM) and should allow accurate, real-time data to provide up-to-date information on pricing and availability to customers and information on incoming orders to the purchasing department, the warehouse, the shop floor, contractors, and to anyone else who needs to use it. In order to compete effectively, organisations must be able to anticipate and adapt to changing market conditions. This means ensuring that relevant information is available to all players in the SC (Oracle, 2020). SCM software solutions can help to manage customer demand, monitor inventory levels and get early warning of production or shipping delays. An up-to-date view of the overall process should be available at any time – it should be possible to observe and manage the whole SC, and also to integrate and automate all important stages of it, from development and design, through planning and sourcing, to production and operation. This will be important in CE as some firms will move from local SCs to complex, multinational SCM. There will be an increasing requirement for accurate SC intelligence.

Regarding SCs in the CE, it is important that firms have a much better grasp of pricing policy in complex CE contracts. Looking further ahead, organisations will need a much broader and deeper insight into the vagaries of national and international trading regulations which are being further complicated by climate change targets. Global treaties to govern the flow of capital, trade and, more recently and into the future, global warming and carbon emissions, have historically been difficult to validate. Given these global changes in SCs, a pressing need for all firms is a requirement to further understand the sociology of consumption. With the international potential and scope of the CE, it would be a positive step for organisations if they took a systems perspective when developing new alliances and markets (Fligstein & Calder, 2015). Historically, we have understood economic values for thousands of years (use of coins/currency), however, we have much less or no understanding of social, aesthetic, or ecological currencies. Despite the wealth of literature in this area over the last 70 years, it is not clear how analysts in the private sector introduce the important element of social responsibility into their design-making equation.

Historically, it has been understood that the manager should try to maximise profits for the firm and shareholders while considering the responsibility of the organisation towards the public, the community, the preservation of the environment, and aligned goals. This has tended to depend on the perceptions of the manager towards different economic and environmental situations. It is often believed that the executive will seek the short- and long-term profit of the company and that he/she will automatically take their responsibility towards wider society into account. This clearly demonstrates the uncertainty of this position. Is it always in the self-interest of the firm to carry out social obligations, and by doing so is it maximising its profits in the long run? This stance leaves the executive open to criticism, uncertain how far to pursue either profits or the welfare of others.

Sustainability targets are powerful governance instruments for making the economy more circular. CE requires actions and policies. The setting of targets in the governance process is crucial, and there is a definite requirement to set CE targets systematically. In this particular study, Morseletto (2020), examined which targets can facilitate an optimum transition towards CE and the analysis focussed on both existing and new targets. The latter complements current targets which are limited to a few discrete cases and only partially address a CE goal. The study clarified that existing targets for recovery and recycling did not necessarily promote CE, even though they were the most commonly applied targets. In view of the lack of efficacy of recovery and recycling, targets should instead favour other more powerful CE strategies. The study proposed an expanded set of brand-new targets for the transition to a CE, together with a fresh view on targets aimed at academics and practitioners alike (Morseletto, 2020). This may add positivity to some CE SCM projects that are currently running with significant uncertainty (Saif et al., 2017). The authors of this book agree that significant risk management must be attached to these initiatives in the early stages of new CE projects. These previous examples show the importance of being able to mitigate risk in resource recovery value chains for CE. This is especially crucial when there are significant supply and demand variations, such as in aggregate concrete (Prakash et al., 2021). Other useful research in this area analysed the risks of adopting CE initiatives in manufacturing SCs (Elia et al., 2020; Ethirajan et al., 2021). Other articles investigate the function of remanufacturing principles and the adoption of green and sustainable manufacturing practices. Improving the capability to influence and reinforce SC resilience in SC networks is a strong possibility. A dynamic remanufacturing capacity can have a positive effect on SC resilience (Bag et al., 2019).

Complex SCs need to determine the optimum amounts of specific elements, such as pricing strategy, remanufacturing (rework) policy, delivery time, and sales effort to reduce the conflicts between different stakeholders. This should enhance the economic and CE objectives of the SC (Alizadeh-Basban & Taleizadeh, 2020). There is a fragmented body of knowledge at the meso-level of SCs. The following authors argue for moving away from a prescriptive set of practices as definitions for CE towards a set of key goals to allow for the inclusion of future practices, technologies, and techniques. It is possible that we do need research to go beyond meso-level to consider a wider social and institutional environment required to solve current challenges (Masi et al., 2017). One recent study covering several organisations focussed on a three-level framework adapted from the CE literature at company (micro), SC (meso), and society (macro) levels (Rovanto & Bask, 2021). Another current research area is the nature-based solutions put forward for resilient cities and communities. Rainwater harvesting (RWH), for example, is a nature-based solution that has the potential to replace non-potable use for toilet flushing. Its integration into a national supply strategy in Ireland has been limited by uncertainty over its reliability as a supply option. These results show that RWH systems can potentially reduce annual mains water consumption by between 12% and 25% (McCarton et al., 2022).

In the future, CE business environments firms will need to build resilient, SSCs that prepare their businesses for the future of work (i.e. circular economies), create greater transparency, and improve employee and customer experiences. Global SC leaders have been forced to fundamentally rethink traditional ways of working, where the greatest threat in navigating disruptions is to act with yesterday's logic – particularly apt for the CE. A recent IBM study, based on interviews with more than 1,500 SC executives from 36 countries and across 45 industries, revealed that organisations are increasing investments in automation, artificial intelligence (AI) and intelligent workflows, ecosystems, and sustainability in order to rebalance and reimagine their SC operations (IBM, 2021). The time is right to put in place circular SC intelligence systems.

4.3. Circular SCM

The recent outcomes from the COP-26 global conference show that change in global sustainability cannot always occur by only issuing edicts and laws; indeed in certain areas of the globe, it would prove more beneficial to rely on conventions rather than laws. A more realistic suggestion may be to develop and implement a set of desirable and feasible international rules and regulations that can facilitate the promotion of an effective CE. Some authors suggest that CE can be given certainty through a mix of laws, policies, risk reduction (tax levies), and strict governance. CE has received global attention because it has the potential to optimise and promote sustainable production and consumption through new models based on continuous growth and limitless production (Govindan & Hasanagic, 2018; Ludeki-Freund, 2019; Tseng et al., 2020). Until recently, it appeared that few practitioners were addressing the CE concept in full, potentially leading to undesirable burden-shifting from reduced material consumption to increased environmental, economic, or social impact. Additionally, new metrics underrepresent the complexities of multiple cycles and the consequences of material down-cycling. CE is perceived as a sustainable economic system where economic growth is decoupled from resource use through the reduction and recirculation of natural resources. Circular metrics intended for sustainable decision-making should be comprehensive enough to avoid burden-shifting and clearly indicate how the benefits of recycling are allocated between the primary and secondary products (Corona & Shen, 2019).

A Circular Performance Indicator (CPI) was developed by Huysman et al. in 2017 and was defined as the ratio of the environmental benefit obtained from a waste treatment option over the ideal environmental benefit that could be achieved according to the material quality. These environmental benefits relate to the reduced consumption of natural resources and are represented by the Cumulative Energy Extraction from the Natural Environment (CEENE). The calculation of the CPI relies on pre-defined quality factors for the analysed factors (e.g. high quality for recycled materials that can substitute virgin materials). There is a particular view that called for building a greater understanding overlapping and conflicting considerations between sustainability principles t informed conceptions of CE and de-growth. It contends that practitioners scholars need to be pragmatic and recognise evident ideological differences, simultaneously acknowledging beneficial similarities and likenesses. The mon aim of both frameworks is to change the status quo and to enable so operate within ecological boundaries which are likely to present opportu formulate new solutions. Management of the inherent tensions, such as and scope of rebound effects, will continue to pose challenges. With positive communication and a commitment to respectful dialogue, a potential for real progress exists. By seeking holistic strategies, the academic community and all key stakeholders can take the global sustainability initiatives forward (Schroder & Bengtsson, 2019).

By employing individual resources more circularly, consumers hope to contribute to more eco-efficient and sustainable resource use. Previously, the link between the circular use of resources at micro- and macro-levels has been under-theorised. The symbiotic relationship between individual resource users enables a reduction in macro-level resource use. Figge et al. (2021) argued that an analogous link exists in finance where desirable investment return is linked to undesirable investment risk, and that, via the generation of efficient portfolios, individual risks are at least partially diversified away. They theorise CE both in its perfect and imperfect forms, using modern portfolio theory. There is scope for future research to deepen and expand the use of portfolio theory to understand the various facets of CE (Figge et al., 2021). Several articles focus on food SCs, and there is a pressing requirement to develop a more detailed understanding of how innovative and flexible solutions can be incorporated into food SCs in order to feed the world (Mahroof et al., 2021; Mehmood et al., 2021). Other recent research in food SCs shows that important learning can be derived from problematical projects when severe challenges impede the smooth development of CE-driven sustainability practices (Sharma et al., 2019). The methodological framework introduced in this chapter allows the identification of circular food waste flows that can maximise the sustainability of food SC (Batista et al., 2021).

Several other articles provide early propositions regarding circular SCs. These are viewed as the embodiment of CE principles and SSCM (De Angelis et al., 2018). A number focus on the individual, though global, organisations which enable scholars to identify different outcomes from circular SC implementations across different continents. An example of this is an in-depth study focussing on packaging ecosystems, by Tetrapak, across China and Brazil (Batista et al., '9). Further research in China focussed on environmental supply chain coop- n (ESCC) practices in their companies. An assessment of CE practice per- e found that there was a significant need to improve SC coordination in mentation of CE. One important conclusion was that effective ESCC ld be beneficial, indeed necessary, for the smooth development of hu et al., 2021). A recent study in the electronics sector has pro- able model using social media analytics, consumer sentiment tics and CE to attain a circular supply regarding sustainabil- urers are trying to focus on getting back old or partially/ and making the best disposition decisions on them. The n tweets using the Twitter Application Programming This industry benchmark relating to CE concepts model across different industries (Shahidzadeh &

t will slow down a SC redesign for the CE. relatively new so we need to develop a set of frameworks that outline the challenges and put forward potential solutions (Bressanelli et al., 2019; Masi et al., 2017; Okorie et al., 2018) although it is probable that linking the CE with SCs will be controversial. Many recent articles do not focus on specific chains but stress the importance of applying SCs in the CE to mitigate the environmental impact of materials and products from production to end consumers (Pereira et al., 2020).

4.4. Incorporating Industry 4.0 within the Circular SC

The industrial world is facing rapidly changing challenges; our resources are finite, and we all need to do more with less. Digitalisation and automation provide the potential transformative capability to meet many of these challenges and thus it is very important that we collect, understands, and use the massive amount of data emanating from the industrial internet of things (IIoT). In theory, the almost infinite amount of data would allow us to use our finite resources efficiently (and effectively) and so make industry more sustainable (new.siemens.com). We must be able to provide our decisionmakers with true business intelligence to ensure they can make accurate decisions for the ultimate good of the planet. One specific claim from a global vendor is that a SC strategy can bring all the Industry 4.0 (I4.0) capabilities together across an ecosystem by combining the power of digital manufacturing in factories and plants with end-to-end business process execution across the SC (sap.com). I4.0 is the subset of digital transformation pertaining to manufacturing. It explains the blending of traditional practices with new technologies, increasing performance with lower costs, improved safety, higher efficiency, better customer retention, and improved quality and consistency. These technologies include Big Data Analytics (BDA), IIoT, cloud computing, additive manufacturing (3D printing), and augmented reality (AR) (KBMax.com). This definition seems to be a million miles away from the sustainability and circularity debate but the central question is whether I4.0, or any particular element of it, can constructively help the global concerns surrounding sustainability.

In today's business world, organisations and policymakers are increasingly utilising the benefits of circular economies to facilitate sustainability. However, it can be argued that there is a certain lack of understanding on how CE systems work, which technologies are used, which partners companies should look for, which agreements are needed to facilitate CE, how CE interfaces with current legislation, and, most pertinently, what benefits they provide. It is generally agreed that further research is required on the challenges and opportunities of CE to ensure stakeholders are sufficiently informed as to all the consequences of these ventures. It is imperative to understand how CE systems are implemented and managed in practice, which strategic alliances companies follow, and how these contracts and agreements are negotiated. It is also important to comprehend the technologies that underpin circular economies, how they are utilised to achieve circularity, and how performance is measured in terms of economic, social and environmental benchmarks. This may include I4.0 developments, such as block-chain technologies, circular business updates, and smart cities (De Giovanni Cases on Circular Economy in Practice, IGI Publishing).

Most definitions of I4.0 consider advanced digital technologies (DTs) as the main business drivers. The Boston Consulting Group identified 9 technologies in particular as being building blocks of I4.0: big data and BDA; autonomous robots and vehicles, additive manufacturing, simulation, augmented and virtual reality, horizontal/vertical system integration, the IoT, cloud, fog, and edge technologies, and block-chain and cyber-security (Rubmann et al., 2015).

Emerging technologies from I4.0 can be integrated with CE practices to establish a business model that reuses and recycles waste materials such as scrap metal or e-waste. The outcome of one study is a recommendation of a circular model to reuse scrap electronic devices, integrating web technologies reverse logistics and AM to support CE practices. Their results suggest a positive influence of improving business sustainability by reinserting waste into the SC to manufacture products on demand. The impact of reusing wasted materials to manufacture new products is relevant to minimising resource consumption and negative environmental impacts. It avoids hazardous materials ending up in landfills or in the oceans which threaten life in ecosystems. Furthermore, the reuse of wasted materials enables the development of local business networks that generate jobs and improve economic performance. It was found that most urban waste is plastic and cast-iron, leaving room for improvement in increasing the recycling of scrap metal and similar materials. The circular business model promotes a culture of reusing and recycling and motivates the development of collection and processing techniques for urban waste through the use of 3D printing techniques. Through this approach, I4.0 involved groups focus on the technical parts of recycling and can be more concerned with research, development, and innovation as many of the procedures will be automated (Nascimento et al., 2019).

DTs such as the IoT, big data and data analytics are considered essential enablers of CE. However, as both CE and DTs are emerging fields, few systematic guidelines exist on how these can be applied to capture the full potential of circular strategies for improving resource efficiency and productivity. There is also sparse insight into the supporting business analytics (BA) capabilities required to accomplish this. Nascimento et al. (2019) produced a Smart CE framework that supports translating circular strategies central to the goals of manufacturing companies to contribute to the UN's SDG 12 – sustainable consumption and production – into the BA requirements of DTs. Both practitioners and scholars may find the framework useful to:

(1)   Create a common language for aligning activities across the boundaries of disciplines such as IS and the CE body of knowledge.
(2)   Identify the gap between the current and entailed BA requirements and identify the strategic initiatives needed to close it.

Additionally, it is suggested that their framework can be used to organise a database of case examples to identify some best practices related to specific smart circular strategies (Kristofferson et al. 2020).

The effects of CE practices on the sustainability performance of firms are manifold, and even more so when both are influenced by drivers such as I4.0 and stakeholder pressure. The current academic literature offers divergent, if limited, views on how to study these dynamics and effects, causing a partial view of the subject in some cases, and confusion and contradictions in understanding this dynamic between sustainability performance, CE practices, and drivers that impact them. This study aimed to analyse the effect of CE practices on the firms' sustainability performance and the external and internal issues that influence both. By utilising snowballing techniques and content analysis, a theoretical framework is presented that articulates, in a systemic way, drivers, practices, CE fields of action, and sustainability performances. The theories that support these relationships can be put forward as a basis for future research on the CE and related fields (Mora-Contreras et al., 2023).

It is argued that the CE and I4.0 represent the two most important industrial paradigms that have driven academia and industry in the last decade (Sassanelli, 2019). CE is an industrial system that is restorative or regenerative by both intention and design. This idea replaces the 'end-of-life' concept with restoration, shifts to the use of renewable energy, eliminates the use of toxic chemicals (which impair reuse) and aims for the elimination of waste through the superior design of materials, products, systems, and within this, business models (Bocken et al., 2016; Okorie et al., 2018; The Ellen MacArthur Foundation, 2013). CE allows the decoupling of economic growth from finite resource constraints by providing opportunities for businesses in new ways of creating value, generating revenue, reducing costs, being resilient, and creating legitimacy (Manninen et al., 2018). Instead, I4.0 is a paradigm referring to a wide range of concepts whose clear classification, as well as their precise distinction, is not possible (Lasi et al., 2014). Yu et al. (2022) also recently examined the role of I4.0 on CE practices and SC capability to improve firm performance.

CE attracts attention from practitioners and academics as expected. The concept has been challenged by claims that it may be viewed as vague or as a new label for old green management practices – old wine in new bottles. Pinheiro and Jugend (2022) propose a new approach to study the effects of CE on company performance: Circular Product Design (CPD). Consequently, this work investigates how I4.0 technologies and stakeholder pressure influence CPD and, in turn, impact company performance. Their research results indicated that: (1) the application of I4.0 technologies favoured CPD, in particular AI and BDA; (2) pressure from stakeholders can encourage the adoption of circular strategies, especially from suppliers because they are responsible for developing and delivering smart components; and (3) the literature might have been viewed as being controversial as there is a positive relationship with regard to the impacts of CE adoption on market performance. The researchers posit a set of design strategies oriented towards the development of products for the CE (Pinheiro & Jugend, 2022).

There are great expectations that I4.0 technologies will enable better CE results at firms, although it is unclear how these technologies might contribute to CE. The authors hypothesised that I4.0 technologies are positively related to the level of integration among actors along the SC and within the firm SC integration (SCI) which, in turn, explains superior CE results. By utilising original survey data from more than 1,200 Italian manufacturing firms and almost 200 adopters, the authors found that disentangling the type of technologies is essential to understanding both their direct and indirect influence on the CE. Smart manufacturing technologies have a stronger impact on CE outcomes than data processing technologies – the mediating effect of SCI is verified for the former but not for the latter type, questioning the possibility of those technologies to support prolonged CE performance in the long run (DiMaria et al., 2022). The integration of these technologies within an industrial context can enable a set of important improvements in competitiveness. This has been highlighted by a number of key articles in this area:

Production and Technologies (Zhou et al., 2015).
Financial Performance (Schuh et al., 2014).
Market Expansion (Sanders et al., 2016).
Supply C.M. (Porter & Heppelmann, 2014).
Product lifecycle Management (Porter & Heppelmann, 2014).
Workforce Empowerment (Oesterreich & Teuteberg, 2016)
Business Models (Lee Kao & Yang, 2014).

While there is a need for businesses and organisations to switch from linear to CE, there are several challenges that require to be addressed such as business models and the criticism of CE projects often being small scale. Technology can be an enabler in scaling up CE, however, the primary challenge is to identify technologies that allow predicting, tracking, and proactively monitoring a product's residual value to motivate businesses to pursue circularity decisions. The writers proposed an IoT enabled Decision Support Systems (DSS) for the CE business model that effectively allows tracking, monitoring, and analysing products in real-time for BDA with a focus on residual value. The following authors addressed the requirement for real-time monitoring of PLCs using I4.0 technologies, namely IoT and 5G (Mboli et al., 2022). Significant research has focussed on waste-to-energy in CE and several articles highlight waste analytics, zero waste, and biowaste products (Akinade & Oyedele, 2019). Several articles focus on BDA, the IoT, and DSSs, and it is posited that CE practices on firm performances for a circular SC can lead to a moderating role that big data-driven SC can play within these relationships (Del Guidice et al., 2020). Several articles highlight the potential benefits of taking a systems thinking and systemic approach to examine topics of this complexity (Iacovidou et al., 2020; Rovanto & Bask, 2021). Theoretical attempts to define what CE is are contributing to the debate in what could be argued is a complex area (Cullen, 2017).

It is claimed that digital SCs enabled by BDA capabilities have become significant in developing a competitive and sustainable SC. CE practices and adaptability in SSC flexibility are significant mediating variables between the BDA capabilities and SSC performance (Cheng et al., 2021). Other authors investigate the possibilities of using DSSs and block-chain to improve CE practices in post COVID-19 SCs (Mboli et al., 2020; Nandi et al., 2021a, 2021b). In these articles, a breadth of theoretical practices and perspectives is considered by academia in addressing future research directions to develop knowledge and understanding about CE operations, principles and theory in areas such as energy analysis and marketing (Alkhuzaim et al., 2021; Batista et al., 2018; Li et al., 2021). The ability to decouple production and consumption will be a positive aspect of CE and should lead to improved resource efficiency. With CE gaining impetus as a concept and practice, the ability to promote closed material processes with strategies for material recycling and product reuse will become more important (Hussain et al., 2020; Moreau et al., 2017). SCs acting as district energy systems should be viewed as a viable method of moving towards a circular industrial economy (Mignacci & Locatelli, 2021; Pan et al., 2015). This framework can be practically transferred to several business and industrial areas, such as construction (Leising, 2018). The formal (contracts and environmental norms) and informal (trust and cooperation) instruments of governance positively influence the induction of green practices within the SC network (Cardoso et al., 2019).

4.5. SSCM Performance Within the CE

SSCM systems should help firms to think and behave in a green way. It is important that organisations capture and effectively use sustainability data across every stage of the SC to align with regulatory and corporate sustainability goals while also balancing profitability. It is crucial to introduce responsible design and production principles to help an organisation prevent waste and pollution, use products and materials longer, and apply circularity principles (sap.com). While the terms 'sustainability' and 'CE' are increasingly gaining traction with academia, industry, and policy-making, the similarities and differences between both concepts remain ambiguous. The relationship between the concepts is not always made explicit in the literature which tends to blur their conceptual contours and constrains the efficacy of using the approaches in research and practice. This research addresses that gap and aims to provide conceptual clarity by distinguishing the terms and synthesising the different types of relationships between them.

CE has been put forward as an economic model that can replace the previous linear model, with an ability to act as a tool for sustainable development (SD) while addressing issues of environmental deterioration, social equity, and long-term economic growth. Despite the individual prominence of SD and CE in the academic and wider literature, the exact relationship between the two concepts has been neither thoroughly defined nor explored. This has resulted in a number of inconsistencies occurring across the literature regarding how CE can serve as a tool for SD and an incomplete understanding of how its long-term effects differ from those of the linear economy. This review highlights numerous challenges concerning conceptual definition, economic growth, and implementation that inhibit the use of CE as a tool for SD (Millar & McLaughlin, 2019).

The concept of a CE is a powerful bridging idea that fosters the fundamental links between resource use, waste, and emissions. It also contributes to integrating environmental (output-related) and economic (input-related) policies. Environmental pressures resulting from the scale and structure of industrial metabolism require concerted action at both ends. Improved collaboration between these currently isolated policy domains could realise co-benefits among environment, employment, and security of supply. Beyond the policy arena, well-attuned concerted actions of policymakers with industries ranging from production to waste management is a further necessary strand for pushing CE. Simultaneously, all these initiatives require monitoring frameworks that provide indicators to assess links between CE and sustainability goals on every scale. The combination of a systematic and balanced approach with regularly published statistical data calls for improvements in data quality, standardising waste statistics, and consolidating these with extraneous data. Such improvements allow a better understanding of not only the level of circularity but the quality of the circularity as well. This could allow for a better understanding of the true contribution to sustainability goals (Mayer & Haas, 2019).

CE represents a major paradigm shift, moving from the concepts of linear to circular SCs across multiple industries. Even though some aspects of CE adoption within industrial SCs have been researched extensively (particularly addressing challenges of design, implementation, and operations), the research that relates CE practices with sustainability performance reveals the current state of practices within small and medium-sized enterprises (SMEs) is in short supply. This research revealed the issues and challenges, strategies and resources, and competencies required for implementing CE in SMEs. The aim was to facilitate SMEs in order to achieve greater sustainability through CE implementation, which resulted in three main research questions: How are CE fields of action related to sustainability performance?; What are the issues, challenges, and opportunities of adopting a CE in SMEs?; What key strategies, resources, and competencies facilitate effective implementation of CE in SMEs? The study of 130 randomly selected SMEs within the UK Midlands revealed that all CE fields of action (take, make, distribute, use, and recover) within SMEs are correlated to economic performance, but only 'make' and 'use' are related to environmental and social performance. The study further derived strategies, resources, and competencies for achieving sustainability across all CE fields of action (Dey et al., 2020).

Intensifying global consumption stipulates the need for the use of sustainable manufacturing and CE concepts to make products while managing available finite resources. Designers must be equipped to design products while considering the economic, environmental, and social impacts of the PLC. This research explored product design in relation to sustainability and circularity principles. It presents fundamental concepts, sets definitions, and proposes a new methodology to incorporate these two principles which synthesises elements of design for sustainability and circularity. The primary stakeholder categories were updated to explicitly include 'society-at-large', a neglected category in typical manufacturer-focussed sustainability evaluations. The methodology promoted a holistic view of the PLC, including end-of-life activity planning, leading to a perpetual resource flow. Performance influencing parameters available for designers were also examined, including the overlooked 'dedicated' and 'incidental' process-induced types, providing a strong basis for future research on product sustainability predictive models (Hapuwatte & Jawahir, 2021).

They identified eight different relationship types in the literature and illustrated evident similarities and differences between both concepts. They define CE as a regenerative system in which resource input and waste, emission, and energy leakage are minimised by slowing, closing, and narrowing material and energy loops. This can be achieved through long-lasting design, maintenance, repair, reuse, remanufacturing refurbishing, and recycling. They then define sustainability as the balanced integration of economic performance, social inclusiveness, and environmental resilience, to the benefit of current and future generations. They found that CE is viewed as a condition for sustainability, a beneficial relation, or a trade-off in the literature. The linkage between CE and emerging concepts such as the performance economy (Stahel, 2010), the sharing economy, and new business forms such as benefit corporations could be investigated (Bocken et al., 2014). The actual impacts of CE need to be analysed – how do these perform against the triple bottom line (Elkington, 1997), and how do they contribute to 'strong sustainability' and slower forms of consumption, that is, closing as well as slowing resource loops (Bocken et al., 2016). Lastly, it is critical to investigate the influence of a better understanding of the relationship between CE and sustainability and their influences on the performance of SCs, business models, and innovation systems (Geissdoerfer et al., 2017).

Once rapid growth of circular businesses has occurred with these firms driving linear players out of the marketplace, the economy may likely be measured in gross domestic product (GDP) terms, smaller than its linear predecessor, if dominant products are ultra-durable and/or more resource efficient. However, this economy may also be larger, after all consumers who tend to reinvest savings induced by CE warn that these savings may be invested unsustainably, thus offsetting any sustainability benefits previously accrued. This has been referred to as the CE rebound effect. It is conceivable that these savings could be reinvested sustainably, setting off a move towards sustainability, ensuring sustainable reinvestments. Academic concern must not focus on whether the economy does or does not grow; rather, it should highlight policies that aim at balancing environmental, economic, and social goals, and thus sustainability. It could be argued circularity is best considered as a means towards sustainability instead of a means towards 'post-growth' which effectively means 'de-growth'. Sound policies that employ circularity principles can help ensure sustainable market offerings en masse, and thus may help in overcoming any CE rebound effects. They may also help ensure that the economy's GDP, circularity, and sustainability are all growing at the same time, the original promise and ambition of the CE idea (Kircherr, 2022).

CE is a popular concept promoted by the European Union (EU), by several national governments and by many businesses across the world; however, its scientific and research content is superficial and lacking in coherence. CE seems to be a collection of vague and separate ideas from many fields and semi-scientific concepts. This particular research aims to define CE from the perspective of the World Commission on Environment and Development (WCED) SD and sustainability science. The WCED's 1987 Brundtland report, Our Common Future, defined SD as:

> development that meets the needs of the present without compromising the ability of future generations to meet their own needs.

A critical analysis of the concept from the perspective of environmental sustainability identifies six challenges, for example, those of thermodynamics and system boundaries that need to be resolved for the CE to be able to contribute to global net sustainability. These challenges also act as research themes and objectives for scholars interested in making progress in SD through its usage. CE is important as it has the power to attract both the business community and the policy-making community towards sustainability work, but it needs scientific research to secure the actual environmental impacts of sustainability (Korkonen et al., 2018). Sustainability and CE concerns have speedily permeated into many sectors of the global economy. A good example of this is construction where sustainability, CE, and circular construction have received increasing attention for over a decade. However, their interpretation is often unclear, as is the way a certain study fits into these research fields. The authors concluded that sustainability is the goal, while CE is a means to achieve a more sustainable economy. At the meso-level, construction in general, is rarely discussed. An in-depth investigation is required to develop specific design strategies for circular bridges; a certain standardisation scheme to facilitate circularity needs to be developed (Anastasiades et al., 2020).

4.6. Optimisation of sustainable reverse SCs

A reverse SC is the series of activities required to retrieve a used product from a customer and either dispose of or reuse it. For a growing number of manufacturers in industries ranging from fashion to technical products, reverse SCs are becoming an essential part of the business (Guide, VDR., and Van Wassenhove, LN., The Reverse Supply Chain – Sustainable Business Practices Harvard Business Review). In an increasing number of instances, organisations are being forced to set up reverse SCs because of environmental regulations or consumer pressures. In 2003, EU legislation required tyre manufacturers operating in Europe to arrange for the recycling of one used tyre for every new tyre they sold. In other examples, firms took the initiative, seeing opportunities to reduce their operating costs by reusing components or products. Kodak remanufactured its single-use cameras after the film had been developed. This resulted in the company recycling over 500 million cameras in over 20 countries (Guide & Van Wassenhove, 2002). Some firms saw reverse SCs as a way of reengineering their business models. Bosch built a successful business selling power hand tools that had been manufactured.

Whether a firm is establishing a reverse SC by choice or necessity, it will face many challenges. It will have to educate customers and staff and establish new points of contact with them, decide which activities to outsource and which to undertake itself, and in general work out how to keep costs to a minimum while finding innovative ways to create value. Increasingly, it will have to meet strict environmental standards. Within a CE, the challenges and complexity in this business area will increase. Reverse Logistics ensures sustainable practices and increases competitiveness for companies, but it also comes with a set of challenges. The implementation of reverse logistics is associated with uncertainties

(Munch et al., 2021). It has been generally accepted that to make rational decisions about the structure of reverse SCs, it is best to divide the chain into five key components to analyse the options, costs, and benefits for each. Within a circular SC, it is highly likely there will be a more complicated cost-benefit analysis to undertake for each option:

Product acquisition: Research suggested that this task – retrieving the used product – is key to creating a profitable chain. The quality, quantity, and timing of product returns need to be carefully managed as, if not, firms may find themselves deluged with returned products of such variable quality that efficient remanufacturing is impossible. Firms will often need to work closely with retailers and other distributors to coordinate collection.

Reverse logistics: Once they have been collected, products need to be transported to appropriate facilities for inspection, sorting, and disposition. It is accepted that there is no one 'best' design for a reverse logistics network; each one must be tailored to the products involved and the economic scenario of their reuse. Bulky products such as tyres will need very different handling techniques than small but fragile products like cameras. Firms should consider not only the costs of shipping and storing but also how quickly the value of the returned products will decline and the need for control. In an increasing number of examples, it will make perfect sense to outsource the logistics to a specialist.

Inspection and disposition: The testing, sorting, and grading of returned products are labour-intensive and time-consuming tasks. However, the process can be streamlined if an organisation subjects the returns to quality standards and uses sensors, bar codes, and other technologies to automate tracking and testing. In general, a business should aim to make disposition decisions based on quality, product configuration, or other variables, at the earliest possible stage in the return process. This can eliminate many logistics costs and get remanufactured products to market quicker.

Reconditioning: Organisations may capture value from returned products by extracting and reconditioning components for reuse or by completely remanufacturing the products for resale. Reconditioning and remanufacturing tend to be much less predictable than traditional manufacturing – there can be a large degree of uncertainty in the timing and quality of returned products. Once again, if clever decisions can be made early in the chain, in particular when returns are accepted and sorted, it will help to reduce manufacturing variability and, therefore, costs.

Distribution and sales: If a firm plans to sell a recycled product it first needs to determine whether there is a demand for it or whether a new market must be created. If the latter, the firm should expect to make substantial investments in consumer education and other marketing efforts, for example, public relations. Potential customers for remanufactured products or components include not just the original purchasers but also new customers in different markets. The firm may want to target customers who cannot afford the new products but who would be keen for the chance to buy used versions at lower prices.

Normally the firms that have the most success with their reverse SCs are those that closely coordinate them with their forward SCs, creating what is called a closed-loop system. In other words, they make product design and manufacturing decisions with eventual recycling, reconditioning, and refurbishment in mind. Bosch is one such example, building sensors into the motors of its power tools which indicate whether the motor is worth reconditioning. The technology dramatically reduces inspection and disposition costs, thus enabling the firm to make a profit on the remanufactured tools. Especially with reverse SCs in a CE, planning can pay big dividends (Guide & Van Wassenhove, Harvard Business School, 2002). The number of miles/kilometres showing on an automobile's milometer has often been used as a raw measure of redundancy.

The following sections will refer to the above five key components with a particular focus on sustainability and CE.

Since production processes have a high environmental impact, it is important to have as few defects as possible. The following section refers to the Water Framework Directive (WFD), a EU Directive concerned with 'measures to protect the environment and human health by preventing or reducing the adverse impacts of the generation and management of waste and by reducing overall impacts of resource use and improving the efficiency of such use' (Wikipedia). This came into force in December 2008 and this legislation has been approached by different countries in different ways. For example, the majority of EU waste management law has been transposed into domestic law in the UK by way of statutory instruments, meaning that the relevant legislation has not been automatically or immediately affected by the UK's exit from the EU: the legislation will remain in place.

The headline target of the EU waste directive is to reduce packaging waste by 15% by 2040 per Member State per capita, compared to 2018. It is hoped that this would lead to an overall waste reduction in the EU of some 37% compared to a scenario without changing the legislation. It will be implemented through both reuse and recycling.

There are four main issues to consider when addressing CE:

(1) Reverse logistics and waste management – This refers directly to the reuse of products and raw materials and refers to the five-step waste hierarchy: waste prevention; preparing waste for reuse; recycling and another recovery; (i.e. backfilling) with disposal (i.e. landfilling) as the last resort (Article 4 of the WFD).
(2) From product to raw material recycling (under Article 3 of the WFD) – In production planning two recycling terms stand out – refurbishment and remanufacturing. Both of these are recovery processes.
(3) Co-products and by-products.
(4) Sustainability and its three pillars (economic, environmental, and social) (Elodie et al., 2020).

Increasingly, research endeavours have focussed on the reverse logistics activities in the food SC that can significantly contribute to green performance management by minimising food waste and loss (Kazancoglu et al., 2021). Several authors have investigated the potential of I4.0 to provide solutions for circular SCM and operational excellence for reverse SC performance (Dev et al., 2020;

Mastos et al., 2021). These approaches to the CE and CSR have been investigated in the Healthcare sector (Dau et al., 2019). An aligned article identifies vulnerabilities, barriers, and challenges to the implementation of sustainable circular practices and suggests ways to overcome them as sustainability, loss prevention, and profit maximisation can go hand-in-hand with the right approach to the organisation of reverse SCs (Frei et al., 2020). Another tranche of empirical research analysed how four Italian firms have incorporated CE as part of their corporate strategy. The findings highlighted that CE can be a true business lever where the corporate strategy complements and supports its development (Maranesi & de Giovanni, 2020).

4.7. Green SC Flexibility Aligned to the CE

Green SC practices incorporate sustainability concepts into traditional SCM. The overall aim is to facilitate the process of firms reducing their carbon emissions and minimise waste while maximising profits. SC flexibility has the power to easily adjust production levels, raw material purchases, and transport capacity and has substantial benefits compared to traditional SCM. To meet this new, dynamic business environment, organisations will need to fundamentally change their sustainability and green business practices. These may be in the areas of attracting and selecting appropriate green-aware staff; incorporating sustainability and green capability competencies into performance management and appraisal systems in the firm; inculcating an environmental management (EM) ethos into staff and, where possible, introducing reward systems for gaining these skills; empowering staff by encouraging environmental suggestion schemes which could be a positive working environment in a CE; and by introducing training programmes in EM.

These green practices can be introduced at all stages of CE, within production and consumption as they are organisational relationships that align with industrial symbiosis perspectives. By incorporating these EM and green practices, organisations will gain a positive reputation in the areas that would attract clients and collaborators. Environmentally aware organisations will want to do business with other environmentally aware organisations in a CE (Renwick et al., 2013). Firms can increase awareness, skills and expertise in environmental issues. Companies can also hire staff who possess green awareness and can take advantage of employees who have tacit knowledge of EM issues. It may be possible to incorporate green targets, goals, and responsibilities into existing business strategies.

At the turn of the millennium, sustainability was a relatively fringe idea. Just over two decades later it exerts a growing influence over decision-making at every level of society. Today, sustainability has become more of a standard practice at the heart of SCM. Consumers increasingly want the firms from whom they purchase goods and services to be taking visible and accountable steps to reduce the negative impacts of their operations and contribute positively to society. It is not just consumers demanding action on sustainability, governments, industry bodies, and regulators are increasingly setting ambitious reduction targets such as requiring firms to report their carbon emissions. The UK's Committee on Climate Change wants the UK to legislate for a net zero emissions goal by 2050, while the International Maritime Organisation wants to reduce global freight green-house gas (GHG) emissions by 50% by 2050. Sustainable procurement requires a high degree of transparency and accountability between buyers and suppliers (Achilles.com).

SC flexibility is an important operations strategy dimension for firms to achieve and maintain a competitive advantage. With increasing greener customer expectations and increasingly strident environmental regulations, green SCs are now viewed as another competitive weapon, being characterised by higher com-plexity and turbulence. Green SC flexibility can help organisations function in these complex and uncertain environments. SC flexibility as a regular operational SC dimension may not be sufficient for green SCs with complex environmental dimensions and operating in more risky and uncertain environments. Given some of their unique characteristics, green flexibility should be an increasingly impor-tant research direction. However, we still need more research in this area.

Understanding which drivers and barriers exist in the development of CE is a relevant and timely endeavour. This chapter aimed to contribute to the ongoing debate by analysing evidence regarding the different factors helping and hamper-ing the development of CE. It focussed on the EI pathway towards CE and tried to coordinate available but fragmented findings regarding how 'transformative innovation' can aid this transition while removing obstacles to sustainability. Tak-ing advantage of a new body of both academic and other research, this chapter offered a framework for analysis as well as an evidence-based survey of the chal-lenges for a green structural change to the economy. We argued that the combina-tion of an innovation-systems view with the more recent 'transformation turn' in innovation studies may provide an appropriate perspective for understanding the transition to CE. It will also facilitate a move towards formulating policy guidelines and organisation strategies (de Jesus Mendonca, 2018). The structural socio-economic changes introduced by the First Industrial Revolution and two world wars changed the way goods were extracted, produced, delivered con-sumed and discarded (Womack et al., 1990). Those fundamental changes, called the 'First Deep Transition' by Schot and Kanger (2016), had severe cumulative consequences for the global environment, including climate change, degradation of ecosystems, and the depletion of natural capital.

Three policy areas that contribute to closing material loops and increasing resource efficiency are thoroughly discussed, and their application challenges were highlighted: (a) policies for reuse; (b) green public procurement and inno-vative procurement; and (c) Policies for improving secondary materials markets all leading to the advancement of the CE. Policy interventions are required at different levels, from local and regional to national and international, to tackle the challenges of CE in the most effective way. Innovators who already embrace CE principles in their business models would need sufficient assistance from the policy environment they operate to scale up and be able to compete in a national/ international context. The 'bottom-up' approach is expected to highlight impor-tant issues for future policy research (Milios, 2017).

We certainly need to move away from the archaic view of making products with built-in obsolescence towards one that changes design and transforms products so that workable relationships can be made between ecological systems and any future economic growth (Genovese et al., 2017). Other academics propose an ambitious, but potentially useful, holistic conceptual GSCM performance assessment framework which integrates environmental, economic, logistical, operational, organisational, and marketing performance (Kazancoglu et al., 2018; Mangers et al., 2021). There is a certain amount of debate concerning the role of institutional pressures and SC integration in shaping the transition towards the adoption of CE in global SCs. A conceptual framework is proposed in order to describe the adoption of CE practices as a SC process (Calzolari et al., 2021). Several articles use institutional theory to construct theoretical models. It is straightforward to use Institutional theory to construct conceptual models according to the paradigm of institution-conduct-performance. As the external sustainability of the SC becomes more difficult, integrating the CE concept into SCM is required to achieve an optimal balance of economic, social, and environmental benefits for a company (Zeng et al., 2017).

New intelligence will need to be rapidly acquired as firms seek to gain an advantage over their rivals. In such business environments, effective routines are those that are highly adaptive to changing circumstances and which allow the firm to move quickly to a more optimum competitive position. Strong DCs alone are unlikely to result in a sustained competitive advantage. Idiosyncratic and intuitive behaviour may be required to navigate these new, dynamic business environments. Constant realignment of resources is likely to be the new norm as executives are confronted with differing sets of clients. The company's strategy needs to be flexible, while still giving staff a course to follow (Teece, 2014). Recent empirical research into the CE advances the literature by recommending that organisations must consider some critical operational level capabilities to develop their dynamic capabilities, that is, SSC flexibility. This capability will ameliorate the competitive market conditions in turbulent business environments (Bag & Rahman, 2021).

Remanufacturing through CE conserves energy and materials while creating economic growth and employment. It is imperative to develop better systems that optimise the use of resources, maximise the value of the product, and minimise total cost. A two-stage stochastic linear model is presented for a make-to-order hybrid manufacturing–remanufacturing production system by integrating capacity and inventory decisions (Reddy & Kumar, 2021). They considered the uncertainty in demand, core returns rate, and yield to impose flexibility as both operations are contemplated with a collective production capacity on the same assembly line. They considered a setting where demand for new and remanufactured products does not cannibalise each other's demand (i.e. new parts for original equipment and remanufactured parts for the independent aftermarket). Additionally, the capacity utilisation by core returns is considered in two ways: less capacity intensive case and increased capacity intensive case. The developed model is solved for optimal inventory and capacity levels along with production quantities by maximising the utilisation of resources and profit. They also presented a closed-form solution by demand space partition to deduce the optimal policy of the firm. Based on their analysis, they present settings where remanufacturing can perfectly substitute manufacturing (Reddy & Kumar, 2021)

4.8. Conclusions

It has become clear during our research that radical change is required regarding the research agenda of SCs and CE. One of the main aims of this book was to clarify the scope of and relationships within SCs in the CE. How and why are the goals of the CE being set? Are these goals underpinned by ethical and ecological standards? Who are the main drivers of CE? Is this a 'push' or 'pull' business scenario? There has been a significant amount of purposeful activity in these research areas in the last few years and there is potential for positive collaboration across many academic disciplines as well as with practitioners in these fields. It is important that executives in these research areas take a wider perspective in planning their activities. Scoping endeavours in a CE will be a difficult, but necessary, ambition. Putting a partial plan in place for single aspects of a CE project could have serious negative repercussions. Executives in these areas will need a concise vision of the whole system. This issue, in itself, may need a radical change in staff competencies and capabilities as firms struggle to envision the bigger, more complex business relationships that will emanate from their new working environments. SCM will move from largely binary contracts towards multi-stakeholder negotiations.

The control that many organisations have over the SC process may seem to disappear as decision-making complexifies. Plans that were being made for the immediate future must now be made for the longer-term. SCM financial negotiations will dramatically change in the CE. Currently, companies and suppliers have a clear idea of their contracts. Many supplier contracts are for several years and a significant number are rolling. There is a certainty within the transaction and process and potentially a complacent attitude. A fee is agreed upon by both parties to provide services at a certain price that can be renegotiated at a pre-defined date.

This is more than the study of national capitalism, systems, and regulations, but another example of where competencies and capabilities within the firm may need to be developed (Fligstein & Calder, 2015). The step proposed here from a Phase 3 managerial focus on social and environmental issues to a Phase 4 CE focus requires a whole-system shift that would require new values, systems, and regulations. Any country, industry, and company moving into Phase 4, requires reeducation and reorientation concerning the recyclability of resources into a CE model. As Blaise Pascal (1958) posited, 'I find it as impossible to know the parts without knowing the whole, as I do to know the whole without specifically knowing the parts'. This shift in thinking, values, and practice is highly likely to require a government-led approach in tandem with industry initiatives and market stimulation to achieve a 'push' and 'pull' element in the requirement to change. Consumer attitudes are certainly evolving towards a CE model throughout the SC for any industry, especially those involving the production and manufacture of physical goods and associated services. Pivotal and high-profile political summits such as COP-26 provide the impetus and a forum for debate and international trade standards and associated barriers to market entry may prove to be highly impactful drivers of Phase 4.

It is important that the key organisational relationships endure and provide an effective increase in industrial symbiosis for the success of the CE. From our previous research we understand the real importance of positive behaviour change in dynamic business environments. It is not only the number of relationships that will increase within a CE but also their complexity. Many organisations will have to move out of their comfort zone as they come to terms with working in sectors that may be new to them. This will have critical human resource issues for even large organisations as a set of new skills will be required.

Increasingly in relation to SCs and CE, it may be necessary to uncouple existing strong links to enable more worthwhile, sustainable relationships to thrive. If this form of industrial symbiosis is to prosper within these new business environments and relationships, organisations need to tailor their technological as well as their business processes. Industrial symbiosis has aligned quite comfortably alongside industrial ecology where the waste, or by-product, of one firm becomes the raw material for another. This is a crucial point as there may be current situations where this is happening but companies are not taking advantage of this possibility. It would be a good idea to undertake a global analysis and audit of these materials, both input and output, to identify if there are any coupling opportunities. This will allow firms to create, change, and share mutually profitable and beneficial interactions.

4.8.1. Case study

An interesting example occurred in the north of England in September 2021. An American-owned firm, CF Fertilisers, Billingham, Teesside, was thinking of closing down their Plant in view of the spiralling costs of natural gas (www.the northern echo.co.uk. 25 August 2022). This may have been another sad situation where several hundred employees become unemployed as production comes to a halt. However, this particular incident became somewhat of a cause celebre owing to the fact its closure would have serious repercussions for the UK's SCs and the wider economy. CF Fertilisers, with its sister site in Cheshire, accounts for 60% of the UK's carbon dioxide (CO_2) supply. CO_2 is used in wide-ranging applications from keeping meat fresh while it is being transported to putting bubbles in beer and soft drinks. When the UK Government realised how interconnected these businesses were – industrial symbiosis – they intervened and 300 jobs were saved in the short term.

This recent case shows how the CE will appear in many different forms that will need to be managed in all their complexities, sometimes almost in real time. If a deal had not been struck with CF Fertilisers, within a very short time there would more than likely have been nationwide food shortages as supermarket shelves emptied when the production process was hampered. This example also shows how important it is for national governments to have greater knowledge of the implications of the CE. We need to identify it in all its forms and demonstrate how important SCs are in its future success. We believe that a major caveat should be inserted here whereby a systems map showing all the linkages and interactions of current and future industrial symbiosis would be formulated. Critical links can then be identified, for example, CF Fertilisers and the food and drinks sector. This will build in true resilience to CE production processes and their aligned SCs. Of course, this will need to be at a global level (and not merely national) for it to be successful.

At the beginning of the chapter, we posited whether there was real virtue in moving to a CE with all its accompaniments and complexity. There is no doubt that we believe this as a beneficial route to take, especially taking the wider global pressures of production and consumption ecosystems into account. We have identified a number of issues of complexity and general system theory that should be considered in order to make the overall transition even more successful. We have attempted to take a more macro, holistic perspective to view the development of the CE. This can be aided by future research in similar or aligned areas, and it would be useful to incorporate a strong lead from all governments in CE enterprise.

References

Akinade, O. O., & Oyedele, L. O. (2019). Integrating construction supply chains within a CE: An ANFIS-based waste analytics system (A-Was). *Journal of Cleaner Production, 229*, 863–873.

Alizadeh-Basban, N., & Taleizadeh, A. A. (2020). A hybrid circular economy-game theoretical approaching a dual-channel green supply chain considering sales effort, delivery time and hybrid remanufacturing. *Journal of Cleaner Production, 250*, 119521.

Alkhuzaim, L., Zhu, Q., & Sarkis, J. (2021). Evaluating energy analysis at the nexus of circular economy and sustainable supply chain management. *Sustainable Production and Consumption, 25*, 413–424.

Anastasiades, K., Blom, J., Buyle, M., & Audenaert, A. (2020). Translating the circular economy to bridge construction: Lessons learnt from a critical literature review. *Renewable and Sustainable Energy Reviews, 117*, 109522.

Bag, S., Gupta, S., & Foropan, C. (2019). Examining the role of dynamic manufacturing capability on SC resilience in circular economies. *Management Decision, 57*(4), 863–885.

Bag, S., & Rahman, M. S. (2023). The role of capabilities in shaping sustainable supply chain flexibility and enhancing circular economy-target performance: An empirical study. *Supply Chain Management: An International Journal, 28*(1), 162–178.

Bai, C., Sarkis, Yin, F., & Don, Y. (2019). Sustainable supply chain flexibility and its relationship to circular economy-target performance. *International Journal of Production Research, 58*(19), 5893–5910.

Baratsas, S. G., Pistikopoulos, E. N., & Avraamidou, S. (2021). A systems engineering framework for the optimisation of food supply chains under circular economy considerations. *The Science of the Total Environment, 794C*, 148726.

Batista, L., Bourlakis, M., Liu, Y., Smart, P., & Sohal, A. (2018). Supply chain operations for a circular economy. *Production Planning and Control, 29*(6), 419–424.

Batista, L., Dora, M., Garza-Reyes, J. A., & Kumar, V. (2021). Improving the sustainability of food supply chains through circular economy practices – A qualitative mapping approach. *Management of Environmental Quality, 32*(4), 752–767.

Batista, L., Gong, Y., Pereira, S., Jia, F., & Bittar, A. (2019). Circular supply chains in emerging economies in China and Brazil. *International Journal of Production Research, 57*(23), 7248–7268.

Bressanelli, G., Pigosso, D. C. A., Saccani, N., & Perona, M. (2021). Enablers, levers, and benefits of circular economies in the electrical and electronic equipment supply chains: A literature review. *Journal of Cleaner Production, 298*, 126819.

Calzolari, T., Genovese, A., & Brint, A. (2021). The adoption of circular economy practices in supply chains – An assessment of European multi-national enterprises. *Journal of Cleaner Production, 312*, 127616.

Cardoso de Oliveira, M. C., Machado, M. C., Chiapetta, J., Charbel, J., Lopes de Sousa, J., & Ana, B. (2019). Paving the way for the circular economy and more sustainable supply chains: Shedding the light on formal and informal governance instruments used to induce green networks. *Management and Environmental Quality, 30*(5), 1095–1113.

Cheng, E. T. C., Kamble, S. S., Benhadi, A., Ndubusi, N. O., Lai, K-H, & Kharat, M. G. (2021). Linkages between big data analytics, circular economies, sustainable supply chains flexibility, and sustainable performance in manufacturing firms. *International Journal of Production Research, 60*(22), 6908–6922.

Cullen, J. M. (2017). CE: Theoretical benchwork or perpetual motion machine?. *Journal of Industrial Ecology, 21*(3), 483–486.

Dau, G., Scavarda, A., Scavarda, L. F., & Portugal, V. J. T. (2019). The healthcare sustainable supply chain 4.0: The circular economy transition conceptual framework with the corporate social responsibility mirror. *Sustainability (Basel), 11*(12), 3259.

De Angelis, R., Howard, M., & Miemczyk, J. (2018). Supply chain management and the circular economy: Towards the circular supply chain. *Production Planning and Control, 29*(6), 425–437.

Del Guidice, M., Chierici, R., Mazzucchelli, A., & Fiano, F. (2020). Supply chain management in the era of circular economy: The moderating effect of big data. *International Journal of Logistics Management, 32*(2), 337–356.

Dev, N. K., Shankar, R., & Qaiser, F. H. (2020). Industry 4.0 and circular economy: Operational excellence for sustainable reverse supply chain performance. *Resources, Conservation and Recycling, 153*, 104583

Dey, P. K., Malesios, C., De, D., Budhwar, P., Chowdhury, S., & Cheffi, W. (2020). Circular economy to enhance sustainability of SMEs. *Business Strategy and the Environment, 29*(6), 2145–2169.

EIB CE Guide. (2020). *The EIB circular economy guide, Supporting the circular transition.* EIB ISBN 9286146728.

Elia, V., Gnoni, M. G., & Tornese, F. (2020). Evaluating the adoption of circular economy practices and industrial supply chains: An empirical analysis. *Journal of Cleaner Production, 273*, 122966.

Elodie S., Absi, N., & Borodin, V. (2020). Towards circular economy in production planning: Challenges and opportunities. *European Journal of Operational Research, 287*(1), 168–190.

Ethirajan, M., Arasu, M. T., Kandasamy, J., Vimal, K. E. K., Nadim, S. P., & Kumar, A. (2021). Analysing the risks of adopting circular economy initiatives in manufacturing supply chains. *Business Strategy and the Environment, 30*(1), 204–236.

Farooque, M., Zhang, A., Thurer, M., Qu, T., & Huising, D. (2019). Circular supply chain management: A definition and structured literature review. *Journal of Cleaner Production, 228*, 882–900.

Figge, F., Thorpe, A. S., & Manzhynski, S. (2021). Between you and I: A portfolio theory of the circular economy. *Ecological Economics, 190*, 107190.

Fligstein, N., & Calder, R. (2015). Architecture of markets. In R. Scott, M. Buchmann & Berkeley Sociology (Eds.), *Emerging trends in the social and behavioural sciences: An interdisciplinary, searchable and linkable resource* (pp. 1–14). John Wiley and Sons, Inc.

Frei, R., Jack, L., & Krzyzanick, S.A. (2020). Sustainable reverse supply chains and circular economies in multi-channel retail returns. *Business Strategy and the Environment, 29*(5), 1925–1940.

Geisdoerfer, M., Morioka, S. N., de Carvalho, M. M., & Evans, S. (2018). Business models and supply chains for the CE. *Journal of Cleaner Production, 190*, 712–721.

Genovese, A., Acquaye, A. A., Figueroa, A., & Koh, S. C. L. (2017). Sustainable supply chain management and the transition towards a circular economy: Evidence and some applications. *Omega,66*(Part B), 344–357.

Georgantzis Garcia, D., Kipnis, E., Vasileiou, E., & Solomon, A. (2021). Modular circular economy in energy infrastructure projects: Enabling factors and barriers. *Journal of Management in Engineering, 37*(5), 04021053.

Govindan, K., & Hasanagic, M. (2018). A systematic review on drivers, barriers, and practices towards circular economy: A supply chain perspective. *International Journal of Production Research, 56*(1–2), 278–311.

Guide, V. D. R., & Van Wassenhove, L. N. (2002). The reverse supply chain – Sustainable business practices. *Harvard Business Review, 80*(2), 25–26.

Hazen, B. T., Russo, I., & Confente, I.. (2020). Circular economy: Recent technology management considerations SC innovation key to business-to-consumer closed loop systems. *Johnson Matthey Technology Review, 64*(1), 69–75.

Hazen, B. T., Russo, I., Confente, I. & Pellathy, D.. (2020). Supply chain management for circular economy: Conceptual framework and research agenda. *The International Journal of Logistics Management, 32*(2), 510–537.

den Hollander, M., Bakker, C. A., & Hultink, E. J. (2017). Product design in a circular economy: Development of a typology of key concepts and terms: Key concepts and terms for circular product design. *Journal of Industrial Ecology, 21*(1), 517–525.

Hussain, Z., Mishra, J., & Vanacore, E. (2020). Waste to energy and circular economy: The case of anaerobic digestion. *Journal of Enterprise Information Management, 33*(4), 817–838.

Hussain, M., & Malik, M. (2020). Organizational enablers for circular economy in the context of sustainable supply chain management. *Journal of Cleaner Production, 256*, 120375.

Iacovidou, E., Hahladakis, J. N., & Purnell, P. (2020). A systems thinking approach to understanding the challenges of achieving the circular economy. *Environmental Science and Pollution Research, 28*, 24785–24806.

Kazancoglu, Y., Ekinci, E., Mangla, S. K., Sezer, M. D., & Kayikci, Y. (2021). Performance evaluation of reverse logistics in food supply chains in a circular economy using systems dynamics. *Business Strategy and the Environment, 30*(1), 71–91.

Kazancoglu, Y., Kazancoglu, I., & Sagnak, M. (2018). A new holistic conceptual framework for green supply chain management performance assessment based on circular economy. *Journal of Cleaner Production, 195*, 1282–1299.

Khajuria, A., Atienza, V. A., Chavanich, S., Henning, W., Islam, I., Kral, U., Liu, M., Liu, X., Murthy, I. K., Oyedotun, T. D. T., Verma, P., Xu, G., & Zeng, X. (2022). Accelerating circular economy solutions to achieve the 2030 agenda for sustainable development goals. *Circular Economy, 1*, 100001.

Kiss, K., Ruszkai, C., & Takacs-Gyorgy, K. (2019). Examination of short supply chains based on circular economy and sustainability aspects. *Resources (Basel), 8*(4), 161.

Kristofferson, E., Blomsma, F., Mikalef, P., & Li, J. (2020). The smart CE: A digital-enabled circular strategies framework for manufacturing companies. *Journal of Business Research, 120*, 241–261.

Leising, E., Quist, J., & Bocken, N. (2018). Circular economy in the building sector: Three cases and a collaboration tool. *Journal of Cleaner Production, 176*, 976–989.

Li, Guo, Wu, H., Sethi, S. P., & Zhang, X. (2021). Contracting green product supply chains considering marketing efforts in the circular economy era. *International Journal of Production Economics, 234*, 108041.

Liu, J., Feng, Y., Zhu, Q., & Sarkis, J. (2018). Green supply chain management and the circular economy: Reviewing theory for advancement of both fields. *International Journal of Physical Distribution and Logistics Management*, *48*(8), 794–817.

Ludeki,-Freund, F., Gold, S., & Bocken, N. M. P. (2019). A review and typology of circular economy business model patterns. *Journal of Industrial Ecology*, *23*(1), 36–61.

Mahroof, K., Omar, A., Rana, N. P., Sivarajah, U., & Weerakkody, V. (2021). Drone as a service (DaaS) in promoting cleaner agricultural production and circular economy for ethical sustainable supply chain development. *Journal of Cleaner Production*, *287*, 125522.

Mangers, J., Minoufeer, M., Plapper, P., & Kobla, S. (2021). An innovative strategy allowing a holistic system change towards circular economy with supply chains. *Energies (Basel)*, *14*, 4375.

Maranesi, C., & de Giovanni, P. (2020). Modern circular economy: Corporate strategy, supply chain and industrial symbiosis. *Sustainability (Basel)*, *12*(22), 1–25.

Masi, D., Day, S., & Godsell, J. (2017). Supply chain configurations in the circular economy: A systematic literature review. *Sustainability (Basel)*, *9*(9), 1602.

Mastos, T. D., Nizanies, A., Terzi, S., Gkortzis, D., Papadopoulis, A., Tsagkalidis, N., Ioannidis, D., Votis, K., & Tvoraras, D. (2021). Introducing an application of an industry 4.0 solution for circular supply chain management. *Journal of Cleaner Production*, *300*, 126886.

Mboli, J. S., Thakker, D., Mishra, J. L. (2018). An internet of things-enabled decision support system for circular economy business model. *Software: Practice and Experience*, *52*(3), 772–787.

Meherishi, L., Narayana, S. A., & Ranjani, K. S. (2019). Sustainable packaging for supply chain management in the circular economy. *Journal of Cleaner Production*, *237*, 117582.

Mehmood, A., Ahmed, S., Viza, E., Bogush, A., & Ayyub, R. M. (2021). Drivers and barriers towards circular economy in agri-food supply chains: A review. *Business Strategy and Development*, *4*(4), 465–481.

Mignacci, B., & Locatelli, G. (2021). Modular circular economy in energy infrastructure projects: Enabling factors and barriers. *Journal of Management in Engineering*, *37*(5), 04021053.

Mishra, J. L., Hopkinson, P. G., & Tidridge, G. (2018). Value creation from circular economy-led closed loop supply chains: A case study of fast-moving consumer goods. *Production Planning and Control*, *29*(6), 509–521.

Moreau, V., Sahakian, M., Griethuysen, P., & Vuille, F. (2017). Coming full circle: Why social and institutional dimensions matter for the circular economy .*Journal of Industrial Ecology*, *21*(3), 497–506.

Munch, C., von der Gracht, H. A. & Hartmann, E. (2021). The future role of reverse logistics as a tool for sustainability in food supply chains: A delphi-based scenario study. *Supply Chain Management*, *28*(2), 262–283.

Nandi, S., Hervani, A., & Helms, M. M. (2020). Circular economy business models – Supply chain perspectives. *IEEE Engineering Management Review*, *48*(2), 193–201.

Nandi, S., Sarkis, J., Hervani, A., & Helms, M. (2021a). Do block-chain and circular economy practices improve post COVID-19 supply chains? A resource-based and resource dependence perspective. *Industrial Management and Data Systems*, *121*(2), 333–363.

Nandi, S., Sarkis, J., Hervani, A. A., & Helms, M. M. (2021b). Redesigning supply chains using block-chain-enabled CE and COVID-19 experiences. *Sustainable Production and Consumption*, *27*, 10–22.

Nasir, M. H. A., Genovese, A., Acquaye, A. A., Koh, S. C. L., & Yamoah, F. (2017). Comparing linear and circular supply chains: A case study from the construction industry. *International Journal of Production Economics*, *183*, 443–457.

Okorie, O., Salonitis, K., Charnley, F., Moreno, M., Turner, C., & Tiwari, A. (2018). Digitisation and the circular economy: A review of current research and future trends. *Energies*, *11*(11), 3009.

Pan, S. Y., Du, M. A., Huang, I. T., Liu, I. H., Chang, E. E., & Chiang, P. C. (2015). Strategies on implementation of waste to energy (WTE) supply chains for circular economy system: A review. *Journal of Cleaner Production*, *108*, 409–421.

Pascal, B. (1958). *Pascal's Pensees*. E.P. Dutton.

Pereira, R., Ferreira, E. A., Alves, J. L., Nadal, J., & de Galvao, G. D. A. (2020). Circular economy and supply chains: A literature review. *Brazilian Journal of Operations and Production Management*, *17*(4), 1–14.

Perry, D. L. (1976). *Social marketing strategies: Conservation issues and analysis* (pp. viii–ix &133–139). Good Year.

Prakash, S., Wijayasundara, M., Pathirana, P. N., & Law, K. (2021). De-risking resource recovery value-chains for a circular economy: Accounting for supply and demand variations in recycled aggregate concrete. *Resources, Conservation and Recycling*, *168*, 105312.

Renwick, D. W. S., Redman, T., & Maguire, S. (2013). Green human resource management: A review and research agenda. *International Journal of Management Reviews*, *15*, 1–14.

Ripanti, E. F., & Tjahjono, B. (2019). Unveiling the potentials of circular economy values in logistics and supply chain management. *The International Journal of Logistics Management*, *30*(3), 723–742.

Rovanto, I. K., & Bask, A. (2021). Systemic circular business model application at the company, supply chains and society levels – A view into CE native and adopter companies. *Business Strategy and the Environment*, *30*(2), 1153–1173.

Rubmann, M., Lorenz, M., Gerbert, P., Waldner, M., Engel, P., Harnisch, M., & Justus, J. (2015). *Industry 4.0: The future of productivity and growth in manufacturing industries*. Boston Consulting Group, Digital Transformation/Focus. Retrieved April 9, 2015, from bcg.com

Russo, I., Confente, I., Scarpi, D., & Hazen, B. T. (2019). From trash to treasure: The impact of consumer perception of bio-waste products in closed-loop supply chains. *Journal of Cleaner Production*, *218*, 966–974.

Saif, Y., Rizwan, M., Almansoori, A., & Elkamel, A. (2017). A circular economy solid waste supply chain management-based approach under uncertainty. *Energy Procedia*, *142*, 2971–2976.

Sawe, F. B., Kumar, A., Garza-Reyes, J. A., & Agrawal, R. (2021). Assessing people-driven factors for circular economy practices in SME supply chains: Business strategies and environmental perspectives. *Business Strategy and the Environment*, *30*(7), 2951–2965.

Sehnem, S., Chiapetta, J., Charbel, J., Faria Pereira, S. C., de Sousa, J., & Lopes, A. B. (2019). Improving sustainable supply chains performance through operational excellence: Circular economy approach. *Resources, Conservation and Recycling*, *149*, 236–248.

Sharma, Y. K., Mangla, S. K., Patil, P. P., & Liu, S. (2019). When challenges impede the process: For circular economy-driven sustainability practices in food supply chains. *Management Decision*, *57*(4), 995–1017.

Tassinari, V. (2020). CE, sustainability, retailers and supply chain collaboration. *Symphony*, (1), 129–135.

Teece, D. J. (2014). The foundations of enterprise performance: Dynamic and ordinary capabilities in an (economic) theory of firms. *Academy of Management Perspectives*, *28*(4), 328–352.

Tseng, M-L., Chiu, A. S. F., Liu, G., & Jantaralolica, T. (2020). Circular economy enables sustainable consumption and production in multi-level supply chain system. *Resources, Conservation and Recycling*, *154*, 104603.

Van Gigch, J. P. (1978). *Applied general systems theory* (2nd ed.). Harper and Row Publishers.

Velis, C. A. (2015). Circular economy and global secondary material supply chains. *Waste Management and Research*, *33*(5), 389–391.

Zeng, H., Chen, X., Xiao, X., & Zhou, Z. (2017). Institutional pressures, sustainable supply chain management and circular economy capability: Empirical evidence from Chinese eco-industrial park firms. *Journal of Cleaner Production*, *155*, 54–65.

Zhu, Q., Geng, Y., & Lai, K-H. (2021). Environmental SC cooperation and its effect on the circular economy practice-performance relationship among Chinese manufacturers. *Journal of Industrial Ecology*, *15*(3), 405–419.

Chapter 5

Business Innovation and Change for Circular Economy

5.1. Introduction

For organisations of any type to move towards circular economy (CE), business models are likely to require transformation based on creative thinking and innovation around technology and partnerships both within the supply chain and with end-users. This chapter explores the role of innovation and technology in a future CE-driven world and looks at some examples in the present that suggest an optimistic outlook.

If we stop and reflect for a moment on the transformation challenge for CE, we can get an insight as to the complexity of its implementation. Practitioners need to effect robust business models – they will need to take a much wider perspective in planning and implementing their business activities. Scoping endeavours in the CE will be a difficult but necessary ambition. Putting a partial plan in place for single aspects of a CE project could have serious negative repercussions and so a holistic mindset is required. Executives in these areas will need a concise vision of the whole system. This issue in itself may need a radical change in staff competences and capabilities as firms struggle to envision the bigger, more complex, business relationships that will emanate from their new working environments. Supply chain management will move from largely binary contracts towards multistakeholder negotiations; the control that many organisations had in the supply chain process may seem to disappear as decision-making becomes much more complex; plans that were being made for the immediate future must now be made for the longer term; supply chain management financial negotiations will dramatically change in the CE. Companies and suppliers currently have a reasonably clear idea of their contracts – many supplier contracts are for several years and a significant number are rolling. The parameters of partnership in supply chains will change, and exchange will not only concern finance and transaction but will involve reuse, recyclables, and the repurposing of resources, data, and materials, in particular, to reduce negative environmental impact and embrace circularity.

This will be the most basic element of the negotiations in these new, turbulent business environments. If firms do not currently have the appropriate capabilities in-house, they will have to set up a training regime to ensure they reach a level of

Sustainable Development Through Global Circular Economy Practices, 113–132
Copyright © 2024 by Stuart Maguire and Ian Robson
Published under exclusive licence by Emerald Publishing Limited
doi:10.1108/978-1-83753-590-320231005

competence sufficient for the new environment. This environment will most likely require a different blend of staff to achieve agreed business objectives. Innovation, creativity, and design will be key drivers of CE as products, processes, materials, and behaviours will need to change fundamentally to align with CE philosophy.

It is important that a coherent set of systems and frameworks is put in place to facilitate the integration of circular business models and circular supply chain management (CSCM) in a way that promotes the growth of sustainable, flexible, and collaborative practices (Bai et al., 2019; Geissdoerfer et al., 2018; Ripanti & Tjahjono, 2019; Tassinari, 2020). However, a comprehensive, integrated view of CSCM is still absent in the extant literature. This prevents a clear distinction when compared to other sustainable supply chain concepts and may be a hindrance to the further development of this field of study (Farooque et al., 2019). Nevertheless, a number of authors have seen the importance of undertaking comparative studies in this area, especially with linear and circular supply chains in the construction and electronics industries. It is posited that an integration of CE principles within green and sustainable supply chain management can provide real advantages from an environmental perspective (Bressanelli et al., 2021; Nasir et al., 2017).

The dynamic of supply chains within the CE will be sufficiently different to make them problematic for a significant number of organisations. CE is likely to open up new business markets for many of these companies. Markets are generally socially constructed arenas where repeated exchanges occur between buyers and sellers under a set of formal and informal rules (conventions) governing relations among competitors, suppliers, and customers. These arenas operate according to local understandings and rules that guide interaction, facilitate trade, define what products are produced – indeed constitute the products themselves – and provide stability for buyers, sellers, and producers. The central role of innovation is clear: through all of this complexity and disruption, innovation and change are required. The old business model and way of organisational operation have led us to an ecological and social disaster. CE is not the solution to a problem of its own making. There is no obvious middle ground here either, despite the reluctance of countries and organisations to transform and embrace the imperative for significant movement towards CE (Geissdoerfer et al., 2018).

This chapter focusses on digital and technological solutions to social and environmental problems. It considers Industry 4.0 and the idea of digitally connected supply chains and markets. It also looks at the concept of resistance to change, including how to lead the strategic change necessary for business model innovation (BMI). We have added some interesting examples to light the way through this complex picture, and we end with an interesting case study of Adidas, a company that has taken great strides towards CE in the effective use of innovation and technology.

5.2. The CE and Innovation

CE is an economic system in which resources are kept in use for as long as possible, waste is minimised, and new products are made from recycled materials

(Kirchherr et al., 2017). We discovered the essence of CE in Chapter 1 and learned that it is gaining momentum as a response to the negative environmental impacts of linear economy models that are based on the 'take, make, use and dispose' approach. One of the earliest forms of circularity in consumer markets is the idea of upcycling – repurposing discarded products (McDonough & Braungart, 2013). However, as short as this journey has been so far, we can see that CE is expected to provide wider solutions for the erosion and depletion of natural resources – air, land, and water pollution, waste management, and climate change (Circular Economy, 2018). Innovation and technology are at the heart of this transformation and much hope is placed on the potential for society to save itself and the planet through significant changes to resource use and waste disposal.

5.3. Introducing Industry 4.0

Industry 4.0 refers to the integration of digital technologies and automation into manufacturing and other industrial processes (Sundin & Lindahl, 2018). These technologies include, among others, the internet of things (IoT), artificial intelligence (AI), robotics, and data analytics. Industry 4.0 has the potential to significantly improve CE outcomes by enabling more efficient resource use, reducing waste, and facilitating closed-loop supply chains. In the Ricoh and H & M examples we have seen in earlier chapters, one key technology that can improve CE outcomes is IoT. By embedding sensors and connectivity into products, components, and equipment, IoT can enable real-time monitoring of resource use, waste generation, and product performance. These data can be used to optimise production processes, reduce waste, and identify opportunities for circular business models such as product-as-a-service (PaaS).

AI and data analytics can also play a critical role in improving CE outcomes. By analysing large amounts of data on resource use, waste, and product performance, it identifies patterns and insights that can inform more efficient and effective CE strategies. For example, AI can be used to optimise material flows and identify opportunities for resource recovery and recycling. Robotics and automation can also support CE outcomes by enabling more precise and efficient manufacturing processes which can reduce waste and improve the quality of products, making them easier to recycle or reuse. Additionally, robotics can enable the disassembly and recovery of valuable materials from end-of-life products, which again reduces waste and supports closed-loop supply chains.

Industry 4.0 technologies have the potential to significantly improve CE outcomes by enabling more efficient resource use, reducing waste, and facilitating closed-loop supply chains. However, the successful implementation of these technologies requires a holistic approach that considers the entire product lifecycle and engages stakeholders across the value chain.

5.4. Technology, Waste, and Resource Efficiency

One of the most important technological developments in recent years is that of 3D printing (Singh et al., 2021). Reducing material wastage to practically nothing and eliminating inventory waste through the supply chain, the use of 3D printing is expected to grow rapidly across the global economy. We saw in Chapter 3 that in the fast fashion industry, RFID is already in use to provide real-time purchase and stock control data to reduce inventory waste and place the right quantity of products in the right marketplaces. Reducing waste and creating lean supply chains are central elements of CE. Sensors and data capture are added to RFID technologies to increase efficiency in supply chains through enhancing decision-making. The IoT has become almost a catchphrase for tech-driven CE transformation where the connectedness of supply chain partners and consumers or end-users can significantly improve efficiency (Zong & Zhao, 2020). The downside of this efficiency concerns reduced numbers of employees through the associated reduction in costs, which then offsets the investment costs for technological development. More efficient supply chains have a huge impact on resource usage and we saw in the H & M case in Chapter 3, how lean supply chains reduced the amount of water and power used in the manufacturing process and the transportation of goods.

5.5. Innovation in Sustainable Design and Product Manufacturing

Creating new materials, new processes and new technologies is essential to implementing CE. Products need to be designed with reuse, repair, and recyclability in mind and all partners in the supply chain as well as end-users/consumers need to adopt a longevity mindset. The current 'throw-away-society' paradigm is not aligned to a CE approach. One interesting area of development and design in CE is biomimicry (Bocken et al., 2018). Natural systems can offer innovative ideas for new materials and new products and thus designers can utilise natural models to create more efficient and sustainable products. The construction industry is one good example of this where sheep wool is now routinely employed in insulation and recycled wood products are widely used. Bioplastics, such as those used in decking and fencing, and wood sourced from sustainable, fast-growing forests help minimise the negative environmental impact while promoting good CE practice. One of the most innovative products to emerge from biomimicry is fungi surfboards (BBC, 2023). A small UK company based in Cornwall has developed the means to grow fungi, harvesting a crop every 20 days to manufacture biodegradable surfboards. This has eliminated the need for plastics and reduced the negative environmental impact associated with fibreglass surfboards to nil. The use of digital design software and computer simulations can help model environmental impacts and optimise production to reduce material waste.

5.6. Digital Technologies and Circular Business Models

There are many recent examples of app-based business models that help increase business efficiency and reduce waste. These technologies are referred to as the sharing economy (Geng et al., 2019) and relate to a wide variety of applications, for example in motor vehicles, equipment, and accommodation. Airbnb, Uber and Zipcar are seen as disruptors in this field and provide sustainable alternatives to traditional offerings. An extension of this form of disruption can be seen in PaaS business models where companies are springing up around the world to offer, for example, the rental of washing machines and clothing for adults and children. In these instances companies retain ownership of products which are then repaired and reused, eliminating the need for consumer ownership and the environmental damage that goes with the current capitalist model. Patagonia, Levi's and Mud Jeans are other examples of PaaS offerings that utilise app technology to access the market.

5.7. Big Data and Blockchain

We previously looked at the fast fashion industry and its use of RFID and generative AI to improve decision-making and supply chain efficiency (Rathore et al., 2019). The IT revolution in CE is already prolific and is gathering pace. Companies are combining sensors, data storage, microprocessors, and software in many different ways to increase network, particularly wireless, connectivity. This in turn provides almost endless possibilities for big data collection and analysis to continuously improve efficient usage and to monitor the effectiveness of design. The disruptive nature of this connectivity, referred to as 'the IoT" above, is the redesign of value chains and internal business processes, creating new competition and markets. The Harvard Business Review (HBR, 2014) reported that connected products constitute a new era of IT-driven business efficiency. Using the example of a car, HBR explains the three elements of connected products: first, physical elements comprise mechanical and electronic parts in a car such as the engine, wheels, seats, and so on; second, smart components are sensors, microprocessors, operating systems, and the user interface (in a car, this would refer to touchscreen displays, rain-sensing windscreens, and windscreen wipers.); third, connectivity components enabling wired or wireless connections (again, in a car these would be Bluetooth interfaces, satellite navigation systems, computer links for engine diagnostics).

A great deal of opportunity exists in connectivity, particularly in supply chain scenarios. Agriculture is a good example of this potential as geolocation data informs seeding patterns and strategies to optimise plant growth. Wind farms and the renewable energy sector are connected to national energy grids, using sensors and weather data to adjust wind turbine direction and blade angles, thus optimising power generation. The immediacy of connected products and industries has huge potential to reduce waste and improve efficiency in almost every imaginable organisational setting.

Blockchain technology is another digital technology that can support circular business models. Blockchain provides a transparent and secure way to track the ownership and transfer of materials and products throughout their lifecycle (Iansiti & Lakhani, 2017). Technology such as sensors and microprocessors are used to collect and store transactional data in sequence to provide a historical record of use, transfer of ownership, expenditure, and other variables (Luthra et al., 2018). This enables companies to manage and manipulate a circular supply chain where materials and products are reused and recycled rather than disposed of. This technology has the potential to revolutionise supply chain management by increasing transparency and accountability. Complex networks of suppliers, manufacturers, distributors, and retailers, in addition to tracing products and materials through these networks can be challenging. Blockchain technology offers a solution by providing a transparent and secure way to track the ownership and transfer of goods and materials. According to Swan (2015), Blockchain offers a radical approach to monitoring and analysing markets and supply chains while maintaining data security and integrity, supporting CE, and leading to significant efficiencies (Truby & Winer, 2018).

That being said, there are also challenges associated with the use of blockchain technology in supply chain management. One of these is the complexity of integrating blockchain with existing supply chain systems and processes. Another is ensuring the security and privacy of sensitive information in a blockchain network. These challenges will need to be addressed to fully realise the potential of blockchain in supply chain management (Christopher & Peck, 2004).

As we saw in Chapter 3, the fashion industry is heavily invested in connecting technologies and is driving efficiencies throughout the supply chain. Fig. 5.1 illustrates the complexity of technology applications from generative AI and blockchain to enhanced online interfaces that augment the customer experience and reduce returns.

Customers benefit from much of the technological development in the industry, through price reductions, better product availability, and a more effective online experience. The sustainability factors are also addressed directly through efficiencies and in the long term, cost reductions and waste reductions coupled with recycle and repair services. These elements of technology in CE transformation are 'push' factors and now we turn to look at 'pull' factors in relation to end-users and consumers.

Fig. 5.1.   CE and Fashion Industry Technology.

5.8. Consumer Behaviour and CE

In Chapter 3, we introduced the challenge of creating end-user or buyer 'pull' to balance against supply chain 'push' in bringing about a CE transformation in any given market, industry, or country. Innovations in technology have historically produced considerable change in buyer behaviour; in CE these innovations are expected to change buying patterns, usage patterns, and crucially, changes in buyer mindsets. Circular consumption refers to the design-led phenomena of creating reuse, refurbish, or recycle behaviour to replace the dominant disposal and single use activity that characterises much of global consumption today. CE aims to keep products and materials in use for as long as possible. The question that remains unanswered is: how long will it take for the vast majority of the world's population to radically change their values and buying behaviour to fully embrace CE? We discovered in Chapter 3 that, to enable this paradigm shift, buyers in any market will require strong incentives, backed up by clear information and education programmes. Technology again has a central role to play in this transformation, through 'push' applications in supply chain management and also through 'pull' initiatives aimed at consumers.

Technology has impacted circular consumption through the use of digital tools to promote sustainable behaviours. For example, mobile apps such as GoodGuide and Buycott allow consumers to scan product barcodes to learn more about the environmental and social impact of the products they are considering purchasing. These tools provide buyers with the information they need to make more sustainable consumption choices and can help drive demand for circular products.

Technology has also played a role in facilitating reuse and recycling. For example, online marketplaces like eBay and Craigslist allow consumers to sell or give away items they no longer need, keeping them in circulation and reducing waste. Similarly, digital platforms like TerraCycle and Freecycle enable consumers to exchange and recycle products in their communities, reducing the amount of waste that ends up in landfills. CE transformation requires consumer-led and consumer-focussed initiatives to enable change. The shift is slow and encounters various barriers and blockages, from regulatory friction to consumer intransigence or fear. We will tackle issues of change and leading change as well as CE adoption or acceptance later in the chapter but for now, we turn our attention to innovation in the design of business models.

5.9. CE Innovation and Business Model Canvas

Business model canvas (BMC) is a popular tool for analysing and designing business models. It consists of nine elements: value proposition, customer segments, channels, customer relationships, revenue streams, key resources, key activities, key partnerships, cost structure. BMI refers to the creation, adoption, or modification of a business model to create new value for customers, stakeholders, and the environment (Geissdoerfer et al., 2018).

Innovation concerning business models is fundamental to achieving a CE-driven transformation and we will look later in this Chapter at how Adidas have begun their journey towards sustainability. Ricoh is another global company who had began this transformation over 30 years ago in the 1990s. Their transformation began with a critical review of their values and practices towards recycling and repair in the office machinery sector. A global market leader, Ricoh decided to switch the business model emphasis from financial gain to a central concept of recycling (CE hub, 2023). In analysing the business model, Ricoh looked at supply chain life cycles across the world and modelled their products against the global market. Circularity was built into the Ricoh supply chain to ensure parts and machines are recycled and that sensors across the supply chain are embedded to provide data to enhance efficiencies wherever they can be made. Taking each element of BMC in turn, we can see how the model underpins CE transformation.

Step 1. The value proposition refers to the products or services that a company offers to its customers (Tukker & Tischner, 2018). In a CE, companies need to rethink their value proposition to focus on designing products that can be reused, repaired, or recycled. BMIs in this area can include using sustainable materials, creating products with modular designs, or offering PaaS models where the company retains ownership of the product, providing maintenance and upgrades to customers (Geissdoerfer et al., 2018).

Step 2. Customer segments. Understanding customer needs and wants is essential for designing products that promote circularity. Companies can segment their customers based on their sustainability preferences and thus design products that meet their specific needs (Lüdeke-Freund & Dembek, 2017). They can also awaken latent needs and promote sustainability to consumers. BMIs in this area might include creating circular communities where customers can share resources, or offering personalised product recommendations based on customers' sustainability preferences (Schaltegger et al., 2016).

Step 3. Channels refer to the ways that a company reaches its customers. In a CE, companies can use channels that promote circularity, such as online marketplaces for second-hand products or take-back programmes for end-of-life products (Niesten & Jolink, 2018). BMIs in this area can include using blockchain technology to track product lifecycles or collaborating with other companies to create closed-loop supply chains (Bhaskar & Manikandan, 2019).

Step 4. Relationships. Customer relationships are the way that a company interacts with its customers. In a CE, companies can engage with customers in new ways, such as by providing repair services, offering warranties, or incentivising customers to return end-of-life products (Geissdoerfer et al., 2020). BMIs in this area can include gamification strategies that encourage customers to engage in circular behaviours or use social media to build communities around circular products (Parguel et al., 2016).

Step 5. Revenue Streams. In a CE, revenue streams can come from a variety of sources, including the sale or leasing of products, or the provision of maintenance and repair services (Bocken et al., 2014). BMIs in this area can include using circular pricing models, such as pay-per-use or subscription models, or developing revenue-sharing models where customers share in the financial benefits of circular products (Tukker, 2015).

Step 6. Key resources refer to the assets that a company needs to create value for its customers. In a CE, companies need to focus on using sustainable resources and reducing waste (Bhupendra et al., 2019). BMIs in this area can include using renewable energy sources, implementing closed-loop production systems, or collaborating with suppliers to create circular supply chains (Singh et al., 2021).

Step 7. Key activities are the processes that a company uses to create value for its customers (Colombo et al., 2017). In a CE, companies need to focus on designing products for circularity and implementing circular processes, such as take-back programmes and refurbishment processes. BMIs in this area can include using 3D printing technology to create customised products or implementing circular design principles such as cradle-to-cradle.

Step 8. Key partnerships refer to the relationships that a company has with suppliers, distributors, and other stakeholders. In a CE, companies need to collaborate with partners to create closed-loop supply chains and promote circularity. BMIs in this area can include partnering with suppliers to source sustainable materials (Casadesus-Masanell & Zhu, 2018).

Step 9. Revenue streams. This step focusses on identifying the ways in which the business generates revenue from its products or services. For a company that is aiming to adopt CE) principles, this may involve identifying new revenue streams that are aligned with CE goals, such as the reuse or recycling of products (Cielens & Blumberga, 2018).

To develop a circular business model using the BMC, the company may need to consider new revenue streams that are based on circular principles. For example, a company that manufactures office furniture could adopt a circular business model by offering a subscription-based service where customers lease furniture and the company takes it back at the end of the lease to refurbish or recycle. This would create a new revenue stream for the company based on the reuse of its products, rather than relying solely on the sale of new products. The following questions could act as a framework or guide as a starting point for CE-driven BMI:

- Can we generate revenue from products that are designed for durability and longevity rather than for disposability?
- What new revenue streams can we create by offering services that support the reuse or recycling of our products?
- Can we create revenue streams based on the data generated by our products or services, such as through data analytics or predictive maintenance services?

5.10. Innovation in CE Business Models

A growing number of companies and organisations exist who have innovated and transformed their business models. While changing values and vision throughout their organisations and, in many cases, throughout the supply chain, a balance between focussing on sustainability and maintaining profitability must be kept. In Chapter 3, we saw how H & M experienced and managed a downturn in profitability, coming through a mini-slump to see profit levels on the rise in recent years. The examples in Table 5.1 present successful CE-focussed innovations in well-known international companies.

Table 5.1.   Business Model Innovation Examples.

1. Closed-loop supply chains: Companies such as H & M, Levi's, and Patagonia have implemented closed-loop supply chains where they take back used products from customers, either in-store or through mail-in programmes, and then reuse or recycle the materials to make new products
2. PaaS models: These models offer customers access to products as a service, rather than owning them outright. This allows companies to retain ownership of the products and take responsibility for their end-of-life management. For example, Philips offers lighting as a service, where customers pay for the use of lighting rather than buying the products
3. Sharing platforms: Platforms, such as Airbnb and Uber, enable the sharing of resources among a community of users. This allows for more efficient use of resources, as well as reduced waste and carbon emissions associated with the production and disposal of new products
4. Design for disassembly: This is a concept where products are designed to be easily disassembled at end-of-life so that the materials can be recovered and reused or recycled. For example, the Fairphone is a modular smartphone that can be easily disassembled and repaired, and the components can be replaced or upgraded as needed
5. Biomimicry. This involves looking to nature for inspiration in design and innovation. For example, the company Sharklet Technologies has developed an antibacterial surface that mimics the texture of shark skin with its natural antibacterial properties. This surface can be used in hospitals, food processing plants, and other settings where hygiene is critical

5.11. Innovation and Adoption in CE

Technology offers a wide range of alternative power sources (e.g. renewable energy), materials (e.g. biomimicry), and analytical platforms (e.g. sensors, RFID, big data, AI, blockchain) that improve efficiency, predict patterns, and persuade consumers and end-users to behave differently. We have discussed the need for 'push' and 'pull' elements to CE transformation and the need for innovation in bringing these values together in new business models. We will look at change and managing change later in the chapter; we now turn our attention to technology adoption and acceptance.

The technology adoption model, also known as the technology adoption curve, is a model that describes the adoption over time of new technologies by individuals or groups. It was first introduced by Everett Rogers in his 1962 book 'Diffusion of Innovation'.

The model suggests that individuals within a population can be divided into five categories based on their readiness to adopt new technologies:

(1) Innovators – the first to adopt a new technology, they are risk takers and willing to try new things.
(2) Early adopters – opinion leaders and influencers who adopt new technologies early after release.
(3) Early majority – will buy into technology once proven and when risks are low.
(4) Late majority – more sceptical buyers who generally do not trust new technologies and products.
(5) Laggards – will adopt new technology as a last resort and may resist change altogether.

Rogers' (1962) model is adapted and presented below in Fig. 5.2. It can be seen as a bell curve with approximate percentages attributed to each of the five categories. The first two groups (innovators and early adopters) represent approximately 16% of the population, the early majority and late majority each representing approximately 34%, and the laggards representing approximately 16%.

Technology acceptance theory assumes a similar reaction to technology as Rogers' modelled in relation to innovation (Hitt & Tamble, 2017). We can assume that a similar response to tech-driven CE developments will be seen in society across the world. The percentages and the shape of Rogers' curve may well differ in CE or Industry 4.0 developments, however, the core logic and concepts remain the same. Technology adoption and technology acceptance models (TAM) are similarly rooted in Rogers' work and have been applied to a wide variety of fields.

TAM have undergone a range of developments over the past 30 years with initial modelling significantly developed to add complexity to our understanding of how technology is diffused throughout societies. TAM focusses on the variables that influence technology acceptance and the most critical are the perceived usefulness and ease of use. In CE, technological developments, and indeed any fundamental proposed changes to consumption and production behaviour, need to satisfy these requirements (Bagozzi et al., 1992). Next, influence will be a key factor in acceptance and communication from government, industry bodies, companies and social media will be required to nudge individuals towards change and acceptance. Education is required to embed new values and behaviours and to instil a sense of environmental imperative in mindsets. Mitigating risk and making technology understandable and accessible will help address resistance (Davis, 1989). In recent years, several authors have offered more holistic models of technology acceptance including Venkatesh et al. (2003).

There are many examples of business failures where CE projects are concerned. One example is the case of P&G's Pampers recycling programme, which aimed to recycle used baby nappies into new products (Weisbrod & Van Hoof, 2012). The programme was launched in the Netherlands in 2002 but was shut down in 2006 due to high costs and a lack of demand. Another example is the failure of the Carpet Recycling UK programme which aimed to recycle carpet waste into new

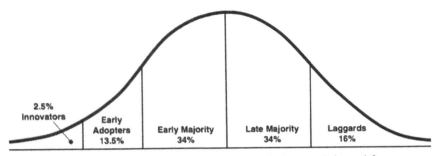

Fig. 5.2.   Roger's Diffusion of Innovation Model. *Source*: Adapted from Rogers (1962).

products. The programme was launched in 2008 but was shut down in 2018 due to a lack of demand and low recycling rates.

These failures highlight the challenges of implementing CE strategies including the need for strong market demand, viable business models, and effective waste management systems. However, they also provide valuable lessons for future initiatives, including the importance of assessing market demand, developing robust business models, and collaborating with stakeholders across the value chain to ensure the success of CE initiatives.

Diffusion of Innovation and TAM give us a sense of the task facing the world if we are to implement CE. We are suggesting a radical change to business models and behaviours in supply chains, coupled with a transformation of values, beliefs, and behaviour in consumer and end-user markets (Shen et al., 2020). We look now at the nature of resistance and ways of overcoming these barriers to change.

5.12. Change and CE

From an organisational point of view, change poses risks and complex problems, especially where wholesale transformation is required to fully embrace CE. There are several well-established models in change management which give us an insight into managing change effectively.

First there is Kurt Lewin's Change Management Model (1951). Developed by the psychologist in the 1950s, this model consists of three stages: unfreezing, changing, and refreezing. In the unfreezing stage, the current situation is evaluated and the need for change is identified. In the changing stage, new behaviours and processes are introduced. In the refreezing stage, the new behaviours and processes are reinforced to ensure they become the new norm. One of the key criticisms of this model is that it fails to accommodate contemporary, dynamic organisational settings where a continuous change in the environment requires constant adjustment to strategy and operations.

The second key change management model is John Kotter's 8-step Change Model (1996). This model consists of creating a sense of urgency, building a coalition, forming a strategic vision and initiatives, enlisting a volunteer army, enabling action by removing barriers, creating short-term wins, sustaining acceleration, and anchoring new approaches in the organisation's culture. Kotter's model is more culturally focussed and is likely to lead to the creation of dynamic capabilities in the workforce as the model prescribes a process that is both iterative and long-term orientated.

Third is the ADKAR model developed by the change consultancy company Prosci (2018) and consists of five elements which inform the acronym: awareness of the need for change, desire to support the change, knowledge of how to change, ability to implement the change, and reinforcement to sustain the change. This model draws on the imperatives and the mechanisms of change. It omits the need for embedded agility to enable change, but does add the external sensing of change drivers to the internal operationalisation of change. These two dimensions of CE-driven change are vital to the partnering concept that is at the heart of sustainability and is expressed by SDG17. Change is needed across the supply chain both in government departments and in consumers or end-users for circularity to be possible.

Fourth is the McKinsey 7-S Framework (2017), developed by management consulting firm McKinsey and Company. The model appears to be more holistic and can be adapted to include the whole supply chain and its seven elements are: strategy, structure, systems, shared values, skills, style, and staff.

Fifth is Bridges' Transition Model (1991), which focusses on the psychological and emotional aspects of change. The model consists of three stages: ending, neutral zone, and new beginning. Building on Lewin's three-stage model, Bridges adds a psychological dimension that recognises elements of resistance to change which might require engaged work to overcome. Although it could be argued that the tipping-point has been reached in the general acceptance that CE is a necessary goal, many individuals will need education, nurturing and support to help them grasp the nature of the required change and the means by which they might achieve it. One of the key elements in bringing about such transformational change is the leadership culture. Next, we turn to look at leading change and consider a selection of the most relevant models.

5.13. Leadership and Change

In these dynamic and turbulent times, adaptability is one of the most important organisational characteristics required to sense, understand and implement change (Teece, 2016). Much of the literature regarding traits and styles is still relevant to understanding individual leaders, and we consider here the context of leadership.

The situational leadership model, developed by Hersey and Blanchard (1977) was one of the first to recognise that leadership and followership are two sides of the same coin. Leaders require followers and organisational culture plays a central role in creating the basis for relationships, conventions for communication and collective behaviour. The role the leader plays comes down to four types in Hersey and Blanchard's situational leadership: directing, coaching, supporting and delegating. Leaders who are looking to garner support in implementing change are required to understand the external environment and to articulate this to colleagues in a compelling way (Uhl Bien, 2021). Next, they are required to work with their teams and individuals to bring about programmes and work streams related to the agreed change. A modern agile leader selects the most appropriate style of leadership to make change happen and will, for example, behave in a more directive manner with some programmes and colleagues and adopt more of a coaching style with other colleagues. This agility may come naturally to some but needs to be developed across the organisation at all levels to be most effective.

Transformational leaders, first posited by Burns (1978), are similar to situational leadership in that it recognises the need for followers. Burns suggests that leaders of change programmes must understand the ways in which colleagues are encouraged and motivated in order to improve and change processes and practices. He also added the dimension of creativity and innovation, suggesting that this is required to stimulate and draw in work colleagues to promote positivity and progression. Servant leadership goes further down the motivational route to suggest that workers require a leader who leads by example and supports colleagues (Greenleaf, 1970). This model advocates open communication and transparency to build trust. Lastly adaptive leadership, as presented by Heifetz in 1994. This model suggests that leaders must be able to adapt to changing circumstances and challenges. Adaptive leaders encourage others to take risks and learn from failure, and they promote experimentation and innovation. In implementing a transformational change programme that moves an organisation and its partners towards a connected CE model, change on a large scale must occur and leadership must be in place to help implement this change. This short review of leadership approaches demonstrates that the organisational setting is likely to be complex and that followership is required to make a successful of CE.

Having identified resistance to change and TAM, as well as organisational leadership approaches to implementing change, we now introduce the concept of transition frameworks (Lieder & Rashid, 2016). These provide a roadmap to transition from a linear to a CE and typically involve several stages or phases that organisations can follow to implement circular business models and practices. There are several transition frameworks available that can be used by organisations looking to make such a transition. An example of a CE transition framework is the Ellen MacArthur Foundation's CE Framework.

This framework is divided into three phases:

(1) Designing out waste and pollution – This phase involves rethinking the design of products and processes to eliminate waste and pollution from the outset. Key strategies here include designing for disassembly, using non-toxic materials, and minimising the use of virgin resources.
(2) Keeping products and materials in use – this phase involves extending the life of products and materials through reuse, repair, refurbishment, and recycling. Key strategies in this phase include designing for durability, developing new business models based on sharing and leasing, and implementing closed-loop material systems.

(3) Regenerating natural systems – This phase involves restoring natural ecosystems and preserving the value of natural resources. Key strategies include regenerative agriculture, sustainable forestry, and the use of renewable energy sources.

The Ellen MacArthur CE framework provides a comprehensive approach to implementing circular business models and practices across the entire value chain, from product design to end-of-life management.

A second example is the Circular Transition Indicators (CTI) framework, developed by Circle Economy (2023). This framework is designed to help organisations measure their circularity and track their progress towards a CE. Consisting of five indicators: Circularity potential, Circularity performance, Circular business models, Enabling conditions, and Circular value chain, the framework provides a structured approach for organisations to measure and improve across a range of dimensions.

In addition to these frameworks, there are also several tools and methodologies available to support organisations in their transition to a CE. These include life cycle assessment (LCA), material flow analysis (MFA), and product environmental footprint (PEF), among others (Levers & Cullen, 2018). These tools can help organisations identify opportunities for resource efficiency, waste reduction, and circular business models.

Transition frameworks provide a structured approach for organisations to implement circular business models and practices. They can help organisations identify opportunities for resource efficiency, waste reduction, and circular business models, and track their progress towards a CE. However, their successful implementation requires a holistic approach that considers the entire product lifecycle and engages stakeholders across the value chain.

5.14. Conclusion

This chapter has explored the nature and importance of innovation in transitioning towards CE. Some members of society will be far more likely to change values and behaviours to engage with CE through a wide range of activities including recycling, reusing, repairing, and repurposing of products. Sharing and rental developments will also facilitate a change in customer and end-user behaviour. We have discovered that resistance to change is a natural phenomenon that needs to be understood and addressed through 'push' factors in the supply chain and through 'pull' factors in end-user environments. Industry 4.0 – the implementation of digital technologies to accelerate efficiency, reduce waste and facilitate careful consumption – is gradually becoming more accepted across the world in a wide variety of industrial settings. We now turn to the Adidas case study to see some of these technologies and innovations in action.

5.15. Adidas Case Study

The sportswear manufacturer Adidas (Adidas Group Corp.) are reportedly making transformational changes to its business model to implement circularity and replace linearity in its supply chain. This is being implemented despite questions surrounding the future profitability of a circular business model and without a full analysis of the implications for the supply chain and customers of the iconic brand (AG, 2022).

The first step in the Adidas sustainability programme has been to analyse the market and assess the segments that are open to circularity and sustainable offerings. This links back to the BMC covered earlier in this chapter. Changing the Adidas value proposition at this point is seen by the executive management group of the company as a positive strategic initiative and is certainly aligned with consumer trends across many markets.

One of the building blocks of the new CE value proposition of Adidas is the in-house development of a 100% recyclable thermoplastic polyurethane. Shoes constructed of this manmade fibre can be melted down (rather than deposited in landfill waste sites) with recycled pellets able to be reintroduced into the manufacturing process (Burgess, 2019). This is an excellent example of innovation and circularity coming together in business model transformation.

One of Adidas's key partnerships in their CE strategy is with Parley For The Oceans (2023), a not-for-profit organisation that collects and recycles discarded fishing nets and ocean plastics for upcycling in the Adidas supply chain. This focus on ocean plastics arises from recent publicity on ocean pollution and a reported five trillion microplastic particles reportedly floating in our oceans, Adidas is leading the way in addressing this problem (van Giezen & Wiegmans, 2020).

Adidas is committed to identifying and implementing upcycling opportunities to further reduce waste in their system and has embedded circularity in their 'Own the game' initiative (AG, 2023). Adidas appears to be investing heavily in a sustainable supply chain that embeds upcycling of waste materials and circularity in every facet of their business.

The Adidas partnership with Stuffstr (Turk, 2019) aims to add buyback options to customers within five years of the initial purchase. Stuffstr takes back used Adidas products and refurnishes (word choice?) them for resale. This project aligns with CE principles in several ways: keeping products in the market for longer; prolonging product life; and recycling at the end-of-life. Adidas have adjusted its supply chain to accommodate recycling and buyback programmes and has costed these to sustain the financial viability of the company.

A high level of investment is required to transform a business model, the supply chain it is part of and the mindsets of the end-users or customers. Profitability seems to dip in the years following such a transformation as investment costs take hold of the company's finances. As with H & M in Chapter 3, many companies would expect to see profitability recover as costs are discounted or accounted for. What is largely ignored in reported cases such as Adidas is the organisational and inter-organisational development work required to frame transformational change, lead and implement change, and manage resistance to change across organisations and stakeholder groups.

Case questions:

(1) Discuss and sketch out a list of challenges and types of resistance that might be expected from Adidas at the outset of their CE project.
(2) Identify the steps that might be taken to outline a transformation plan.
(3) As CEO, how would you address inconsistencies in the beliefs and values of the workforce in relation to this new CE vision?
(4) What logistical problems might Adidas face in gathering in used products for recycling?
(5) What proportion of the market will constitute innovators and those ready to accept recyclability, reuse and repair? What would their likely segmentation profiles be?

References

AG. (2022). *Own the Game, Our Strategy 2025*. Retrieved March 30, 2023, from https://www.adidas-group.com/en/sustainability/focus-sustainability/our-targets/

Bagozzi, R. P., Davis, F. D., & Warshaw, P. R. (1992). Development and test of a theory of technological learning and usage. *Human Relations, 45*(7), 659–686.

Bai, C., Sarkis, J., Yin, F., & Don, Y. (2019). Sustainable SC flexibility and its relationship to CE-target performance. *International Journal of Production Research, 58*(19), 5893–5910.

BBC. (2023). *Fungi surfboards show there's mush-room for innovation*. Retrieved February 18, 2023, from https://www.bbc.co.uk/news/av/uk-wales-64680249

Bhaskar, R., & Manikandan, S. (2019). Blockchain-based circular economy: A comprehensive review. *Journal of Cleaner Production, 230*, 560–571.

Bhupendra, K., Wadhwa, V., & Kumar, R. (2019). Circular economy for sustainable development: A review. *Journal of Cleaner Production, 12*(23), 10109.

Bocken, N. M., Bakker, C., & Pauw, I. (2018). Product dsesign and business model strategies for a circular economy. *Journal of Industrial and Production Engineering, 35*(7), 449–464.

Bocken, N. M. P., Short, S. W., Rana, P., & Evans, S. (2014). A literature and practice review to develop sustainable business model archetypes. *Journal of Cleaner Production, 65*, 42–56.

Bressanelli, G., Pigosso, D. C. A., Saccani, N., & Perona, M. (2021). Enablers, levers, and benefits of CE in the electrical and electronic equipment SC: A literature review. *Journal of Cleaner Production, 298*, 126819.

Bridges, W. (1991). *Managing transitions: Making the most of change*. Addison-Wesley.

Burgess, M. (2019). A new Adidas shoe uses just one material – and it's fully recyclable. *Wired UK*. Retrieved January 12, 2023, from https://www.wired.co.uk/article/adidas-futurecraft-looprunning-shoe-recycle

Burns, J. M. (1978). *Leadership*. Harper & Row.

Casadesus-Masanell, R., & Zhu, F. (2018). Business model innovation and competitive imitation: The case of sponsor-based business models. *Strategic Management Journal, 39*(3), 729–749.

Christopher, M., & Peck, H. (2004). Building the resilient supply chain. *The International Journal of Logistics Management, 15*(2), 1–13.

Cielens, I., & Blumberga, A. (2018). The sharing economy: A comprehensive approach. *Baltic Journal of Management, 13*(2), 143–163.

Circular Economy Hub. (2023). *Case Study: Ricoh Circular Economy Hub (2023)*. Retrieved February 20, 2023, from https://ce-hub.org/knowledge-hub/case-study-ricoh/

Circular Economy. (2018). *Circular transition indicators*. Retrieved March 20, 2023, from https://www.circle-economy.com/circular-transition-indicators/

Colombo, G., Piva, E., & Rossi-Lamastra, C. (2017). How external and internal sources of knowledge contribute to firms' innovation performance. *Research Policy, 46*(5), 905–920.

Davis, F. D. (1989). Perceived usefulness, perceived ease of use, and user acceptance of information technology. *MIS Quarterly, 13*(3), 319–340.

Ellen MacArthur Foundation. (2013). *Towards the circular economy: Economic and business rationale for an accelerated transition*. Retrieved January 23, 2023, from https://www.ellenmacarthurfoundation.org/assets/dowloads/publications/TCE_Report-2013.pdf

Farooque, M., Zhang, A., Thurer, M., Qu, T., & Huising, D. (2019). Circular SCM: A definition and structured literature review. *Journal of Cleaner Production, 228*, 882–900.

Geissdoerfer, M., Morioka, S. N., de Carvalho, M. M., & Evans, S. (2020). Business models and value propositions for a circular economy: An integrative review. *Journal of Cleaner Production, 272*, 122806.

Geissdoerfer, M., Savaget, P., Bocken, N. M., & Hultink, E. J. (2017). The circular economy – A new sustainability paradigm? *Journal of Cleaner Production, 143*, 757–768.

Geissdoerfer, M., Vladimirova, D., & Evans, S. (2018). Sustainable business model innovation: A review. *Journal of Cleaner Production, 198*, 401–416

Geng, Y., Zhang, P., Sun, L., & Tian, X. (2019). The impact of sharing economy on circular consumption behavior. *Resources, Conservation and Recycling, 149*, 166–173.

Ghisellini, P., Cialani, C., & Ulgiati, S. (2016). A review on circular economy: The expected transition to a balanced interplay of environmental and economic systems. *Journal of Cleaner Production, 114*, 11–32.

Greenleaf, R. K. (1970). *The servant as leader*. Robert K. Greenleaf Publishing Center.

Harvard Business Review. (2014, November). *Spotlight on managing the internet of things*. https://hbr.org/2014/11/spotlight-on-managing-the-internet-of-things

Heifetz, R. A. (1994). *Leadership without easy answers*. Harvard University Press.

Hersey, P., & Blanchard, K. H. (1977). *Management of Organizational Behavior: Utilizing Human Resources*. Prentice-Hall.

Hitt L. M., & Tambe, P. (2017). Broadening the scope of sociotechnical systems: Toward a theoretical basis for technology adoption in complex settings. *IEEE Transactions on Engineering Management, 64*(4), 384–398.

Kahn, M. E., & Matsusaka, J. G. (2019). Technology, consumer behavior, and environmental policy. *Journal of Public Economics, 177*, 104036.

Kircherr, J., Reike, D., & Hekkert, M. (2017). Conceptualizing the circular economy: An analysis of 114 definitions. *Resources, Conservation and Recycling, 127*, 221–232.

Kjaer, L. L., Pigosso, D. C. A., McAloone, T. C., & Roos Lindgreen, M. (2020). Digital technology and the circular economy: Drivers, challenges and opportunities. *Journal of Cleaner Production, 244*, 118676.

Kotter, J. P. (1996). *Leading change*. Harvard Business Review Press.

Leal Filho, W., Mifsud, M., Shiel, C., & do Paco, A. (2020). The use of digital technologies to facilitate the adoption of circular business models. *Journal of Cleaner Production, 261*, 121156.

Levers, A., & Cullen, J. M. (2018). Industry 4.0: The role of raw materials in the future of manufacturing. *Annual Review of Materials Research, 48*(1), 1–29.

Lewin, K. (1951). *Field theory in social science: Selected theoretical papers* (D. Cartwright, Ed.). Harper & Row.

Lieder, M., & Rashid, A. (2016). Towards circular economy implementation: A comprehensive review in context of manufacturing industry. *Journal of Cleaner Production, 115,* 36–51.

Lüdeke-Freund, F., & Dembek, K. (2017). Sustainable business model research and practice: Emerging field or passing fancy? *Journal of Cleaner Production, 168,* 1668–1678.

Ludeke-Freund, F., Gold, S., & Bocken, N. M. (2019). A review and typology of circular economy business model patterns. *Journal of Industrial Ecology, 23*(1), 36–61.

Luthra, S., Garg, D., Haleem, A., Kumar, A., & Rahman, Z. (2018). Blockchain-based framework for secure and efficient supply chain management in the automotive industry. *International Journal of Production Research, 56*(14), 4894–4916.

McDonough, W., & Braungart, M. (2013). *The upcycle: Beyond sustainability—Designing for abundance.* North Point Press.

McKinsey & Company. (2017). *The 7-S model.* McKinsey & Company.

Mont, O. (2002). Clarifying the concept of product–service system. *Journal of Cleaner Production, 10*(3), 237–245.

Nasir, M. H. A., Genovese, A., Acquaye, A. A., Koh, S. C. L., & Yamoah, F. (2017). Comparing linear and circular SCs: A case study from the construction industry. *International Journal of Production Economics, 183,* 443–457.

Niesten, E., & Jolink, A. (2018). Towards a circular economy: The role of Dutch frontrunner businesses and implications for the business community. *Environmental Innovation and Societal Transitions, 27,* 1–15.

Osterwalder, A., & Pigneur, Y. (2010). *Business model generation: A handbook for visionaries, game changers, and challengers.* John Wiley & Sons.

Osterwalder, A., Pigneur, Y., Bernarda, G., & Smith, A. (2014). *Value proposition design: How to create products and services customers want.* John Wiley & Sons.

Parguel, B., Benoit-Moreau, F., & Russell, C. A. (2016). Can social media advertising enhance advertising effectiveness? *Journal of Advertising, 45*(2), 178–192.

Parley For The Oceans. (2023). *Adidas X Parley.* Retrieved February 4, 2023, from https://parley.tv/initiatives/adidasxparley

Pigosso, D. C., Rozenfeld, H., & McAloone, T. C. (2018). Circular business model innovation: Lessons from the field. *Journal of Cleaner Production, 190,* 712–725.

Rathore, S. M., Maheshwari, K., & Jain, S. (2019). Fast moving H&M: An analysis of supply chain management. *International Journal of Advance Research and Innovative Ideas in Education, 5*(4), 1557–1568.

Ripanti, E. F., & Tjahjono, B. (2019). Unveiling the potentials of CE values in logistics and SCM, *The International Journal of Logistics Management, 30*(3), 723–742.

Rogers, E. M. (1962). *The diffusion of innovation.* Free Press.

Schaltegger, S., Hansen, E. G., & Lüdeke-Freund, F. (2016). Business models for sustainability: Origins, present research, and future avenues. *Organization & Environment, 29*(1), 3–10.

Shen, B., Li, Y., & Dai, W. (2020). Promoting consumers' circular consumption behavior: The role of mobile applications, advancements, and challenges. *International Journal of Production Research.*

Singh, J., Singh, N., & Singh, R. (2021). A comprehensive review on 3D printing technology: Applications, advancements, and challenges. *International Journal of Production Research.*

Sundin, E., & Lindahl, M. (2018). Industry 4.0 and the circular economy: A proposed research agenda and original roadmap for sustainable operations. *Journal of Manufacturing Technology Management, 29*(5), 910–929.

Swan, M. (2015). *Blockchain: Blueprint for a new economy.* O'Reilly Media, Inc.

Tassinari, V. (2020). CE, sustainability, retailers and SC collaboration. *Symphonya,* (1), 129–135.

Teece, D. J. (2016). Dynamic capabilities and entrepreneurial management in large organizations: Toward a theory of the (entrepreneurial) firm. *European Economic Review*, *86*, 202–216.

Truby, J., & Winer, R. S. (2018). The blockchain carrot to encourage environmentally sustainable behavior. *Yale Journal of International Affairs*, *13*(1), 107–125.

Tukker, A. (2015). Product services for a resource-efficient and circular economy – A review. *Journal of Cleaner Production*, *97*, 76–91.

Tukker, A., & Tischner, U. (2018). *New business for old Europe: Product-service development, competitiveness and sustainability*. Routledge.

Turk, R. (2019). *Adidas introduces "Infinite Play" trade-in program*. FashionUnited. Retrieved March 15, 2023, from https://fashionunited.ie/news/fashion/adidas-introduces-infinite-play-trade-inprogram-1571385321/20191017107382

Uhl Bien, M. (2021). Complexity leadership and followership: Changed leadership in a changed world. *Journal of Change Management*, *21*, 144–162.

van Giezen, A., & Wiegmans, B. (2020). Spoilt – ocean cleanup: Alternative logistics chains to accommodate plastic waste recycling: A economic evaluation. *Transportation Research Interdisciplinary Perspectives*, *5*, 100115.

Venkatesh, V., Morris, M. G., Davis, G. B., & Davis, F. D. (2003). User acceptance of information technology: Toward a unified view. *MIS Quarterly*, *27*(3), 425–478.

Weisbrod, A. V., Van Hoof, G. (2012). LCA-measured environmental improvements in Pampers® diapers. *International Journal of Life Cycle Assessment*, *17*, 145–153. https://doi.org/10.1007/s11367-011-0343-1

Zong, W., He, H., & Zhao, X. (2020). Internet of things based resource efficiency in manufacturing: A review. *Journal of Cleaner Production*, *246*, 119076.

Chapter 6

A Review and Research Agenda for the Circular Economy

6.1. Introduction

Moving to a circular economy (CE) at a time of increased global ecological awareness may require a change of ethical and moral standards in existing and future staff. This may manifest itself in different ways across a range of organisations and circumstances and may include: a different sense of personal responsibility, possibly deriving from one's own beliefs; a sense of official responsibility, including corporate social responsibility (CSR); acting with the interest of one's employees, customers, and shareholders; standards stemming from personal loyalties, including organisational loyalties; technical morality dictated by standards set by one's professional enterprise; and legal responsibility to abide by the law, court decisions, and administrative orders (adapted from Steiner, 1975, chapter 13). However, this list does not go far enough towards the ethical and moral standards required by employees and companies to meet the obligations of business and ecological change in the CE into the 2030s.

It must be stated that this is not an academic discipline as such, but rather a major industrial, business, and management initiative with global consequences. However, there is no doubt that the academic community can play an important role in its effective development. New intelligence will need to be rapidly acquired as firms seek to gain an advantage over their rivals. In such business environments, effective routines are those that are highly adaptive to changing circumstances, giving the firm the opportunity to move quickly to a more optimum competitive position. It has become clear during our preparation for this book that radical change is required regarding the research agenda for the CE. One of the main rationales for this book, in fact, was to clarify the scope of, and relationships within, the future CE. How and why are the goals of the CE being set? Are these goals underpinned by ethical and ecological standards? Who are the main drivers of the CE? Is this a 'push' or 'pull' business scenario? There has been a significant amount of purposeful activity in these research areas over the last few years which offers potential for positive collaboration across many academic disciplines as well as with practitioners in these fields.

Sustainable Development Through Global Circular Economy Practices, 133–156
Copyright © 2024 by Stuart Maguire and Ian Robson
Published under exclusive licence by Emerald Publishing Limited
doi:10.1108/978-1-83753-590-320231006

6.2. Embedding CE Concepts into Mainstream Business and Management

The modern idea of regenerative and responsible product design, typified by the concept of the CE, stems from a number of whole system design concepts. Influences on this concept come from renowned architect Walter R. Stahel, sustainability pioneer Gunter Pauli and Natural Step founder Karl-Hendrik Robert including other accomplished researchers. Among the influences on the concept are the criteria outlined in the Hannover Principles, published in 1991, compiled and written by William McDonough and chemist Michael Braungart, the founders of Cradle to Cradle. These principles are a set of statements concerning the design of buildings and objects with forethought about their environmental impact, their effect on sustainable growth, and their overall impact on society (innovationnewsnetwork.com).

The Hannover Principles:

- Insist on the right of humanity and nature to co-exist in a healthy, supportive, diverse, and sustainable condition.
- Recognise interdependence.
- Accept responsibility for the consequences of design decisions upon human well-being, the viability of natural systems, and their right to co-exist.
- Create safe objects of long-term value.
- Eliminate the concept of waste.
- Rely on natural energy flows.
- Understand the limitations of design.
- Seek constant improvement by sharing knowledge.

Over the last 30 years, these principles have been expanded upon and evolved into what is now termed the Cradle to Cradle (C2C) design protocols or standards. The C2C standard evaluates and assesses product design, processing, and manufacturing criteria and administers a certification of end products which are specifically designed to flow effectively through the various channels of the CE system.

The importance of the key concepts of CE cannot be exaggerated. As a result of the 2007 McKinsey study into the next evolution in global socio-economics, the concept came into reality and was defined as a practice to adopt for global sustainable economic development. In 2009, Dame Ellen MacArthur founded the Ellen MacArthur Foundation (EMF), an organisation wholly focussed on educating and supporting CE efforts worldwide and fostering pioneering education and global principles of CE implementation. Highly influential companies such as Google, Unilever, Phillips, Renault, Nike, ECOR, Stella McCartney, and many more high-profile organisations, are part of the Foundation's CE 100 initiative which aims to encourage and support CE practices throughout supply chains (SCs), bringing the socio-economic, ecological, and financial benefits of CE activity to businesses and customers worldwide.

CE is a vital system to facilitate a reduction in the depletion of finite resources. For example, a 'circular' designed phone would be one that is designed for disassembly at the end of use, made with approved high-quality materials that can be safely reutilised, either into another phone or other suitable products. The reuse of resources includes their reclamation by the original manufacturer for use in new products, allowing the manufacturers substantial financial benefits. This activity retains material value and can dramatically reduce undesirable ecological impacts. In some instances, CE is understood as responsible recycling or effective and efficient waste management/reduction. While these activities do add to and improve CE outcomes, they are not an adequate or accurate definition (innovationnewsnetwork.com).

Through the lens of CE, Sehnem and Queiroz (2022) seek to identify the intellectual contours of this emerging field, conducting a review of the basic conceptual framework with an analysis of articles published on the topic of CE and innovation. The results of the study show that eco-innovation and innovation in business models are highlighted in this field and are operationalised, mainly by activating dynamic, relational, and absorptive capabilities. The most important innovation practices in this context are waste management, eco-design business models, product leasing, and collaborative commerce. The main output is to pave the way for new conceptual developments in organisational capabilities to make transition sustainable and serve as a support arsenal for the maturation of CE studies supported by the theory of innovation. It is also to link management practices to operational processes in the business and production environment, favouring the transition to a circular business model (CBM). Sehnem and Queiroz (2022) claim that it generates insights into the scientific progression of studies and shows propositions that can be validated in future quantitative studies.

However, evaluation tools for CBMs include environment and business management tools which are products of the linear economy, thus raising concerns around their applicability in CE. CBMs have been receiving even greater attention in both the business sector and academia while the existing literature is scattered and fragmented. This work offers an integrated firm-level framework to link CBM typologies, CE, a transition process, and relevant tools for CBM development and clarifies the positioning and roles of those tools in the process. In response to any fragmentation issues, the results of Chen et al.'s study were presented in three sub-topics: (a) CBM typologies and archetypes, (b) transition guidelines, and (c) major analytical tools for CBM research. The roles and functions of CBM typologies and tools were integrated into different stages of the transition process, and the challenges and shortfalls for CBM research in the various stages were identified. Their work can lay the foundation for future operational studies (Chen et al., 2021).

6.3. Developing Critical Assessment of the CE

Even though the CE has been recognised as a powerful integrative framework, believed to be able to solve certain societal problems, its overall introduction may need to be put under greater scrutiny. CE may not always be effective, or even desirable, owing to the spatio-temporal dimensions of the environmental risk of material flows. These flows involve toxic materials and may impose a high risk to the environment and public health, to such an extent that an overemphasis on anthropogenic (environmental change caused or influenced by people, either directly or indirectly) circularity may not be desirable. Groundwater abstraction, chemical explosions, vegetation removal, and subsurface mining are good examples of anthropogenic processes, and we subsequently need to factor in the lack of stability in the geo-political situation across the globe. Recent attempts to introduce a carbon neutrality strategy at the global level are likely to propel CE further into additional economic sectors. However, significant challenges remain in implementing and enforcing these international policies across national and political boundaries. The United Nations (UN) Basel Convention on the Transboundary Movement of Hazardous Waste and their Disposal is a good example of anthropogenic circularity (Zeng et al., 2022).

Several critics claim that the CE has diffused limits, and unclear theoretical grounds and that its implementation faces structural obstacles. They argue that the CE is based on an ideological agenda which is dominated by technical and economic accounts brings uncertain contributions to sustainability and de-politicises sustainable growth. Bringing these critiques together demonstrates that CE is far from being as promising as its advocates claim, rather it emerges as a theoretically, practically, and ideologically questionable notion (Corvellec et al., 2022; Foucault, 1982). Critics also claim that CE literature includes ambiguous definitions and we therefore need these to be more precise. We propose a metric that is derived from maximising the value to society of materials used in the production of commodities that provide services to consumers. It can then cater to recycling and alternative strategies, such as lifetime extension and new business models. In turn, this may provide unambiguous definitions for the linear economy, CE, and circular economic growth (Garcia-Barragan et al., 2019).

If the desire is for an equitable and truly sustainable economy that is circular, the critiques stress that a radical shift is essential to confront conventional neo-liberal governance regimes (Flynn & Hacking, 2019). There is a potential danger in the myths which surround CE – if they become normalised the space for critical reflection will decrease (Lazarevic & Valve, 2017). Examples of this include the 'risk of increased polarisation between city and country and that the countryside is left out with poorer access to welfare services as a result' (Hagbert et al., 2013). Other issues include the lack of a global approach encouraging neo-colonialism by either side-stepping developing countries, not giving agency to people with problems outside the Global North, or engaging with the informal sectors (Genovese & Pansera, 2021; Velis, 2018).

To put it succinctly, CE stands as a discourse that focusses on the economy excludes social dimensions, and simplifies its environmental consequences (Geisendorf & Pietrulla, 2018). These critiques point to the need to question how CE is currently conceived, consented, and implemented. A renewed, enlarged, and transdisciplinary research agenda on CE is needed in order to support the future policy process and CE requires research, policy, and managerial attention (Corvellec et al., 2022). There is clearly a need for conceptual coherence about definitions, plans, implementations, and modes of evaluation, because without coherence the expansion of knowledge could be obstructed by deadlocked debates or could, in fact, collapse entirely (Kirchherr et al., 2017). The work following focusses on a better understanding of economic development in the Global South, where a significant share of material extraction occurs. A clearer understanding of the technology, industrial structure, and development pathways in these regions may have a strong impact on understanding the dynamics of global supply/demand relationships. We stress that in a resource-constrained world, with an estimated 10 billion people in 2050 having the same material aspirations of today's high-income nations, there is no question that the future economy will need to be circular. From a policy perspective, the question we need to answer is whether averting catastrophic environmental impacts through an accelerated transition to global CE can also deliver sustained growth and jobs (Wiebe et al., 2019).

CE is a popular concept promoted by the European Union (EU), by several national governments and by many businesses across the world, however, its scientific and research content is superficial and lacking in coherence. Several academics and practitioners claim that CE seems to be a collection of vague and separate ideas from many fields and semi-scientific concepts. This work aims to define the concept of CE from the perspective of the World Commission on Environment and Development (WCED, refer to Chapter 4.4), sustainable development, and sustainability science and is a critical analysis of the concept from the perspective of environmental sustainability. The analysis identifies six challenges, for example, those of thermodynamics and system boundaries that need to be resolved for CE to be able to contribute to global net sustainability. The challenges also act as research themes and objectives for scholars interested in making progress in sustainable development through the employment of CE. CE is important for its power to attract both the business and policy-making communities towards sustainability but it needs scientific research to ensure that the actual environmental impacts of CE work effectively (Korkonen et al., 2018).

In reality, the research undertaken by industry and practitioners into CE remains limited. In view of this, in 2018 they undertook a systematic review of 46 corporate sustainability reports in the fast-moving consumer goods (FMCG) sector. They explored how these firms incorporated CE into their sustainability agenda. They focussed on: companies' uptake of CE; the relationship between CE and sustainability; and the CE practices presented. This work revealed that CE had started to be integrated into the corporate sustainability agenda. Most reported activities were oriented towards the main product and packaging, focussing on end-of-life management and sourcing strategies, and, to a lesser extent, on circular product design (CPD) and business model strategies. Most of the identified collaborations were with businesses while most of the initiatives focussed on consumers were largely missing although considered a critical part of the move towards CE (Stewart & Niero, 2018). While the terms 'sustainability' and 'CE' are increasingly gaining traction with academia, industry, and policy-making, the similarities and differences between both concepts remain ambiguous.

The relationship between the concepts is not made explicit in the literature which effectively blurs their conceptual contours and constrains the efficacy of using the approaches in research and practice. This research addresses that gap and aims to provide conceptual clarity by distinguishing the terms and by synthesising the different types of relationships between concepts. Through the use of an extensive literature review Geissdoerfer et al. identified eight different relationship types in the research output and illustrated the most evident similarities and differences between both concepts. They define CE as a regenerative system in which resource input and waste, emission, and energy leakage are minimised by slowing, closing, and narrowing material and energy loops. This can be achieved through long-lasting design, maintenance, repair, reuse, remanufacturing refurbishing, and recycling. Geissdoerfer et al. then define sustainability as the balanced integration of economic performance, social inclusiveness, and environmental resilience, to the benefit of current and future generations. They found that the CE is viewed as a condition for sustainability, a beneficial relation, or a trade-off in the literature (Geissdoerfer et al., 2017).

Previous research appeared to reveal that very few CE stakeholders are addressing the concept in full, potentially leading to an undesirable burden-shifting from reduced material consumption to increased environmental, economic, or social impact. Additionally, new metrics under-represent the complexities of multiple cycles and the consequences of material down-cycling. CE is perceived as a sustainable economic system where economic growth is decoupled from resource use through the reduction and recirculation of natural resources. Circularity metrics intended for sustainable decision-making should be comprehensive enough to avoid burden-shifting and clearly indicate how the benefits of recycling are allocated between the primary and secondary products.

The circular performance indicator (CPI) was developed by Huysman et al. (2017) and is defined as the ratio of the environmental benefit obtained from a waste treatment option over the ideal environmental benefit that could be achieved according to the material quality. These environmental benefits relate to the reduced consumption of natural resources and are represented by the Cumulative Energy Extraction from the Natural Environment (CEENE). The calculation of CPI relies on predefined quality factors for the analysed factors (e.g. high-quality recycled materials that can substitute virgin materials; Corona & Shen, 2019).

There has always been pressure to see concise and focussed research in the area of CE. The linkage between CE and emerging concepts such as the performance economy (Stahel, 2010), the sharing economy, and new business forms such as benefit corporations, have been investigated (Bocken et al., 2014). The actual impact of CE needed to be analysed: how does its output perform against the triple bottom line? (Elkington, 1997); and how does it contribute to 'strong sustainability' and slower forms of consumption, that is, closing as well as slowing resource loops (Bocken et al., 2016). Lastly, it is critical to investigate the consequences of better understanding the relationship between CE and sustainability and their influences on the performance of SCs, business models, and innovation systems.

6.3.1. The UN Basel Convention on the Transboundary Movement of Hazardous Waste and Their Disposal

The overarching objective of the Basel Convention was to protect human health and the environment against the adverse effects of hazardous wastes. Its scope of application covers a wide range of 'hazardous wastes' based on their origin and/ or composition and their characteristics, as well as two types of wastes defined as 'other wastes', namely household waste and incinerator ash.

This convention was adopted on 22 March 1989 by the Conference of Plenipotentiaries in Basel, Switzerland, in response to a public inquiry following the discovery of deposits of toxic wastes imported from abroad in Africa and other parts of the developing world in the 1980s. Insightful environmental awareness aligned with a tightening of environmental regulations in the industrialised world in the 1970s and 1980s had led to increasing public resistance to the disposal of hazardous wastes. This became known as the 'Not in My Back Yard' syndrome (NIMBY) and resulted in an escalation of disposal costs. This consequently led to some operators seeking cheap disposal options for hazardous wastes in Eastern Europe and the developing world, where environmental awareness was not as well developed, and regulations (including enforcement regulations) were deficient. This was the background to the negotiated Basel Convention; was to combat 'toxic trade', as it was referred to, and the Convention came into force in 1992. Its provisions centred around the following principal aims:

- The reduction of hazardous waste generation and the promotion of environmentally sound management of such wastes, wherever the place of disposal.
- The restriction of transboundary movements of hazardous wastes except where it is perceived to be in accordance with the principles of environmentally sound management.
- A regulatory system applying to cases where transboundary movements are permissible.

6.4. New Managerial and Policy Implications for the CE

In 2015, the UN adopted the 2030 development agenda entitled 'Transforming our World: The 2030 Agenda for Sustainable Development'. It outlined 17 sustainable development goals (SDGs) linked with 169 sub-targets that are structured around 5 pillars – people, planet, prosperity, peace, and partnership (the 5Ps). It aims to shift the world onto a sustainable and resilient development path, ensuring no one is omitted. The first pillar, 'people', focusses on ending poverty and hunger; the second, 'planet', identifies the need to protect the planet from destruction and degradation; third 'prosperity' makes certain that all human beings can enjoy prosperous and fulfilling lives; 'peace' aims to foster peaceful, just, and inclusive societies; and finally the fifth pillar, 'partnership', helps to establish a network and mobilise the means to implement this agenda (Khajuria et al., 2022). It is fair to state that without the fifth P, and the coordination of all the key stakeholders around the world, it will be very difficult to implement this agenda. Similarly, the EU's transition to a CE will reduce pressure on natural resources and will create sustainable growth and jobs. It is also a prerequisite to achieve the EU's 2050 climate neutrality target and to halt biodiversity loss. This new action plan announces initiatives along the entire life cycle of products; however, waste flows on a global scale might result in an uneven and spasmodic distribution of the risks and costs usually associated with CE. For CE to be successful in the long run it needs to generate significant environmental benefits, energy savings, and reductions in greenhouse gas emissions (Zeng et al., 2022).

There are several directions research on CE could travel, and there are positive indicators that this future work can be concise and coherent. Combining sustainable consumption (SC) with CE could help tackle challenges such as resource scarcity and climate change by reducing resource throughput and increasing recycling (Tunn et al., 2019). SC patterns are necessary to realise a sustainable society and economy (Druckman & Jackson, 2010). A major role of SC entails satisfying consumer needs while reducing the negative impacts caused by material extraction, production, and consumption. Within CE, companies are potential enablers of SC through changing production processes and consumption patterns, thus satisfying consumer needs in new ways through new business models (Bocken, 2017). Over the last 15 years, new forms of sustainability-focussed organisations have emerged, one such example being the 'Benefit Corporation', a specific type of firm certified to purposely generate positive impact for stakeholders, the environment, and society as part of its corporate structure (B Lab, 2018).

This approach called for building a greater understanding of overlapping and conflicting considerations between the sustainability principles informing ideas of CE and de-growth. Schroder and Bengtsson (2019) contend that practitioners and scholars need to be pragmatic and recognise evident ideological differences, while simultaneously acknowledging beneficial similarities and likenesses. The common aim of both frameworks would lead to a change in the status quo, enabling society to operate within ecological boundaries and giving opportunities to formulate new solutions. It has always been expected that management of the inherent tensions, such as the scale and scope of rebound effects, would continue to pose challenges. It was hoped there would be progress given positive communication and commitment to respectful dialogue, and, additionally, by seeking holistic strategies the academic community and all key stakeholders could move forward with the global sustainability initiatives (Schroder & Bengtsson, 2019).

Detailed and comprehensive accounts of waste generation and treatments which form the quantitative basis of designing and assessing policy instruments for CE have also been viewed as a research focus. Tisserant et al. (2017) presented a harmonised multi-regional solid waste account, covering 48 world regions, 11 types of solid waste, and 12 waste treatment processes for the year 2007. Patterns of waste generation differ across countries, but a significant potential for closing material cycles exists in both high and low-income countries. The EU needs to increase recycling by approximately 100 megatonnes per year (Mt/yr) and reduce landfilling by approximately 35 Mt/yr by 2030 to meet the targets set by the Action Plan for the CE (Tisserant et al., 2017).

It is argued that once rapid growth of circular businesses has occurred with these firms, linear players will be driven out of the marketplace. The economy could then be measured with a gross domestic product (GDP), smaller than its linear predecessor, especially if dominant products are ultra-durable and/or more resource efficient. However, this economy may also be larger as consumers tend to reinvest savings induced by CE. The caveat is that these savings may be invested in unsustainable projects and portfolios, thus offsetting any sustainability benefits previously accrued. This is known as the CE rebound (CER) effect. It is also possible, of course, that CE savings are reinvested sustainably, thus stimulating an economic move towards sustainability. In an effort to ensure sustainable reinvestments academic concern must not be focussed on whether the economy does or does not grow. However, it should focus on policies which aim at balancing environmental, economic, and social goals, resulting in sustainability (S). The book's authors believe this is a very important discussion for the future effectiveness of sustainability and CE policy implementation. Thus, it could be argued that circularity (C) is best considered as a means towards sustainability rather than a means towards 'post-growth' which is effectively de-growth. Through sound and resilient S policies that employ C principles, it can help to ensure sustainable market offerings en masse and thus may help over-come any CER effect. They may also help ensure that the economy's GDP, circularity, and sustainability are all growing at the same time – the original promise and ambition of CE (Kircherr, 2022).

CE is a powerful bridging concept that fosters the fundamental links among resource use, waste, and emissions and contributes to integrating environmental (output-related) and economic (input-related) policies. Environmental pressures resulting from the scale and structure of the industrial metabolism required concerted action at both ends. Improved collaboration between these currently isolated policy domains could realise co-benefits among environment, employment, and security of supply. Beyond the policy arena, well-attuned concerted actions of policymakers with industries ranging from production to waste management is a further necessary strand for formulating CE opportunities. Simultaneously, all these initiatives require monitoring frameworks, which provide indicators to assess links between CE and S goals at all levels (Mayer & Haas, 2019).

The combination of a systematic and comprehensive, balanced approach with regularly published statistical data calls for improvements in data quality, the standardising of waste statistics, and consolidation with extraneous data. Such improvements should allow a greater insight into not only the level of circularity but the quality of C as well. Consequently, it should also allow for a better understanding of the true contribution towards sustainability goals (Mayer & Haas, 2019). Making the transition to CE is an important goal for society and individual companies, particularly in resource-intensive manufacturing industries. The complexities and interdependencies of such an undertaking could mean that no single company can achieve it in isolation; thus, ecosystem-wide coordination is necessary. Using the findings from six large manufacturing firms, Parida & Burstrom developed a model that described the scarcely understood process of ecosystem transformation towards a CE paradigm. This process model had two stages: the first stage was an ecosystem readiness assessment; the second consisted of an ecosystem transformation, involving mechanisms and their purpose, use, and interdependencies, all moving towards CE (Parida & Burstrom, 2019).

6.5. Organisational and Dynamic Capabilities for the Enhancement of Sustainability and the CE

This work by De Los Rios & Charnley (2017) proposed a holistic and systemic process for CE-oriented business model innovation (BMI) by integrating available approaches from the academic literature and practice that should largely benefit organisations that are planning to engage in CE and need to define their strategy. By systematically reviewing 92 approaches, a new process was consolidated based on the integration of the unique elements of 16 existing process models for sustainability/CE-oriented BMI. It is fair to say that there is a wide range of dynamic capabilities required to play an active role in the formulation and development of the CE. The essence of this process model contains 33 activities, 21 deliverables, 88 techniques/tools, and 13 enablers for change. The debate surrounding the competences, skills, and capabilities for sustainability and CE is still under discussion. Change in production and consumption is needed alongside CE – when changes in design processes are identified they could reveal that the industry needs new proficiencies that support the closure of material loops, leading to a deeper knowledge of material composition and a rich understanding of social behaviour. These learning goals can act as guidance for manufacturing firms tackling climate change and this recalibration could end with a rethinking of education and knowledge in design and engineering (De Los Rios & Charnley, 2017). Besides enabling a holistic view of processes and procedures to guide all stages of BM innovation, it also allows for a systemic view with an indication of the behaviour and learning skills required to stimulate CE-thinking or circularity-oriented innovation, formalised decision-making processes, and activities to integrate sustainability thinking (i.e. sustainability performance assessments) and product innovation strategies with the BMI activities (Pieroni et al., 2019).

Another interesting concept is the CER effect, comprised of the capability of CE to achieve its intended sustainability benefits. The CER issue may potentially lead firms engaged with circular strategies to overstate environmental and sustainability performance. There is the potential to indulge in 'greenwashing' and therefore undermine their economic prosperity and sustainability. Within the science literature, there are examples of CER management being reduced at the micro-economic level so as not to jeopardise the effectiveness of circular transition. Using a contingency theory lens, guidelines are put forward to manage the causes of the CER effect. It is necessary to balance the trade-off between economic and environmental performance (Zerbino, 2022).

Several recent works have focussed on redesigning SCs by taking advantage of blockchain-enabled CE. This specific research also puts the work through a COVID-19 lens as the COVID-19 pandemic exposed businesses and societies to shortfalls in their normal patterns of production and consumption. It also had a long-lasting impact on SCs with a requirement to make them more resilient, transparent, and sustainable. It is generally agreed that SCs need to develop 'localisation', agility, and digitisation (LAD) characteristics. They could link LAD to a potential solution using blockchain technology and CE principal capabilities which would lead to SC tracking, tracing, and responsiveness. It is argued that blockchains can facilitate business at multiple levels with different stakeholders at individual, organisational, SC, governmental, and community levels (Nandi et al., 2021a, 2021b).

Many consumer-facing corporations (CFCs) are setting ambitious CE goals requiring firms' innovators to question what they can do to meet these targets, but a more pressing question is how they can change their business practices to align them with circularity requirements. A significant proportion of the Circular business model innovation (CBMI) literature has focussed on business-to-business contexts, efficiency, and recycling, but it may lack insight into the innovation activities within consumer-facing organisations. To follow different strategies in the waste hierarchy, such as repair and reuse, even firms of this scale and potential may require a different set of competences. This research used a dynamic capabilities lens to review the literature on innovation activities according to the CBMI stages of visioning, sensing, seizing, and transforming (Bocken & Konietzko, 2022).

Firms face multiple challenges in developing sustainable business models. Evaluating the sustainability impacts of various business model designs is of crucial importance, and several assessment tools and processes have been developed, each fitting different organisational needs in the SBM innovation process. This research is underpinned by a systematic literature review (SLR), using a qualitative meta-synthesis approach, to design principles for integrating sustainability assessments into the BMI process (Bhatnagar et al., 2022). Their classification helps to distinguish how concepts are situated in dimensions such as industry/service oriented, efficiency/zero waste target, or micro-/macro-scope. The revised definition distinguishes between CE's core characteristics and the framing conditions enabling its implementation. It has the potential to support both practitioners and researchers in developing clearer guidelines for the path to CE (Geisendorf et al., 2017). Very recently, a survey examined the role of Industry 4.0 (I4.0) on CE practices and SC capability to improve firm performance (Yu et al., 2022).

6.6. Drivers, Barriers, and Practices Towards an Effective CE Implementation

CE attracts attention from both practitioners and academics. The concept has been challenged by claims that it may be viewed as a vague concept or a new label for old green management practices – old wine in new bottles. Pinheiro and Jugend (2022) proposed a new approach to study the effects of CE on company performance: CPD and, consequently, this work investigates how I4.0 technologies and stakeholder pressure influence CPD and, in turn, impact on company performance. Their research results indicated that: (1) the application of I4.0 technologies favoured CPD, in particular, artificial intelligence (AI) and big data analytics (BDA); (2) pressure from stakeholders can encourage the adoption of circular strategies, especially from suppliers because they are responsible for developing and delivering smart components; and (3) even though the literature might have been viewed as being controversial, there is a positive relationship with regard to the impact of CE adoption on market performance. These researchers posit a set of design strategies oriented towards the development of products for CE (Pinheiro & Jugend, 2022).

Even though CE has been widely discussed within the EU, it has been argued quite recently that only limited progress has been made with regard to its introduction/implementation. The following research did not agree that progress is being held up due to technological barriers, instead we found that cultural barriers, particularly a lack of consumer interest and awareness as well as a hesitant company culture, were considered the main CE barriers by policymakers and businesses. These are driven by market barriers which, in turn, are induced by a lack of synergistic governmental interventions to accelerate the transition towards CE. However, not a single technological barrier is ranked among the most urgent CE barriers. It was suggested that CE was a niche discussion among sustainable development professionals in 2019, however, we considered that significant efforts needed to be undertaken for the concept to maintain its momentum (Kircherr et al., 2019).

Given the complexity of CE implementation, it is argued that the literature is missing a strategic standpoint. Unal and Shao (2019) investigated the taxonomy of CE implementation strategies at the managerial level by linking them to the strategy literature. The taxonomy incorporated 391 C2C product scorecards of 187 companies from 10 different industries. Their analysis was based on the relative importance assigned to each competitive capability that defines CE, namely material health, material reutilisation, renewable energy, water stewardship, and social fairness. They observed three distinct clusters of CE implementation strategy groups: (1) founding (recyclers); (2) development (all-decent circulars); and (3) maturity (toxicity fighters). All clusters have been present in various industries, although there is an industry effect. The results indicated that each cluster has a different strategy and they contradict the general assumption and expectation of simultaneous improvement at all CE dimensions. They suggest that the maturity degree of a competitive capability may determine the implementation strategy (Unal & Shao, 2019).

The following chapter has the main goal of developing tools for CE implementation. Two tools are discussed:

(1) The first is a CE strategies database which includes 45 CE strategies that are applicable to different parts of the value chain.
(2) The second is a CE implementation database, which includes over 100 case studies categorised by Scope. Parts of the value chain, as well as those used at the strategy and implementation level, are viewed as prerequisites for the CE to achieve a more sustainable society (Kalmykova et al., 2018).

The development of what we refer to as the CE has been ongoing for many years; indeed, it is reasonable to say that the definition of CE has been adapted and changed over the years. The distinction of historic phases, from CE 1.0 to CE 3.0, shows the evolutionary nature of CE and its relations to predecessors. Is it reasonable to state that CE 3.0 is CE refurbished or possibly a transformational upgrade? It is argued that CE 3.0 stagnates on low-value resource retention options (ROs). The revival of CE has been accompanied by controversies and confusion across different stakeholders in science and practice. There has been a focus on the historical development of the CE concept and value ROs for products and materials aiming for increased circularity. The three phases in the evolution of CE are proposed and it is argued that this concept, in its dominant framing, is not as new as frequently claimed. How far have we travelled globally with respect to CE implementation? High levels of circularity have already been reached in areas of the globe where longer-loop value ROs are possible, such as energy recovery and recycling (Reike et al., 2018).

While there is a need for businesses and organisations to switch from linear to CE, there are several challenges that need to be addressed, such as business models and the criticism that CE projects are often small scale. Technology can be an enabler towards scaling up, however, the primary challenge is to identify technologies that can allow predicting, tracking and proactively monitoring a product's residual value which will in turn motivate businesses to pursue circularity decisions. Mboli et al. (2022) propose an Internet of Things (IoT) enabled decision support system (DSS) for the CE business model that effectively allows tracking, monitoring, and analysing products in real-time for business analytics with the focus on residual value. These authors addressed the requirement of real-time monitoring of a product's lifecycle using I4.0 technologies, namely through the use of IoT and 5G technology (Mboli et al., 2022).

CE activities mainly focus on the meso- and macro-levels, and only the micro-level has been limited. This chapter concentrates on how organisations have implemented what has been termed the four Rs: reducing, repairing, remanufacturing and recycling. Certain organisations that engage with the four Rs do not do so under the CE umbrella while others that profess to apply CE have low levels of engagement with the four Rs. It is claimed that firms are using the four Rs to contribute to CE, but not all of them are aware that they are applying CE principles. Organisations need to improve their 4R efforts by better linking their theory with practice – CE has to be implemented outside organisational environments in a more holistic way through better collaboration with stakeholders on efforts and activities. Results show that organisations favour reducing and recycling from an internal focus. In this, as in other contexts, organisations are not islands but must collaborate with their stakeholders in order to achieve the goals of sustainability and CE (Barriero & Lazano, 2020). It is generally accepted that CE can only be successful if all the key stakeholders in its environment work collectively to bring the relevant strands together effectively. A recent addition to the debate was aimed at evaluating the relative influence of socio-demographic and psychological features of CE. This identified the various criteria that ruled the extent to which consumers engaged in CE purchased waste-to-value (WTV) food enriched with ingredients otherwise wasted in the SC. A significant amount of attention was given to aspects related to the generalised aversion to new foods, that is, food neophobia (FN), and the aversion to food processed in new ways, that is, food technology neophobia (FTN) (Coderoni & Perito, 2020).

One of the observations from the plethora of analyses is that while such parts of the value chain as recovery/recycling and consumption/use are prominently featured, others, including manufacturing and distribution, are rarely involved in CE. On the other hand, the implementation levels of the used strategies indicate that many market-ready solutions exist already. The scope of current CE implementation considers selected products, materials, and sectors, while system changes to the economy are seldom suggested. Finally, CE monitoring methods and suggestions for future development, including the analysis of theoretical approaches, can serve as an introduction to the CE concept, while developed tools can be instrumental in designing new CE cases (Kalmykova et al., 2018). Recent research has identified challenges to the implementation of the CE in a large city. It showed the implementation difficulties when low-value, circular activities encounter a lack of space in large conurbations such as London, highlighting the imbalance between local supply and demand for circular products which prevents potential scaling-up. At the moment, a lack of data, monitoring the benefits of adopting circular development, has undermined political support (Williams, 2022).

6.7. Frameworks for Embedding and Ensuring the Longevity of Sustainability and CE Principles

Intensifying global consumption stipulates the need to use sustainable manufacturing and CE concepts to make products while managing available finite resources. Designers must be equipped to design products considering the economic, environmental, and social impacts of the product life cycle. A recent interesting piece of research explored product design in relation to sustainability and circularity principles. Hapuwatte et al. (2021) presented fundamental concepts, putting forward set definitions and proposing a new methodology to incorporate these principles. This new methodology synthesised elements of design for sustainability and circularity. The primary stakeholder categories were updated to explicitly include the concept of 'society-at-large', a neglected category in typical manufacturer-focussed sustainability evaluations. The methodology promoted a holistic view of the product life cycle, including end-of-life activity planning, leading to a perpetual resource flow. Performance-influencing parameters available for designers were also examined, including the overlooked 'dedicated' and 'incidental' process-induced types, providing a strong basis for future research on product sustainability predictive models (Hapuwatte et al., 2021).

Further relevant research focussed on what was required to explicitly address and understand complementarities and incompatibilities between green, circular, and bioeconomy solutions. It identified that there is a need to develop coherent decision-making strategies, actions, and tools, as well as indicators that take into consideration solutions based on multiple sustainability narratives including Green Economy (GE), CE, and Bioeconomy (BE). D'Amato and Korhonen (2021) concluded that none of the three narratives offer a comprehensive 'package' of solutions individually. However, when considered jointly as collaborative narratives, they direct us towards a society and economy based on renewable/reproductive and biodiversity-based/benign processes, delivering material and immaterial benefits that fulfil the economic and social requirements of all people now and in the future. This certainly appears to fit the requirements of the sustainability and CE agenda (D'Amato & Korhonen, 2021).

Closing the loop is a key aspect of much debate surrounding CE. To move towards circularity, this particular chapter argued that brands must integrate and fuse these strategies across SCs rather than limiting them to only the waste stage. The fashion industry is recognised as one of the most wasteful consumer industries in the world – since the advent of fast fashion and 'trendy', low-cost clothing produced by global fashion brands, clothing has evolved from a durable good to a daily purchase. In recent years, the concept of CE as a framework for a more efficient, closed-loop economy has emerged as a fundamental way forward in the transition to a more sustainable and less wasteful fashion industry. For the industry to move towards circularity, this chapter argued that brands must integrate these strategies across SCs rather than limiting them to the waste stage. Brydges (2021) explored the gaps between CE principles and practice identifying particular challenges inherent in fashion brand approaches.

This next study did not find any consensus regarding the importance of environmental management certifications or eco-labels in measuring the circularity of a company or a product because (Delphi) experts were divided on environmental certifications. In these challenging times when an environmental crisis is threatening social and economic sustainability, it is crucial that practitioners, policymakers, and academics share their knowledge and intelligence and interact with each other to design eco-innovative solutions that move industry towards real sustainable development (Prieto-Sandoval et al., 2018). CE has been put forward as a paradigm that aims to generate economic prosperity, protect the environment, and prevent pollution. Within this, resources are taken from nature, transformed into products, distributed in the marketplace, consumed, and then recovered through biological and technical cycles (Prieto-Sandoval et al., 2018). It is also possible for the flow of material to be closed, waste in industrial ecosystems can be minimised, and symbiosis can be fostered (Stahel, 2016). The extensive growth in man-made material turnover has resulted not only in a significant increase in wealth and convenience for a large proportion of the global population, it has also led to the exploitation of resource deposits in almost all parts of the globe along with the generation of huge amounts of waste. Ever-increasing resource extraction and waste generation are associated with major environmental problems which range from climate change and marine littering to land misuse. The following authors suggest a set of metrics for measuring and fostering the CE. Besides a recycling rate-based evaluation, they recommended including a substitution factor describing the share of primary resources replaced by the establishment of a CE (Fellner & Lederer, 2020).

It is argued that remanufacturing throughout CE conserves energy and materials while creating economic growth and employment. It is seen as imperative that we develop better systems to optimise the use of resources, maximise the value of the product, and minimise the total cost. The following two authors present a two-stage stochastic linear model for a make-to-order hybrid manufacturing–remanufacturing production system by integrating capacity and inventory decisions. They consider the uncertainty in demand, core returns rate, and yield, to impose flexibility as both operations are considered with a collective production capacity on the same assembly line. They also considered a setting where demand for new and remanufactured products does not mutually cannibalise (i.e. new parts for original equipment and remanufactured parts for the independent after-market (Reddy & Kumar, 2021). Additionally, the capacity utilisation by core returns is considered in two ways: less capacity intensive case and increased capacity intensive case. The developed model is solved for optimal inventory and capacity levels along with production quantities by maximising the utilisation of resources and profit. They also presented a closed-form solution by demand-space partition to deduce the optimal policy of the firm. Based on their analysis, they present settings where remanufacturing can perfectly substitute manufacturing.

It is argued that an optimum methodology for the measurement of performance related to the ecological and ethical transition is still missing from the sustainability armoury. Therefore, this methodology or framework can have true relevance in several key areas:

(a)   With the integration of sustainability, CE, and industrial symbiosis paradigms.
(b)   The possibility it can be applied at different levels of application, that is, firm-level, the SC, or the district.
(c)   Adaptability to firms with different characteristics (firm size and awareness), thanks to the development of two different (full and core) scalable systems.

The framework has been tested in four manufacturing firms against its capacity to represent each paradigm, its usefulness, and ease of use. The utility of the framework could be in its ability to overcome tensions among the three paradigms and encourage firms to consider performance beyond their own boundaries, including SC or district, and its scalability for different sizes. It should also be beneficial to increase knowledge on ecological and ethical transition (Cagno et al., 2023).

In CE the economic and environmental value of materials is preserved for as long as possible by keeping them in the economic system, either by lengthening the life of the products formed from them or by looping back into the system to be reused. The notion of waste no longer exists in CE because products and materials are, in principle, reused and cycled indefinitely. Taking this description as a starting point, Hollander et al. (2017) asked which guiding principles, design strategies, and methods are required for circular product design (CPD) and to what extent these differ from the principles, strategies, and methods of eco-design. They argue that there is a fundamental distinction to be made between eco-design and CPD and proceed to develop, based on an extensive literature review, a set of new concepts and definitions, starting from a redefinition of product lifetime and introducing new terms such as pre-source and recovery horizon. Walter Stahel's Inertia Principle (2016) was taken as a key to CPD, allowing the development of a typology of approaches as a design for product integrity. With a focus on tangible, durable consumer products, this should lead to a deeper understanding of CE as a concept, as well as its broader aspects of product design (Hollander et al., 2017).

In the last 15 years, the expression 'CE' has increasingly gained interest with practitioners and academics, now in greater focus with the advent of a plethora of environmental regulations all around the world. In Europe, the Waste Framework Directive (2008); in the United States, the Enactment of the

Resource Conservation and Recovery Act (1984) and the Pollution Prevention Act (amended in 2002); in China the CE Promotion Law (2008); in Japan, the Law for establishing a Material Cycles Society; in Vietnam the Environmental Protection Law (2005), in Korea, the Waste Control Act (amended in 2007), and the Act on Promotion of Resources Saving and Recycling (amended in 2008). A side effect of the rising popularity of the concept of CE among political, industrial, and academic communities is the lack of consistency around its definition and the ensuing scope of action. These various schools of thought regarding CE include production and operations management, C2C manufacture of products, and industrial ecology (Elodie et al., 2020).

Since production processes can often have a high impact on carbon emissions this has led to short product life cycles on supply, resource use, and waste generation. This has been synthesised into four main topics dealing with CE:

(1) Reverse logistics and waste management: This focusses on the reuse of products and raw materials and a 5-step waste hierarchy – waste prevention; preparing waste for reuse; recycling and other recovery (i.e. back-filling) with disposal (i.e. landfilling) as the last resort (Article 4 of the Waste Framework Directive).
(2) From product to raw material recycling: Under Article 3 of the Waste Framework Directive – in production planning two recycling terms stand out – refurbishment and remanufacturing. Both of these are recovery processes.
(3) Co and by-products.
(4) Sustainability and its three pillars (economic, environmental, and social).

Rising technologies such as those within I4.0 can be integrated with CE practices to establish a business model that is capable of reusing and recycling waste materials such as scrap metal or e-waste. The outcome of this study is the recommendation of a circular model to reuse scrap electronic devices, integrating web technologies, reverse logistics and additive manufacturing (AM) to support CE practices. Nascimento et al.'s (2019) results suggest a positive influence of improving business sustainability by reinserting waste into the SC to manufacture products on demand. The impact of reusing waste materials to manufacture new products is relevant to minimising resource consumption and negative environmental impacts. It also avoids hazardous materials ending up in landfills or in the world's oceans seriously threatening life in ecosystems. Furthermore, the reuse of wasted materials enables the development of local business networks that generate jobs and improve economic performance. It was also revealed in this particular study that most urban waste is plastic and cast iron, thus leaving room for improvement in increasing the recycling of scrap metal and similar materials. In theory, the CBM promotes a culture of reusing and recycling and motivates the development of collection and processing techniques for urban waste through the use of 3D printing techniques and I4.0. Using this approach, groups involved are focussed on the technical parts of recycling and it is hoped they can be more focussed on research, development and innovation, as many of these procedures will be automated (Nascimento et al., 2019).

By employing resources more circularly, individual users can contribute to more eco-efficient and sustainable resource use. Whether resources are used sustainably is evaluated at the macro-level. However, it is usually the efficiency of the circular use of resources at the micro-level that aggregates to the macro-level. There appears to be a general consensus that the link between the circular use of resources at micro- and macro-levels is under theorised. The symbiotic relationship between individual users enables a reduction in resource use at a macro-level. The following researchers argued that an analogous association exists in finance where desirable investment return is linked to undesirable investment risk and that via the generation of efficient portfolios, individual risks are at least partially diverted away. They theorise CE both in its perfect and imperfect forms, using modern portfolio theory. Portfolio Theory states that, given a desired level of risk, an investor can optimise the expected returns of a portfolio through diversification. The researchers' theory identified the drivers of circular resource use, showing under which conditions individual use contributes to the circular use of resources. There is obviously plenty of scope for future research to deepen and expand on the use of portfolio theory to understand CEs various facets (Figge et al., 2021).

6.8. Conclusions

One of the most exciting aspects of planning the CE is to address the potential methodological impasse that exists in its design. We believe that the future design of CE may need to be radically changed as the moral compass for choosing such systems is reset. Churchman (1968), describing Singer's philosophy, stated that the best solution must also satisfy optimum social costs. The morality of a system's design is to evaluate the effects of the planner's intervention on those for whom the plan is intended. This should be a positive, not negative, outcome from the future design of the CE. The move to a CE is undoubtedly a major sociological change.

Fligstein and McAdam (2014) undertook some important research, underpinned by social management theory and the political theory of markets, into business structures and fields that give an insight into how CE may develop. They state that social order is constructed through a process of interactions among stakeholders who are competing for advantageous business positions, identifying the dynamic of how new systems and institutions emerge, remain stable, and are transformed. They also investigated how individuals and groups come to compete with each other in social arenas where something important is at stake.

The dynamic of SCs within the CE will be sufficiently different to make them problematic for a significant number of organisations. CE is likely to open up new business markets for many of these companies. Markets are generally socially constructed arenas where repeated exchanges occur between buyers and sellers under a set of formal and informal rules (conventions) governing relations among competitors, suppliers, and customers. These arenas operate according to local understandings and rules that guide interaction, facilitate trade, define what products are produced, indeed constitute the products themselves, and provide stability for buyers, sellers, and producers. However, with governments signing up to ambitious targets in areas such as carbon reduction across the globe, it is more than likely that this stability will disappear. Marketplaces are also dependent on governments, laws, and cultural understandings supporting marketing activity. If we add ethical and ecological aims and goals to this list the future is certain to be more complex and uncertain in SC and CE transactions.

Values held by managers on the subject of CSR can be viewed of as 3 phases over the last 50 years, but we posit a fourth phase that may become the norm over the next 20 years. This fourth phase is important as it is likely to provide a more suitable business environment in which sustainability and CE will thrive. It is imperative that all key stakeholders – those who can facilitate improvement in sustainability within the world and who can formulate an effective CE – work in unison to bring about its fruition. This can be achieved by viewing all the different elements of sustainability and CE in a systemic way.

This model is presented in Fig. 6.1.

We believe it fits with the ethos of this book to analyse the dynamics of sustainable production and consumption ecosystems and associated organisational relationships. This analysis will be aligned with the industrial symbiotic perspectives of the CE.

Phase 1 – the manager believed that 'raw self-interest should prevail in our society', rationalising that 'making as much profit as it is possible would be good (for the firm and) for society'. In this phase, profit maximisation and economic goals are fundamental.

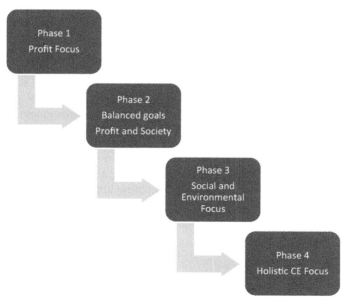

Fig. 6.1.   Towards the CE – Four-Phase Development Model.
Source: Based on the book by Hay et al. (1976).

Phase 2 – is referred to as trustee management – the manager is a profit 'satisficer' – he/she tries to balance the goals and contributions of the main participants and claimants to the organisation welfare. The executive recognises the need to balance social values with economic values.

Phase 3 – the manager believes in 'enlightened self-interest'. This position can be interpreted as one which considers that it is in the interest of firms to pursue socially-oriented goals over and beyond those strictly dictated by law, in order to participate in the shaping of an environment that is favourable to the short and long-term interests of the corporation. The maxim is: 'What is good for society is good for the company'. People may be considered as more important than money. Whereas profit is necessary for the firm's survival, businesses must cooperate and spearhead the movement towards 'quality of life' management (Hay et al., 1976).

This book extends the model of a developing managerial focus from Phase 3, social and environmental focus, to Phase 4, which embodies a significant further paradigm shift towards a sustainability and CE model.

Phase 4 – The manager/executive knows that green and sustainable policies will be beneficial to the organisation. However, the autonomy of the decision-maker has disappeared, leaving no certainty that the firm will survive by following this strategy. Executives will hope for alignment between following CSR policies and making the organisation resilient in a totally different business environment. The organisation will need to 'buy time' as they may not have the staff with the right competences to move the company forward in the current climate. The range of dynamic capabilities within the firm may be out of balance. Working practices, such as those in CE, will change as collaborative contracts alter the dynamics of the tendering process. Cost-benefit analysis, the usual way of deciding on projects, becomes more complex as the normal currency for contract negotiations, that is, financial transactions, may be complemented/replaced by carbon reduction vouchers, meeting sustainability targets, product resilience, etc.

The usual binary negotiations in the SC will be replaced by multi-stakeholders with different goals. Some will be negotiating SC and CE contracts with the aim of profit maximisation; others will be focussed on deals where carbon reduction or neutrality is of paramount importance. The business environment of SC and the CE will rapidly move from one of reasonably constant medium and long-term contracts to high-velocity markets with multiple stakeholders negotiating short-term contracts. Being locked into relatively long contracts may mean tying up valuable and scarce resources in projects that are not delivering the required business or ecological outcomes. This change in tempo appears to mimic the machinations of freight forwarding.

References

Barriero-Gen, M., & Lazano, B. (2020). How circular is the CE? Analysing the implementation of CE in organisations. *Business Strategy and the Environment, 29*(8), 3484–3494.

Bhatnagar, R., Keskin, D., Kirkels, A., Romne, A., Georges, L., & Huijben, J. C. C. M. (2022, December). Design principles for sustainability assessments in the business model innovation process. *Journal of Cleaner Production, 377*, 134313.

Bocken, N. M. P., de Pauw, I., Bakker, C., & van der Grinten, B. (2016). Product design and business model strategies for a circular economy. *Journal of Industrial and Production Engineering, 33*(5), 308–320.

Bocken, N. M. P., & Konietzko, J. (2022). Circular business model innovation in consumer-facing corporations. *Technological Forecasting and Social Change, 185*, 122076.

Bocken, N. M. P., Ritala, P., & Huotari, P. (2017). The circular economy: Exploring the introduction of the concept among S & P 500 firms. *Journal of Industrial Ecology, 21*(3), 487–490.

Bocken, N. M. P., Short, S. W., Rana, P., & Evans, S. (2014, February). A literature and practice review to develop sustainable business model archetypes.*Journal of Cleaner Production, 65*, 42–56.

Brydges, T. (2021, April). Closing the loop on take, make, waste: Investigating circular economy practices in the Swedish fashion industry. *Journal of Cleaner Production, 293*, 126245.

Cagno, E., Negri, M., Neri, A., & Giambone, M. (2023). One framework to rule them all: An integrated, multi-level and scalable performance measurement framework of sustainable, circular economy and industrial symbiosis. *Sustainable Production and Consumption, 35*, 55–71.

Chen, X., Memon, H. A., & Tebyetekerwa, M. (2021). Circular economy and sustainability of the clothing and textile industry. *Materials Circular Economy, 3*, 12.

Churchman, C. W. (1968). *Challenge to Reason*. McGraw-Hill.

Coderoni, S., & Perito, M. A. (2020, April). Sustainable consumption in the circular economy: An analysis of consumers' purchase intentions for waste-to-value food. *Production, 252*, 119870.

Corona, B., Shen, L., Reike, D., Carreon, J. R., & Worrell, E. (2019, December). Towards sustainable development through the circular economy – A review and critical assessment on current circularity metrics. *Resources, Conservation and Recycling, 151*, 104498.

Corvellec, H., Stowell, A. F., & Johansson, N. (2022). Critiques of the circular economy. *Journal of Industrial Ecology, 26*, 421–432.

D'Amato, D., & Korhonen, J. (2021, October). Integrating the green economy, circular economy, and bio-economy in a strategic sustainability framework. *Ecological Economics, 188*, 107143.

De Los Rios, I. C., & Charnley, F. (2017, September). Skills and capabilities for a sustainable and circular economy: The changing role of design. *Journal of Cleaner Production, 160*, 109–122.

Druckman, A., & Jackson, T. (2010). The bare necessities: How much carbon do we really need?. *Ecological Economics, 69*(9), 1794–1804.

EIB CE Guide. (2020). *The EIB Circular Economy Guide: Supporting the Circular Transition* (pp. 98–100). European Investment Bank, Luxembourg.

Elkington, J. (1997). *Cannibals with forks: The triple bottom line of 21st century business*. Oxford.

Elodie S., Absi, N., & Borodin, V. (2020, November). Towards circular economy in production planning: Challenges and opportunities. *European Journal of Operational Research, 287*(1), 168–190.

Fellner, J., & Lederer, J. (2020, July) Recycling rate – The only practical metric for a circular economy?. *Waste Management, 113*, 319–320.

Figge, F., Thorpe, A. S., & Manzhynski, S. (2021). Between you and I: A portfolio theory of the circular economy. *Ecological Economics, 190*, 1–9.

Fligstein, N., & McAdam, D. (2014). *A theory of fields*. Oxford University Press.

Flynn, A., Hacking, N., & Xie, L. (2019, August). Governance of the circular economy: A comparative examination of the use of standards by China and the United Kingdom. *Environmental Innovation and Societal Transitions, 33*, 1566.

Foucault, M. (1982). The subject and power. *Critical Inquiry, 8*(4, Summer), 777–795.

Garcia-Barragan, J. F., Eyckmans, J., & Rousseau, S. (2019). Defining and measuring the circular economy: A mathematical approach. *Ecological Economics, 157*(C), 369–372.

Genovese, A., & Pansera, M. (2021). The circular economy at a crossroads: Technocratic eco-modernism or convivial technology for social revolution?. *Capitalism Nature Socialism, 32*(2), 95–113.

Geisendorf S., & Pietrulla, F. (2017). The circular economy and circular economic concepts – A literature analysis and redefinition. *Thunderbird International Business Review, 60*(3), 771–782.

Geissdoerfer, M., Morioka, S. N., de Carvalho, M. M., & Evans, S. (2018). Business models and supply chains for the CE. *Journal of Cleaner Production, 190*, 712–721.

Hagbert, P., Mangold, M., & Femenias, P. (2013). Paradoxes and possibilities for a 'Green' housing sector: A Swedish case. *Sustainability, 5*(5), 2018–2035.

Hapuwatte, B. M., & Jawahir, I. S. (2021, May). Closed-loop sustainable product design for circular economy. *Journal of Industrial Ecology, 25*(2), 1430–1446.

Hay, R. D., Gray, E. R., & Gates, J. E. (1976). *Business and society* (pp. 4–16). South Western.

den Hollander, M., Bakker, C. A., & Hultink, E. J. (2017). Product design in a circular economy: Development of a typology of key concepts and terms: Key concepts and terms for circular product design. *Journal of Industrial Ecology, 21*(1), 517–525.

Huysman, S., de Schaepmeester, J., Ragaert, K., Dewulf, J., & De Meester, S. (2017). Performance indicators for a circular economy: A case study on post-industrial plastic waste. *Resources, Conservation and Recycling, 120*, 46–54.

Kalmykova, Y., Sadagopan, M., & Rosado, L. (2018). CE: from review of theories and practices to development of implementation tools. *Resources, Conservation and Recycling, 135*, 190–201.

Khajuria, A., Atienza, V. A., Chavanich, S., Henning, W., Islam, I., Kral, U., Liu, M., Liu, X., Murthy, I. K., Oyedotun, T. D. T., Verma, P., Xu, G., & Zeng, X. (2022). Accelerating circular economy solutions to achieve the 2030 agenda for sustainable development goals. *Circular Economy, 1*, 100001.

Kircherr, J., Reike, D., & Hekkert, M. (2017, December). Conceptualizing the circular economy: An analysis of 114 definitions. *Resources, Conservation, and Recycling, 127*, 221–232.

Kircherr, J., Pisielli, I., Bour, R., Kostense-Smit, E., Muller, J., Huibrechtse-Truijens, A., & Hekkert, M. (2019). Barriers to the circular economy: Evidence from the European Union (EU). *Ecological Economics, 150*, 264–272.

Kircherr, J. (2022). Bullshit in the sustainability and transitions literature: A provocation. *Circular Economy and Sustainability, 3*, 167–172.

Korhonen, J., Nuur, C., Feldmann, A., & Birkie, S. E. (2018, February). Circular economy as an essentially contested concept. *Journal of Cleaner Production, 175*, 544–552.

Lazarevic, D., & Valve, H. (2017, September). Narrating expectations for the circular economy: Towards a common and contested European transition. *Energy Research and Social Science, 31*, 60–69.

Mayer, A., Haas, W., Wiedenhofer, D., Krausmann, F., Nuss, P., & Blengini, G. A. (2019). Measuring progress towards a circular economy: A monitoring framework for economy-wide material loop closing in the EU28. *Journal of Industrial Ecology, 23*(1), 62–76.

Mboli, J. S., Thakker, D., & Mishra, J. L. (2022). An internet of things-enabled decision support system for circular economy business model. *Software: Practice and Experience, 52*(3), 772–787.

Nandi, S., Sarkis, J., Hervani, A., & Helms, M. (2021a). Do blockchain and CE practices improve post Covid-19 SCs? A resource-based and resource dependence perspective. *Industrial Management and Data Systems, 121*(2), 333–363.

Nandi, S., Sarkis, J., Hervani, A. A., & Helms, M. M. (2021b). Redesigning SCs using blockchain-enabled CE and Covid-19 experiences. *Sustainable Production and Consumption, 27*, 10–22.

Nascimento, D. L. M., Alencastro, V., Quelhas, O. L. G., Caiado, R. G. G., Garza-Reyes, J. A., Lona, L. R., & Tortorello, G. (2019). Exploring industry 4.0 technologies to enable CE practices in a manufacturing context: A business model proposal. *Journal of Manufacturing Technology Management, 30*(3), 607–627.

Parida, V., Burstrom, T., Visnjic, I., & Wincent, J. (2019, August). Orchestrating industrial ecosystem in circular economy: A two-stage transformation model for large manufacturing companies. *Journal of Business Research, 101*, 715–725.

Pieroni, M., McAloone, T. C., & Pigosso, D. C. A. (2019). Business model innovation for circular economy: Integrating literature and practice into a conceptual process model. *Proceedings of the Design Society International Conference on Engineering Design, 1*(1), 2517–2526.

Pinheiro, M. A. P., Jugend, D., Jabbour, A. B. L. S., Jabbour, C. J. C., & Latan, H. (2022). Circular economy-based new products and company performance: The role of stakeholders and industry 4.0 technologies. *Business Strategy and the Environment, 31*(1), 483–499.

Prieto-Sandoval, V., Ormazabal, M., Jaca, C., & Viles, E. (2018). Key elements in assessing circular economy implementation in small and medium-sized enterprises. *Business Strategy and the Environment, 27*(8), 1525–1534.

Reddy, K. N., & Kumar, A. (2021). Capacity investment and inventory planning for a hybrid manufacturing – Remanufacturing system in the circular economy. *International Journal of Production Research, 59*(8), 2450–2478.

Reike, D., Vermeulen, W. J. V., & Witjes, S. (2018). The circular economy: New or refurbished a C.E. 3.0? Exploring controversies in the conceptualisation of the CE through a focus on history and resource value retention options. *Resources, Conservation and Recycling, 135*, 246–264.

Renwick, D. W. S., Redman, T., & Maguire, S. (2013). Green human resource management: A review and research agenda. *International Journal of Management Reviews, 15*, 1–14.

Schroder, P., Bengtsson, M., Cohen, M., Dewick, P., Hofstetter, J., & Sarkis, J. (2019, July). Degrowth within – Aligning circular economy and strong sustainability narratives. *Resources, Conservation and Recycling, 146*, 190–191.

Sehnem, S., Queiroz, A. A. F. S. L., Pereira, S. C. F., & dos Santos Correia, G. (2022). Circular economy and innovation: A look from the perspective of organizational capabilities. *Business Strategy and the Environment, 31*(1), 236–250.

Stahel, W. R. (2010). *The performance economy*. Palgrave Macmillan.

Stahel, W. R. (2016). The circular economy. *Nature, 531*, 435–438.

Steiner, G. A. (1975). *Business and society* (2nd ed.). Random House.

Stewart, R., & Niero, M. (2018). Circular economy in corporate sustainability strategies: A review of corporate sustainability reports in the fast-moving consumer goods sector. *Business Strategy and the Environment, 27*(7), 1005–1022.

Tisserant, A., Pauliuk, S., Merciai, S., Schmidt, J., Fry, J., Wood, R., & Tukker, A. (2017). Solid waste and the circular economy: A global analysis of waste treatment and waste footprints. *Journal of Industrial Ecology, 21*(3), 628–640.

Tunn, V. S. C., Bocken, N. M. P., van den Hende, E. A., & Schoormans, J. P. L. (2019, March). Business models for sustainable consumption in the circular economy: An expert study. *Journal of Cleaner Production, 212*, 324–333.

Unal, E., & Shao, J. (2019, March). A taxonomy of circular economy implementation strategies for manufacturing firms: Analysis of 391 cradle-to-cradle products. *Production, 212*, 754–765.

Velis, C. (2018). No circular economy if current systemic failures are not addressed. *Waste Management and Research, 36*(9), 757–759.

Wiebe, K. S., Harsdorff, M., Montt, G., Simas, M. S., & Wood, R. (2019). Global circular economy scenario in a multiregional input–output framework. *Environmental Science and Technology, 53*, 6362–6373.

Williams, J. (2022). Challenges to implementing circular development – Lessons from London. *International Journal of Urban Sustainable Development, 14*(1), 287–303.

Yu, Z., Khan, S. A. R., & Umar, M. (2022). Circular economy practices and industry 4.0 technologies: A strategic move of automobile industry. *Business Strategy and the Environment, 31*(3), 796–809.

Zeng, X., Ogunseitan, O. A., Nakamura, S., Suh, S., Kral, U., Li, J., & Geng, Y. (2022). Reshaping global policies for circular economy. *Circular Economy, 1*(1), 100003.

Zerbino, P. (2022, December). How to manage the circular economy rebound effect: A proposal for contingency-based guidelines. *Journal of Cleaner Production, 378*, 134584.

Index

Printed and bound by CPI Group (UK) Ltd, Croydon, CR0 4YY

04/02/2024

08231246-0003